YOU ARE NOT SO SMART

YOU ARE NOT SO SMART

Why You Have Too Many Friends on Facebook,
Why Your Memory Is Mostly Fiction, and
46 Other Ways You're Deluding Yourself

DAVID McRANEY

GOTHAM BOOKS

DUTTON

Published by Penguin Group (USA) Inc.

375 Hudson Street, New York, New York 10014, U.S.A.

Penguin Group (Canada), 90 Eglinton Avenue East, Suite 700, Toronto, Ontario M4P 2Y3, Canada (a division of Pearson Penguin Canada Inc.) · Penguin Books Ltd, 80 Strand, London WC2R 0RL, England · Penguin Ireland, 25 St. Stephen's Green, Dublin 2, Ireland (a division of Penguin Books Ltd) · Penguin Group (Australia), 250 Camberwell Road, Camberwell, Victoria 3124, Australia (a division of Pearson Australia Group Pty Ltd) · Penguin Books India Pvt Ltd, 11 Community Centre, Panchsheel Park, New Delhi–110 017, India · Penguin Group (NZ), 67 Apollo Drive, Rosedale, Auckland 0632, New Zealand (a division of Pearson New Zealand Ltd) · Penguin Books (South Africa) (Pty) Ltd, 24 Sturdee Avenue, Rosebank, Johannesburg 2196, South Africa

Penguin Books Ltd, Registered Offices: 80 Strand, London WC2R 0RL, England

Published by Dutton, a member of Penguin Group (USA) Inc.

First printing, November 2011

1   3   5   7   9   10   8   6   4   2

Copyright © 2011 by David McRaney
All rights reserved

REGISTERED TRADEMARK—MARCA REGISTRADA

LIBRARY OF CONGRESS CATALOGING-IN-PUBLICATION DATA
has been applied for.

ISBN 978-1-592-40659-3

Printed in the United States of America
Set in Granjon
Designed by Elke Sigal

For Jerry, Evelyn, and Amanda

CONTENTS

YOU ARE NOT SO SMART

INTRODUCTION

You

THE MISCONCEPTION: *You are a rational, logical being who sees the world as it really is.*

THE TRUTH: *You are as deluded as the rest of us, but that's OK, it keeps you sane.*

You hold in your hands a compendium of information about self-delusion and the wonderful ways we all succumb to it.

You think you know how the world works, but you really don't. You move through life forming opinions and cobbling together a story about who you are and why you did the things you did leading up to reading this sentence, and taken as a whole it seems real.

The truth is, there is a growing body of work coming out of psychology and cognitive science that says you have no clue why you act the way you do, choose the things you choose, or think the thoughts you think. Instead, you create narratives, little stories to explain away why you gave up on that diet, why you prefer Apple over Microsoft, why you clearly remember it was Beth who told you the story about the clown with the peg leg made of soup cans when it was really Adam, and it wasn't a clown.

Take a moment to look around the room in which you are reading this. Just for a second, see the effort that went into not only what you see, but the centuries of progress leading to the inventions surrounding you.

Start with your shoes, and then move to the book in your hands, then look to the machines and devices grinding and beeping in every corner of your life—the toaster, the computer, the ambulance wailing down a street far away. Contemplate, before we get down to business, how amazing it is humans have solved so many problems, constructed so much in all the places where people linger.

Buildings and cars, electricity and language—what a piece of work is man, right? What triumphs of rationality, you know? If you really take it all in, you can become enamored with a smug belief about how smart you and the rest of the human race have become.

Yet you lock your keys in the car. You forget what it was you were about to say. You get fat. You go broke. Others do it too. From bank crises to sexual escapades, we can all be really stupid sometimes.

From the greatest scientist to the most humble artisan, every brain within every body is infested with preconceived notions and patterns of thought that lead it astray without the brain knowing it. So you are in good company. No matter who your idols and mentors are, they too are prone to spurious speculation.

Take the Wason Selection Task as our first example. Imagine a scientist deals four cards out in front of you. Unlike normal playing cards, these have single numbers on one side and single colors on the other. You see from left to right a three, an eight, a red card, and a brown card. The shifty psychologist allows you to take in the peculiar cards for a moment and poses a question. Suppose the psychologist says, "I have a deck full of these strange cards, and there is one rule at play. If a card has an even number on one side, then it must be red on the opposite side. Now, which card or cards must you flip to prove I'm telling the truth?"

Remember—three, eight, red, brown—which do you flip?

As psychological experiments go, this is one of the absolute simplest. As a game of logic, this too should be a cinch to figure out. When psychologist Peter Wason conducted this experiment in 1977, less than 10 percent of the people he asked got the correct answer. His cards had vowels instead of colors, but in repetitions of the test where colors were used, about the same number of people got totally confused when asked to solve the riddle.

So what was your answer? If you said the three or the red card, or said only the eight or only the brown, you are among the 90 percent of people whose minds get boggled by this task. If you turn over the three and see either red or brown, it does not prove anything. You learn nothing new. If you turn over the red card and find an odd number, it doesn't violate the rule. The only answer is to turn over both the eight card and the brown card. If the other side of the eight is red, you've only confirmed the rule, but not proven if it is broken elsewhere. If the brown has an odd number, you learn nothing, but if it has an even number you have falsified the claims of the psychologist. Those two cards are the only ones which provide answers. Once you know the solution, it seems obvious.

What could be simpler than four cards and one rule? If 90 percent of people can't figure this out, how did humans build Rome and cure polio? This is the subject of this book—you are naturally hindered into thinking in certain ways and not others, and the world around you is the product of dealing with these biases, not overcoming them.

If you replace the numbers and colors on the cards with a social situation, the test becomes much easier. Pretend the psychologist returns, and this time he says, "You are at a bar, and the law says you must be over twenty-one years old to drink alcohol. On each of these four cards a beverage is written on one side and the age of the person drinking it on the other. Which of these four cards must you turn over to see if the owner is obeying the law?" He then deals four cards which read:

23—beer—Coke—17

Now it seems much easier. Coke tells you nothing, and 23 tells you nothing. If the seventeen-year-old is drinking alcohol, the owner is breaking the law, but if the seventeen-year-old isn't, you must check the age of the beer drinker. Now the two cards stick out—beer and 17. Your brain is better at seeing the world in some ways, like social situations, and not so good in others, like logic puzzles with numbered cards.

This is the sort of thing you will find throughout this book, with explanations and musings to boot. The Wason Selection Task is an example of how lousy you are at logic, but you are also filled with beliefs that look good on paper but fall apart in practice. When those beliefs fall apart, you tend not to notice. You have a deep desire to be right all of the time and a deeper desire to see yourself in a positive light both morally and behaviorally. You can stretch your mind pretty far to achieve these goals.

The three main subjects in this book are cognitive biases, heuristics, and logical fallacies. These are components of your mind, like organs in your body, which under the best conditions serve you well. Life, unfortunately, isn't always lived under the best conditions. Their predictability and dependability have kept confident men, magicians, advertisers, psychics, and peddlers of all manner of pseudoscientific remedies in business for centuries. It wasn't until psychology applied rigorous scientific method to human behavior that these self-deceptions became categorized and quantified.

Cognitive biases are predicable patterns of thought and behavior that lead you to draw incorrect conclusions. You and everyone else come into the world preloaded with these pesky and completely wrong ways of seeing things, and you rarely notice them. Many of them serve to keep you confident in your own perceptions or to inhibit you from seeing yourself as a buffoon. The maintenance of a positive self-image seems to be so important to the human mind you have evolved mental mechanisms designed to make you feel awesome about yourself. Cognitive biases lead to poor choices, bad judgments, and wacky insights that are often totally incorrect. For example, you tend to look for information that confirms your beliefs and ignore information that challenges them. This is called confirmation bias. The contents of your bookshelf and the bookmarks in your Web browser are a direct result of it.

Heuristics are mental shortcuts you use to solve common problems. They speed up processing in the brain, but sometimes make you think so fast you miss what is important. Instead of taking the long way around and deeply contemplating the best course of action or the most logical train of thought, you use heuristics to arrive at a conclusion in record time. Some heuristics are learned, and others come free with every copy of the human brain. When they work, they help your mind stay frugal. When they don't, you see the world as a much simpler place than it really is. For example, if you notice a rise in reports about shark attacks on the news, you start to believe sharks are out of control, when the only thing you know for sure is the news is delivering more stories about sharks than usual.

Logical fallacies are like math problems involving language, in which you skip a step or get turned around without realizing it. They are arguments in your mind where you reach a conclusion without all the facts because you don't care to hear them or have no idea how limited your information is. You become a bumbling detective. Logical fallacies can also be the result of wishful thinking. Sometimes you apply good logic to false premises; at other times you apply bad logic to the truth. For instance, if you hear Albert Einstein refused to eat scrambled eggs, you might assume scrambled eggs are probably bad for you. This is called the argument from authority. You assume if someone is super-smart, then all of that person's decisions must be good ones, but maybe Einstein just had peculiar taste.

With each new subject in these pages you will start to see yourself in a new way. You will soon realize you are not so smart, and thanks to a plethora of cognitive biases, faulty heuristics, and common fallacies of thought, you are probably deluding yourself minute by minute just to cope with reality.

Don't fret. This will be fun.

1

Priming

THE MISCONCEPTION: *You know when you are being influenced and how it is affecting your behavior.*

THE TRUTH: *You are unaware of the constant nudging you receive from ideas formed in your unconscious mind.*

You are driving home from the grocery store and you realize you forgot to buy spinach dip, which was the only reason you went there in the first place. Maybe you could buy some at a gas station. Nah, you'll just get it next trip. Thoughts of dip lead to ruminations on the price of gas, which lead to excogitation over bills, which leads to thoughts about whether you can afford a new television, which reminds you of the time you watched an entire season of *Battlestar Gallactica* in one sitting—what the hell? You are home already and have no recollection of the journey.

You drove home in a state of highway hypnosis, your mind and body seemingly floating along in parallel. When you stopped the car and turned the key, you snapped out of a dreamlike state sometimes called line hypnosis when describing the dissociative mental world of an assembly line worker stuck in a repetitive grind. In this place, consciousness drifts as one mental task goes into autopilot and the rest of the mind muses about less insipid affairs, floating away into the umbra.

You split your subjective experience into consciousness and sub-consciousness all the time. You are doing it right now—breathing, blinking, swallowing, maintaining your posture, and holding your mouth closed while you read. You could pull those systems into conscious control or leave them to the autonomic nervous system. You could drive cross-country consciously adjusting your foot on the gas pedal, shifting your hands on the wheel, mulling over the millions of micro decisions needed to avoid gnashing metallic death at high speeds, or you could sing along with your friends while the other parts of your mind handle the mundane stuff. You accept your unconscious mind as just another weird component of the human experience, but you tend to see it as a separate thing—a primal self underneath consciousness that doesn't have the keys to the car.

Science has learned otherwise.

A great example of how potent a force your unconscious can be was detailed by researchers Chen-Bo Zhong at the University of Toronto and Katie Liljenquist at Northwestern in a 2006 paper published in the journal *Science*. They conducted a study in which people were asked to remember a terrible sin from their past, something they had done which was unethical. The researchers asked them to describe how the memory made them feel. They then offered half of the participants the opportunity to wash their hands. At the end of the study, they asked subjects if they would be willing to take part in later research for no pay as a favor to a desperate graduate student. Those who did not wash their hands agreed to help 74 percent of the time, but those who *did* wash agreed only 41 percent of the time. According to the researchers, one group had unconsciously washed away their guilt and felt less of a need to pay penance.

The subjects didn't truly wash away their emotions, nor did they consciously feel as though they had. Cleansing has meaning beyond just avoiding germs. According to Zhong and Liljenquist, most human cultures use the ideas of cleanliness and purity as opposed to filth and grime to describe both physical and moral states. Washing is part of many religious rituals and metaphorical phrases used in everyday language, and referring to dastardly deeds as being dirty or to evil people as scum is also common. You even make the same face when feeling disgusted about a person's actions as you do when seeing something gross. Unconsciously, the people in the study connected their hand washing with all the interconnected ideas associated with the act, and then those associations influenced their behavior.

When a stimulus in the past affects the way you behave and think or the way you perceive another stimulus later on, it is called priming. Every perception, no matter if you consciously notice, sets off a chain of related ideas in your neural network. Pencils make you think of pens. Blackboards make you think of classrooms. It happens to you all the time, and though you are unaware, it changes the way you behave.

One of many studies that have revealed how much influence your subconscious mind has over the rest of your thinking and behavior and how easily it can be influenced by priming was conducted in 2003 by Aaron Kay, Christian Wheeler, John Barghand, and Lee Ross. People were separated into two groups and asked to draw lines between photos and text descriptions. One group looked at neutral photos. They drew lines to connect kites, whales, turkeys, and other objects to descriptions on the other side of the paper. The second group connected lines to descriptions for photos of briefcases, fountain pens, and other items associated with the world of business. Participants were then moved into isolated rooms and told they had been paired off with another subject. The other person was actually in on the experiment. Each person was then told they were now going to play a game in which they could earn up to $10. The researchers presented the subject with a cup and explained two strips of paper waited inside, one with the word "offer" written on it and another with the word "decision." The subject was then given a choice—blindly pluck a slip of paper from the cup, or allow the other person to blindly select. The catch? Whoever pulled out the "offer" slip would get the $10 and choose how it was divided between both parties. The partner would then choose to accept or reject the offer. If the partner rejected, both received nothing. This is called the ultimatum game, and its predictability has made it a favorite tool of psychologists and economists. Offers below 20 percent of the total amount are usually turned down.

Most people chose to do the picking. They didn't know both slips had "offer" written on them. If they instead let the other person do the picking, the actor pretended to get the "decision" slip. So everyone in the study was put in the position of making a reasonable offer, knowing if they did not, they would miss out on some free cash. The results were bizarre, but confirmed the scientists' suspicions about priming.

So how did the two groups differ? In the group who connected neutral photos to their descriptions before the ultimatum game, 91 percent chose to split the money evenly—$5 each. In the group who connected the business photos, only 33 percent offered to split the money evenly; the rest tried to keep a little more for themselves.

The researchers ran the experiment again with real objects instead of photos. They had participants play the ultimatum game in a room with a briefcase and leather portfolio on the far end of a table along with a fountain pen in front of the participant's chair. Another group sat in a room with neutral items—a backpack, a cardboard box, and a wooden pencil. This time, 100 percent of the neutral group chose to split the money evenly, but only 50 percent of those in the group sitting in a room with business-related items did the same. Half of the business-primed group tried to stiff the other party.

All of the subjects were debriefed afterward as to why they behaved as they did, but not one person mentioned the objects in the room. Instead, they confabulated and told the researchers about their own feelings on what is and is not fair. Some described their impressions of the people they were playing the game with and said those feelings influenced them.

Mere exposure to briefcases and fancy pens had altered the behavior of normal, rational people. They became more competitive, greedier, and had no idea why. Faced with having to explain themselves, they rationalized their behavior with erroneous tales they believed were true.

The same researchers conducted the experiment in other ways. They had subjects complete words with some of the letters omitted, and again those who first saw business-related images would turn a word like "c—p—tive" into "competitive" 70 percent of the time while only 42 percent of the neutral group did. If shown an ambiguous conversation between two men trying to come to an agreement, those who first saw photos of business-related objects saw it as a negotiation, whereas the neutral group saw an attempt at compromise. In every case, the subjects' minds were altered by unconscious priming.

Just about every physical object you encounter triggers a blitz of associations throughout your mind. You aren't a computer connected to two cameras. Reality isn't a vacuum where you objectively survey your surroundings. You construct reality from minute to minute with memories and emotions orbiting your sensations and cognition; together they form a collage of consciousness that exists only in your skull. Some objects have personal meaning, like the blow-pop ring your best friend gave you in middle school or the handcrafted mittens your sister made you. Other items have cultural or universal meanings, like the moon or a knife or a handful of posies. They affect you whether or not you are aware of their power, sometimes so far in the depths of your brain you never notice.

Another version of this experiment used only smell. In 2005, Hank Aarts at Utrecht University had subjects fill out a questionnaire. They were then rewarded with a cookie. One group sat in a room filled with the faint smell of cleaning products while another group smelled nothing. The group primed by the aroma in the clean-smelling room cleaned up after themselves three times more often.

In a study by Ron Friedman where people were merely shown but not allowed to drink sports beverages or bottled water, those who just looked at sports drinks persisted longer in tasks of physical endurance.

Priming works best when you are on autopilot, when you aren't trying to consciously introspect before choosing how to behave. When you are unsure how best to proceed, suggestions bubble up from the deep that are highly tainted by subconscious primes. In addition, your brain hates ambiguity and is willing to take shortcuts to remove it from any situation. If there is nothing else to go on, you will use what is available. When pattern recognition fails, you create patterns of your own. In the aforementioned experiments, there was nothing else for the brain to base its unconscious attitudes on, so it focused on the business items or the clean smells and ran with the ideas. The only problem was the conscious minds of the subjects didn't notice.

You can't self-prime, not directly. Priming has to be unconscious; more specifically, it has to happen within what psychologists refer to as the adaptive unconscious—a place largely inaccessible. When you are driving a car, the adaptive unconscious is performing millions of calculations, predicting every moment and accommodating, adjusting your mood and manipulating organs. It does the hard work, freeing up your conscious mind to focus on executive decisions. You are always of two minds at any one moment—the higher-level rational self and the lower-level emotional self.

Science author Jonah Lehrer wrote extensively about this division in his book *How We Decide*. Lehrer sees the two minds as equals who communicate and argue about what to do. Simple problems involving unfamiliar variables are best handled by the rational brain. They must be simple because you can juggle only four to nine bits of information in your conscious, rational mind at one time. For instance, look at this sequence of letters and then recite them out loud without looking: RKFBIIRSCBSUSSR. Unless you've caught on, this is a really difficult task. Now chunk these letters into manageable portions like this: RK FBI IRS CBS USSR. Look away now and try to recite them. It should be much easier. You just took fifteen bits and reduced them to five. You chunk all the time to better analyze your world. You reduce the complex rush of inputs into shorthand versions of reality. This is why the invention of written language was such an important step in your history—it allowed you to take notes and preserve data outside the limited capacity of the rational mind. Without tools like pencils, computers, and slide rulers, the rational brain is severely hampered.

The emotional brain, Lehrer argues, is older and thus more evolved than the rational brain. It is better suited for complex decisions and automatic processing of very complex operations like somersaults and break dancing, singing on key and shuffling cards. Those operations seem simple, but they have too many steps and variables for your rational mind to handle. You hand those tasks over to the adaptive unconscious. Animals with small cerebral cortices, or none at all, are mostly on autopilot because their older emotional brains are usually, or totally, in charge. The emotional brain, the unconscious mind, is old, powerful, and no less a part of who you are than the rational brain is, but its function can't be directly observed or communicated to consciousness. Instead, the output is mostly intuition and feeling. It is always there in the background co-processing your mental life. Lehrer's central argument is "you know more than you know." You make the mistake of believing only your rational mind is in control, but your rational mind is usually oblivious to the influence of your unconscious. In this book I add another proposition: You are unaware of how unaware you are.

In a hidden place—your unconscious mind—your experience is always being crunched so suggestions can be handed up to your conscious mind. Thanks to this, if a situation is familiar you can fall back on intuition. However, if the situation is novel, you will have to boot up your conscious mind. The spell of highway hypnosis on a long trip is always broken when you take an exit into unfamiliar territory. The same is true in any other part of your life. You are always drifting back and forth between the influence of emotion and reason, automaticity and executive orders.

Your true self is a much larger and more complex construct than you are aware of at any given moment. If your behavior is the result of priming, the result of suggestions as to how to behave handed up from the adaptive unconscious, you often invent narratives to explain your feelings and decisions and musings because you aren't aware of the advice you've been given by the mind behind the curtain in your head.

When you hug someone you love and then feel the rush of warm emotions, you have made an executive decision which then influenced the older parts of your brain to deliver nice chemicals. Top-down influence makes intuitive sense and isn't disturbing to ponder.

Bottom-up influence is odd. When you sit next to a briefcase and act more greedy than you usually would, it is as if your executive brain centers are nodding in agreement to hidden advisers whispering in your ear. It seems mysterious and creepy because it's so clandestine. Those who seek to influence you are sensitive to this, and try to avoid creating in you the uncomfortable realization that you have been duped. Priming works only if you aren't aware of it, and those who depend on priming to put food on the table work very hard to keep their influence hidden.

Let's look at casinos, which are temples to priming. At every turn there are dings and musical notes, the clatter of coins rattling in metal buckets, symbols of wealth and opulence. Better still, casinos are sensitive to the power of the situation. Once you are inside, there are no indications of the time of day, no advertisements for anything not available inside the box of mutually beneficial primes, no reason to leave, whether to sleep, eat, or anything else—no external priming allowed.

Coca-Cola stumbled onto the power Santa Claus has to prime

you during the holidays. Thoughts of childhood happiness and wholesome family values appear in your subconscious as you choose between Coke or a generic brand of soda. Grocery stores noticed an increase in sales when the smell of freshly baked bread primed people to buy more food. Adding the words "all natural" or including pictures of pastoral farms and crops primes you with thoughts of nature, dissuading thoughts of factories and chemical preservatives. Cable channels and large corporations prime potential audiences by adopting an image, a brand, so as to meet you halfway before you decide how to engage and judge them. Production companies spend millions of dollars to create trailers and movie posters to form first impressions so you are primed to enjoy their films in a certain way right up until the opening titles. Restaurants decorate their interiors to communicate everything from fine dining to psychedelic hippie communes in order to prime you to enjoy their cheese sticks. From every corner of the modern world advertisers are launching attacks on your unconscious in an attempt to prime your behavior to be more favorable for the bottom lines of their clients.

Businesses discovered priming before psychologists did, but once psychology started digging into the mind, more and more examples of automaticity were uncovered, and even today it isn't clear how much of your behavior is under your conscious control.

The question of who is truly in the driver's seat was made far more complex in 1996 by a series of studies published by John Bargh in the *Journal of Personality and Social Psychology*.

He had New York University students unscramble thirty separate five-word sentences. He told them he was interested in their language abilities, but he was really studying priming. He assembled three groups. One unscrambled sentences with terms associated with aggression and rudeness such as "brazen," "disturb," and "bluntly." Another group unscrambled words from a bank of polite terms like "courteous" and "behaved." A third group served as a control with words like "gleefully," "prepares," and "exercising."

The experimenters told the students how to complete the task and once they were done to come find them to receive the second assignment, but this was the real experiment. When each student approached the researcher he or she found him already engaged in a conversation with an actor who was pretending to be having trouble understanding the word puzzles. The researcher completely ignored the student until he or she interrupted the conversation or ten minutes passed.

The results? The polite-word group waited on average 9.3 minutes to interrupt; the neutral group waited about 8.7 minutes; and the rude-word group waited around 5.4 minutes. To the researchers' surprise, more than 80 percent of the polite-word group waited the full 10 minutes. Only 35 percent of the rude-word group chose not to intrude. The subjects were interviewed after the experiment and couldn't pinpoint why they chose to wait or to interrupt. The question never entered their minds because as far as they knew, their behavior had not been influenced. The scrambled sentences, they believed, had not affected them.

In a second experiment, Bargh had participants unscramble sentences that contained words associated with old age, like "retired," "wrinkled," and "bingo." He then clocked participants' speed as they walked down a hall to an elevator and compared it to the speed they walked when they first strolled in. They took about one to two extra seconds to reach their destination. Just as with the rude-word groups, the old-word groups were primed by the ideas and associations the words created. To be sure this was really a result of priming, Bargh repeated the experiment and got the same results. He ran it a third time with a control group who unscrambled words related to sadness to be sure he hadn't simply depressed people into walking slower. Once again, the old-age group tottered along the longest.

Bargh also conducted a study in which Caucasian participants sat down at a computer to fill out boring questionnaires. Just before each section began, photos of either African-American or Caucasian men flashed on the screen for thirteen milliseconds, faster than the participants could consciously process. Once they completed the task, the computer flashed an error message on the screen telling the participants they had to start over from the beginning. Those exposed to the images of African-Americans became hostile and frustrated more easily and more quickly than subjects who saw Caucasian faces. Even though they didn't believe themselves to be racist or to harbor negative stereotypes, the ideas were still in their neural networks and unconsciously primed them to behave differently than usual.

Studies of priming suggest when you engage in deep introspection over the causes of your own behavior you miss many, perhaps most, of the influences accumulating on your persona like barnacles along the sides of a ship. Priming doesn't work if you see it coming, but your attention can't be focused in all directions at once. Much of what you think, feel, do, and believe is, and will continue to be, nudged one way or the other by unconscious primes from words, colors, objects, personalities, and other miscellany infused with meaning either from your personal life or the culture you identify with. Sometimes these primes are unintended; sometimes there is an agent on the other end who plotted against your judgment. Of course, you can choose to become an agent yourself. You can prime potential employers with what you wear to a job interview. You can prime the emotions of your guests with how you set the mood when hosting a party. Once you know priming is a fact of life, you start to understand the power and resilience of rituals and rites of passage, norms and ideologies. Systems designed to prime persist because they work. Starting tomorrow, maybe with just a smile and a thank-you, you can affect the way others feel—hopefully for the best.

Just remember, you are most open to suggestion when your mental cruise control is on or when you find yourself in unfamiliar circumstances. If you bring a grocery list, you'll be less likely to arrive at the checkout with a cart full of stuff you had no intention of buying when you left the house. If you neglect your personal space and allow chaos and clutter to creep in, it will affect you, and perhaps encourage further neglect. Positive feedback loops should improve your life, not detract from it. You can't prime yourself directly, but you can create environments conducive to the mental states you wish to achieve. Just like the briefcase on the table, or the clean aroma in the room, you can fill your personal spaces with paraphernalia infused with meaning, or find meaning in the larger idea of owning little. No matter, when you least expect it, those meanings may nudge you.

2

Confabulation

THE MISCONCEPTION: *You know when you are lying to yourself.*

THE TRUTH: *You are often ignorant of your motivations and create fictional narratives to explain your decisions, emotions, and history without realizing it.*

When a movie begins with the words "Based on a True Story," what crosses your mind? Do you assume every line of dialogue, every bit of clothing and song in the background is the same as it was in the true event on which the film was based? Of course you don't. You know movies like *Pearl Harbor* or *Erin Brockovich* take artistic license with facts, shaping them so a coherent story will unfold with a beginning, middle, and end. Even biopics about the lives of musicians or politicians who are still alive are rarely the absolute truth. Some things are left out, or some people are fused into single characters. The details, you think when watching, are less important than the big picture, the general idea.

If only you were so savvy when it came to looking back on the biopic in your head, but you are not so smart. You see, the movie up there is just as dramatized, and scientists have known this for quite a while.

It all starts with your brain's desire to fill in the gaps.

Take your thumbs and place them side by side in front of you. Close your left eye and slowly move your right thumb away in a horizontal line to your right. Notice anything? Probably not. Somewhere along the line is your blind spot, the point where your optic nerve breaks into the retina. You have one per eye, and in this area of your vision you can't see anything. It is larger than you think too—roughly 2 percent of your eyesight. If you want to see for yourself, take a blank sheet of paper and draw on it a dot about the size of a dime. Now, about two inches to the right, draw another. Close your left eye and focus on the left-hand dot. Move the paper closer to you until the right-hand dot disappears. There it is, one of your blind spots.

Now look around the room with your eye closed. Try the same trick above with some words on this page. Notice anything? Is there a giant gap in your vision? Nope. Your brain fills it in with a bit of mental Photoshopping. Whatever surrounds the blind spot is copied and pasted into the hole in an automatic imaginary bit of visual hocus-pocus. Your brain lies to you, and you go about your business none the wiser.

Just as the brain fills in your blind spot every moment of the day without your consciously noticing, so do you fill in the blind spots in your memory and your reasoning.

Have you ever been telling a story about something you and someone else did long ago, and then they stop you to say, "No, no, no. That's not how it happened," just as you get on a roll? You say it was at a Christmas party when you acted out the final episode of *Lost* with stockings on your hands; they say it was Easter. You remember opening presents and drinking eggnog, but they promise it was eggs and it wasn't even you. It was your cousin, and they used a chocolate bunny to represent the smoke monster.

Consider how often this seems to happen, especially if you are in a relationship with someone who can call you out in this way all the time. Is it possible if you had a recording of everything you've ever done it would rarely match up with how you remember it? Think of all the photographs that have blown your mind when you saw yourself in a place you had completely deleted from memory. Think of all the things your parents bring back up about your childhood that you have zero recollection of, or which you remember differently. But you still have a sense of a continuous memory and experience. The details are missing, but the big picture of your own life persists. But the big picture is a lie, nurtured by your constant and unconscious confabulation, adding up to a story of who you are, what you have done, and why.

You do this so much and so often that you can't be sure how much of what you consider to be the honest truth about your past is accurate. You can't be sure how you came to be reading these words at this moment instead of languishing on a street corner or sailing around the world. Why didn't you go in for the kiss? Why did you say those horrible things to your mother? Why did you buy that laptop? Why are you really angry with that guy? What is the truth about who you are and why you are here?

To understand confabulation, we have to head into surgery. Every once in a while, in extreme cases where nothing else will work, doctors resort to splitting a patient's brain right down the middle. And what they discover is fascinating.

To get a rough idea of how large and how halved your brain is, hold your hands out in front of you and form two fists. Now bring them together so that if you were wearing rings they would be facing upward. Each fist represents a hemisphere. Your two hemispheres communicate with each other via a dense series of nerve fibers called the corpus callosum. Imagine when you made those fists you grabbed two handfuls of yarn—the yarn is your corpus callosum. In a corpus callosotomy (which is sometimes performed when a case of epilepsy becomes so severe and unmanageable that no drug will bring relief and normalcy) that yarn is cut. The two halves of the brain are disconnected in a careful way that allows the patients to live out their lives with as much normalcy as possible.

Split-brain patients seem fine from the outside. They are able to hold down jobs and carry their weight in conversation. But researchers who have looked deeper have discovered the strengths and weaknesses of the separate hemispheres with the help of split-brain patients. Since the 1950s, studies with those who have undergone this procedure have revealed a great deal about how the brain works, but the insight most germane to the topic at hand is how quickly and unflinchingly these patients are capable of creating complete lies which they then hold to as reality. This is called split-brain confabulation, but you don't have to have a split brain to confabulate.

You feel like a single person with a single brain, but in many ways, you really have two. Thoughts, memories, and emotions cascade throughout the whole, but some tasks are handled better by one side than the other. Language, for example, is usually a task handled by the left side of the brain, but then bounced back and forth between the two. Strange things happen when a person's brain hemispheres are disconnected, making this transfer impossible.

Psychologist Michael Gazzaniga at the University of California at Santa Monica was one of the first researchers, along with Roger Sperry, to enlist the help of split-brain patients in his work. In one experiment subjects looked at a cross in the center of a computer screen, and then a word like "truck" was flashed on only the left side. They were then asked what they saw. Those with connected brains would, of course, say "truck." Those with split brains would say they didn't know, but then, amazingly, if they were asked to draw with their left hand what they had seen, they easily doodled a truck.

Oddly enough, your right hand is controlled by your left brain and your left hand by the right. What the left eye sees travels diagonally through the cranium into the right hemisphere and vice versa, and these nerves are not severed when the brains are split.[1]

Normally this isn't a problem, because what one side of the brain perceives and thinks gets transmitted to the other, but a split-brain can't say what they see when a scientist shows an image to the left visual field. The language centers are in the other hemisphere, across from where the image is being processed. The part of their brain in charge of using words and sending them to the mouth can't tell the other side, the one holding the pencil, what it is looking at. The side that saw the image can, however, draw it. Once the image appears, the split-brain person will then say, "Oh, a truck." The communication that normally takes place across the corpus callosum now happens on the paper.

This is what goes on in the world of a split-brain patient. The same thing happens in your head too. The same part of your brain is responsible for turning thoughts into words and then handing

---

1 To be precise, the right hemisphere gets information from the left visual field, not just the left eye. The opposite is true for the right. A portion of the left visual field can be seen by the right eye, just around the nose.

those words over to the mouth. All day long, the world appearing in your right hemisphere is being shared with your left in a conversation you are unaware of. At the biological level, this is a fundamental source of confabulation, and it can be demonstrated in the lab.

If split-brain people are shown two words like "bell" on the left and "music" on the right and then asked to point out with their right hand in a series of four photos what they saw, they will point to the image with a bell in it. They will ignore other photos of a drummer, an organ, and a trumpet. The amazing confabulatory moment happens when they are asked why they chose the image. One split-brain patient said it was because the last music they heard was coming from the college's bell towers. The left eye saw a bell, and told the right hand to point to it, but the right side saw music and was now concocting a justification for ignoring the other pictures that were also related to the idea.

The side of the brain in charge of speaking saw the other side point out the bell, but instead of saying it didn't know why, it made up a reason. The right side was no wiser, so it went along with the fabrication. The patients weren't lying, because they believed what they were saying. They deceived themselves and the researcher but had no idea they were doing so. They never felt confused or deceptive; they felt no different than you would.

In one experiment a split-brain person was asked to perform an action only the right hemisphere could see, and the left hemisphere once again explained it away as if it knew the cause. The word "walk" was displayed; the subject stood. When the researcher asked why he got up, the subject said, "I need to get a drink." Another experiment showed a violent scene to only the right hemisphere. The subject said she felt nervous and uneasy and blamed it on the way the room was decorated. The deeper emotional centers could still talk to both sides, but only the left hemisphere had the ability to describe what was bubbling up. This split-brain confabulation has been demonstrated many times over the years. When the left hemisphere is forced to explain why the right hemisphere is doing something, it often creates a fiction that both sides then accept.

Remember though, your brain works in the same way—you just have the benefit of a connection between the two halves to help buffer against misunderstandings, but they can still happen from time to time. Psychologist Alexander Luria compared consciousness to a dance and said the left hemisphere leads. Since it does all the talking, it sometimes has to do all the explaining. Split-brain confabulation is an extreme and amplified version of your own tendency to create narrative fantasies about just about everything you do, and then believe them. You are a confabulatory creature by nature. You are always explaining to yourself the motivations for your actions and the causes to the effects in your life, and you make them up without realizing it when you don't know the answers. Over time, these explanations become your idea of who you are and your place in the world. They are your self.

The neuroscientist V. S. Ramachandran once encountered a split-brain patient whose left hemisphere believed in God, but whose right hemisphere was an atheist. Essentially, as he put it, there were two people in one body—two selves. Ramachandran believes your sense of self is partly the action of mirror neurons. These complex clusters of brain cells fire when you see someone hurt themselves or cry, when they scratch their arm or laugh. They put you in the other person's shoes so you can almost feel that person's pain and itches. Mirror neurons provide empathy and help you learn. One of the greatest discoveries in recent years was to find that mirror neurons fire also when *you* do things. It is as if part of your brain is observing yourself as an outsider.

You are a story you tell yourself. You engage in introspection, and with great confidence you see the history of your life with all the characters and settings—and you at the center as protagonist in the tale of who you are. This is all a great, beautiful confabulation without which you could not function.

As you move through your day, you imagine a wide range of potential futures, potential situations outside your senses. When you read news articles and nonfiction books, you create fantasy worlds for situations that actually did happen. When you recall your past, you create it on the spot—a daydream part true and part fantasy that you believe down to the last detail. If you were to lie back and imagine yourself sailing around the world, seeing all the wonders of the planet from one port to the next, you could with varying levels of detail imagine the entire globe from Paris to India, from Cambodia to Kansas, but you know you haven't actually taken this trip. And there are severe brain disorders where sufferers cannot sort out their own confabulations:

- Patients with Korsakoff's syndrome have amnesia surrounding recent events but can recall their past. They make up stories to replace their recent memories and believe them instead of becoming confused. If you were to ask someone with Korsakoff's syndrome where they had been over the last few weeks, they might say they worked in the hospital's garage and need to get back to work when in reality they are patients receiving daily treatment in that same hospital.
- Anosognosia sufferers are paralyzed but won't admit it. They tell their doctors and loved ones they have severe ar-

thritis or need to watch their weight if asked to move their incapacitated arm to take a piece of candy. They lie, but they don't know they are lying. The deception is only directed inward. They truly believe the fiction.

- A person with Capgras delusion believes their close friends and family have been replaced by impostors. The part of the brain that provides an emotional response when you see someone you know stops functioning properly in those with this dysfunction. They recognize their loved ones, but don't feel the spark. They make up a story to explain their confusion and accept it entirely.

- Those with Cotard's syndrome believe they have died. Those with this affliction will assume themselves to be spirits in an afterlife and believe the delusion so strongly they sometimes die of starvation.

Psychologists have long assumed that you aren't aware of your higher cognitive processes, as Richard Nisbett and Timothy De-Camp Wilson at the University of Michigan suggested in their 1977 article for *Psychological Review*. In their paper they shot holes in the idea of introspection, saying you are rarely aware of the true stimuli that have led to your responses over the years, even from one day to the next. In one study, they write, subjects were asked to think of their mother's maiden name.

Go ahead. You try. What is your mother's maiden name?

The next question in the study was "How did you come up with that?"

So how did you?

You don't know. You just thought it. How your mind works is something you can never access, and although you often believe you understand your thoughts and actions, your emotions and motivations, much of the time you do not. The very act of looking inward is already several steps removed from the thoughts you are remembering. This, however, doesn't prevent you from assuming you really do know, you really can recall in full detail, and this is how narratives begin. This is how confabulation provides a framework from which to understand yourself.

As the psychologist George Miller once said, "It is the result of thinking, not the process of thinking, that appears spontaneously in consciousness." In other words, in many ways you are only reporting on what your mind has already produced instead of directing its performance. The flow of consciousness is one thing; the recollection of its course is another, yet you usually see them as the same. This is one of the oldest concepts in psychology and philosophy—phenomenology. It was one of the first debates among researchers over just how deep psychology could delve into the mind. Since the early 1900s, psychologists have wrestled with the conundrum of how, at a certain level, subjective experience can't be shared. For instance, what does red look like? What do tomatoes smell like? When you stub your toe, what does it feel like? What would you say if you had to explain any of these to someone who had never experienced them? How would you describe red to a person blind from birth or the scent of a fresh tomato to someone who had never smelled before?

These are qualia, the deepest you can tunnel down into your experience before you hit rock. Most everyone has seen red but can't explain what it is like to do so. Your explanations of experience can build up from qualia but can't go any lower. These are the ineffable building blocks of consciousness. You can explain them only in relation to other experiences, but you can never completely describe the experience of qualia to another person, or yourself.

There is more at work in your mind than you can access; beneath the rock there is more complexity to your thoughts and feelings than you can directly behold. For some behaviors, the antecedent is something old and evolved, a predilection passed down through thousands of generations of people like you trying to survive and thrive. You want to take a nap on a rainy afternoon because perhaps your ancestors sought shelter and safety in the same conditions. For other behaviors, the impetus may have come from something you simply didn't notice. You don't know why you feel like leaving in the middle of Thanksgiving dinner, but you come up with an explanation that seems to make sense at the time. Looking back, the explanation may change.

Philosopher Daniel Dennett calls seeing yourself in this way heterophenomenology. Basically, he suggests when you explain why you feel the way you do, or why you behaved as you did, to take it with a grain of salt, as if you were listening to someone tell you about their night out. When you listen to someone else tell a story, you expect some embellishment and you know they are only telling you how the events seemed to transpire to them. In the same way, you know how reality seems to be unfolding, how it seems to have unfolded in the past, but you should take your own perception with a grain of salt.

In the Miller and Nisbett paper, they cited many studies in which people were aware of their thoughts but not how they arrived at them. Despite this, subjects usually had no problem providing an explanation, an introspection, which failed to address the true cause. In one, two groups were given electric shocks while they performed memory tasks. Both groups were then asked to run through the tasks again after the experiment ended. One group was told the second set of shocks was important in the pursuit of understanding the human mind. The other group was told the new round of shocks was just being used to satisfy the scientist's curiosity. The second group then performed better on the memory tasks, because they had to come up with their own motivation for continuing, which was to believe the shocks didn't hurt. In their minds the shocks really didn't hurt as much as they did for the first group, at least they said as much when interviewed later.

In another study, two groups of people who said they were very afraid of snakes were shown slides of snakes while listening to what they believed was their heart rate. Occasionally one group would see a slide with the word "shock" printed on it. They were given a jolt of electricity when they saw this slide, and the researchers falsely increased the sound of the beating of their hearts in the monitor. When they later were asked to hold a snake, they were far more likely to give it a shot than the group who didn't see the shock slide and hear a fake increase in heart rate. They had convinced themselves they were more afraid of being shocked than of snakes and then used this introspection to truly be less afraid.

Nisbett and Miller set up their own study in a department store where they arranged nylon stockings side by side. When people came by, they asked them to say which of four items in a set was the best quality. Four-to-one, people chose the stocking on the right-hand side even though they were all identical. When the researchers asked why, people would comment on the texture or the color, but never the position. When asked if the order of the presentation influenced their choice, they assured the scientists it had nothing to do with it.

In these and many other studies the subjects never said they didn't know why they felt and acted as they did. Not knowing why didn't confuse them; they instead found justification for their thoughts, feelings, and actions and moved on, unaware of the machinery of their minds.

How do you separate fantasy from reality? How can you be sure the story of your life both from long ago and minute to minute is true? There is a pleasant vindication to be found when you accept that you can't. No one can, yet we persist and thrive. Who you think you are is sort of like a movie based on true events, which is not necessarily a bad thing. The details may be embellished, but the big picture, the general idea, is probably a good story worth hearing about.

3

Confirmation Bias

THE MISCONCEPTION: *Your opinions are the result of years of rational, objective analysis.*

THE TRUTH: *Your opinions are the result of years of paying attention to information that confirmed what you believed, while ignoring information that challenged your preconceived notions.*

Have you ever had a conversation in which some old movie was mentioned, something like *The Golden Child*, or maybe even something more obscure?

You laughed about it, quoted lines from it, wondered what happened to the actors you never saw again, and then you forgot about it.

Until . . .

You are flipping channels one night and all of the sudden you see *The Golden Child* is playing. Weird.

The next day you are reading a news story, and out of nowhere it mentions forgotten movies from the 1980s, and holy shit, there are three paragraphs about *The Golden Child*. You see a trailer that night at the theater for a new Eddie Murphy movie, and then you see a billboard on the street promoting Charlie Murphy doing stand-up in town, and then one of your friends sends you a link to a post at TMZ showing recent photos of the actress from *The Golden Child*.

What is happening here? Is the universe trying to tell you something?

No. This is how confirmation bias works.

Since the conversation with your friends, you've flipped channels plenty of times; you've walked past lots of billboards; you've seen dozens of stories about celebrities; you've been exposed to a handful of movie trailers.

The thing is, you disregarded all the other information, all the stuff unrelated to *The Golden Child*. Out of all the chaos, all the morsels of data, you noticed only the bits that called back to something sitting on top of your brain. A few weeks back, when Eddie Murphy and his Tibetan adventure were still submerged beneath a heap of pop culture at the bottom of your skull, you wouldn't have paid any special attention to references to it.

If you are thinking about buying a particular make of new car, you suddenly see people driving that car all over the roads. If you just ended a longtime relationship, every song you hear seems to be written about love. If you are having a baby, you start to see babies everywhere. Confirmation bias is seeing the world through a filter.

The examples above are a sort of passive version of the phenomenon. The real trouble begins when confirmation bias distorts your active pursuit of facts.

Punditry is an industry built on confirmation bias. Rush Limbaugh and Keith Olbermann, Glenn Beck and Arianna Huffington, Rachel Maddow and Ann Coulter—these people provide fuel for beliefs, they pre-filter the world to match existing worldviews.

If their filter is like your filter, you love them. If it isn't, you hate them. You watch them not for information, but for confirmation.

> Be careful. People like to be told what they already know. Remember that. They get uncomfortable when you tell them new things. New things . . . well, new things aren't what they expect. They like to know that, say, a dog will bite a man. That is what dogs do. They don't want to know that man bites a dog, because the world is not supposed to happen like that. In short, what people think they want is news, but what they really crave is olds . . . Not news but olds, telling people that what they think they already know is true.
>
> —TERRY PRATCHETT THROUGH THE CHARACTER
> LORD VETINARI FROM HIS *The Truth: a Novel of Discworld*

During the 2008 U.S. presidential election, researcher Valdis Krebs at orgnet.com analyzed purchasing trends on Amazon. People who already supported Obama were the same people buying books that painted him in a positive light. People who already disliked Obama were the ones buying books painting him in a negative light. Just as with pundits, people weren't buying books for the information, they were buying them for the confirmation. Krebs has researched purchasing trends on Amazon and the clustering habits of people on social networks for years, and his research shows what psychological research into confirmation bias predicts: you want to be right about how you see the world, so you seek out information that confirms your beliefs and avoid contradictory evidence and opinions.

Half a century of research has placed confirmation bias among the most dependable of mental stumbling blocks. Journalists looking to tell a certain story must avoid the tendency to ignore evidence to the contrary; scientists looking to prove a hypothesis must avoid designing experiments with little wiggle room for alternate outcomes. Without confirmation bias, conspiracy theories would fall apart. Did we really put a man on the moon? If you are looking for proof we didn't, you can find it.

In a 1979 University of Minnesota study by Mark Snyder and Nancy Cantor, people read about a week in the life of an imaginary woman named Jane. Throughout the week, Jane did things that showcased she could be extroverted in some situations and introverted in others. A few days passed. The subjects were asked to return. Researchers divided the people into groups and asked them to help decide if Jane would be suited for a particular job. One group was asked if she would be a good librarian; the other group was asked if she would be a good real estate agent. In the librarian group, people remembered Jane as an introvert. In the real estate group, they remembered her being an extrovert. After this, when each group was asked if she would be good at the other profession, people stuck with their original assessment, saying she wasn't suited for the other job. The study suggests even in your memories you fall prey to confirmation bias, recalling those things that support even recently-arrived-at beliefs and forgetting those things that contradict them.

An Ohio State study in 2009 showed people spend 36 percent more time reading an essay if that essay aligns with their opinions. Another study at Ohio State in 2009 showed subjects clips of the parody show *The Colbert Report,* and people who considered themselves politically conservative consistently reported "Colbert only pretends to be joking and genuinely meant what he said."

Over time, by never seeking the antithetical, through accumulating subscriptions to magazines, stacks of books, and hours of television, you can become so confident in your worldview that no one can dissuade you.

Remember, there's always someone out there willing to sell eyeballs to advertisers by offering a guaranteed audience of people looking for validation. Ask yourself if you are in that audience. In science, you move closer to the truth by seeking evidence to the contrary. Perhaps the same method should inform your opinions as well.

4

Hindsight Bias

THE MISCONCEPTION: *After you learn something new, you remember how you were once ignorant or wrong.*

THE TRUTH: *You often look back on the things you've just learned and assume you knew them or believed them all along.*

"I knew they were going to lose."

"That's exactly what I thought was going to happen."

"I saw this coming."

"That's just common sense."

"I had a feeling you might say that."

How many times have you said something similar and believed it?

Here's the thing: You tend to edit your memories so you don't seem like such a dimwit when things happen you couldn't have predicted. When you learn things you wish you had known all along, you go ahead and assume you *did* know them. This tendency is just part of being a person, and it is called the Hindsight Bias.

Take a look at the results of this study:

A recent study by researchers at Harvard shows as people grow older they tend to stick to old beliefs and find it difficult to accept conflicting information about topics they are already familiar with. The findings seem to suggest you can't teach an old dog new tricks.

Of course the study showed this. You've known this your whole life; it's common knowledge.

Consider this study:

A study out of the University of Alberta shows older people, with years of wisdom and a virtual library of facts from decades of exposure to media, find it much easier to finish a four-year degree ahead of time than an eighteen-year-old who has to contend with an unfinished, still-growing brain. The findings show you are never too old to learn.

Wait a second. That seems like common knowledge too.

So which is it—you can't teach an old dog new tricks, or you are never too old to learn?

Actually, I made both of these up. Neither one is a real study. (Using fake studies is a favorite way of researchers to demonstrate hindsight bias.) Both of them seemed probable because when you learn something new, you quickly redact your past so you can feel the comfort of always being right.

In 1986, Karl Teigen, now at the University of Oslo, did a study in which he asked students to evaluate proverbs. Teigen gave participants famous sayings to evaluate. When participants were given adages, like "You can't judge a book by its cover," they tended to agree with the wisdom. What would you say? Is it fair to say you can't judge a book by its cover? From experience, can you remember times when this was true? What about the expression "If it looks like a duck, swims like a duck, and quacks like a duck, then it probably is a duck?" Seems like common sense too, huh? So which is it?

In Teigen's study, most people agreed with all the proverbs he showed them, and then agreed once again when he read to them proverbs that stated opposing views. When he asked them to evaluate the phrase "Love is stronger than fear," they agreed with it. When he presented them the opposite, "Fear is stronger than love," they agreed with that too. He was trying to show how what you think is just common sense usually isn't. Often, when students and journalists and laypeople hear about the results of a scientific study, they agree with the findings and say, "Yeah, no shit." Teigen showed this is just hindsight bias at work.

You are always looking back at the person you used to be, always reconstructing the story of your life to better match the person you are today. You have needed to keep a tidy mind to navigate the world ever since you lived in jungles and on savannas. Cluttered minds got bogged down, and the bodies they controlled got eaten. Once you learn from your mistakes, or replace bad info with good, there isn't much use in retaining the garbage, so you delete it. This deletion of your old, incorrect assumptions de-clutters your mind. Sure, you are lying to yourself, but it's for a good cause. You take all you know about a topic, all you can conjure up on the spot, and construct a mental model.

Right before President Nixon left for China, a researcher asked people what they thought the chances were for certain things to happen on his trip. Later, once the trip was over, knowing the outcomes, people remembered their statistical assumptions as being far more accurate than they were. The same thing happened with people who felt that another terrorist attack was likely after 9/11. When no attack happened, these people recalled having made much lower estimates of the risk of another attack.

Hindsight bias is a close relative of the availability heuristic. You tend to believe anecdotes and individual sensational news stories are more representative of the big picture than they are. If you see lots of shark attacks in the news, you think, "Gosh, sharks are out of control." What you should think is "Gosh, the news loves to cover shark attacks." The availability heuristic shows you make decisions and think thoughts based on the information you have at hand, while ignoring all the other information that *might* be out there. You do the same thing with Hindsight Bias, by thinking thoughts and making decisions based on what you know now, not what you *used* to know.

Knowing hindsight bias exists should arm you with healthy skepticism when politicians and businessmen talk about their past decisions. Also, keep it in mind the next time you get into a debate online or an argument with a boyfriend or girlfriend, husband or wife—the other person really does think he or she was never wrong, and so do you.

5

The Texas Sharpshooter Fallacy

THE MISCONCEPTION: *You take randomness into account when determining cause and effect.*

THE TRUTH: *You tend to ignore random chance when the results seem meaningful or when you want a random event to have a meaningful cause.*

Abraham Lincoln and John F. Kennedy were both presidents of the United States, elected one hundred years apart. Both were shot and killed by assassins who were known by three names with fifteen letters, John Wilkes Booth and Lee Harvey Oswald, and neither killer would make it to trial. Spooky, huh? It gets better. Kennedy had a secretary named Lincoln. They were both killed on a Friday while sitting next to their wives, Lincoln in the Ford Theater, Kennedy in a Lincoln made by Ford. Both men were succeeded by a man named Johnson—Andrew for Lincoln and Lyndon for Kennedy. Andrew was born in 1808, Lyndon in 1908. What are the odds?

In 1898, Morgan Robertson wrote a novel titled *Futility*. Given that it was written fourteen years before the *Titanic* sank, eleven years before construction on the vessel even began, the similarities between the book and the real event are eerie. The novel describes a giant boat called the *Titan* which everyone considers unsinkable. It is the largest ever created, and inside, it seems like a luxury hotel—just like the as yet unbuilt *Titanic*. *Titan* had only twenty lifeboats, half of what it would need should the great ship sink. The *Titanic* had twenty-four, also half what it needed. In the book, the *Titan* hits an iceberg in April four hundred miles from Newfoundland. The *Titanic*, years later, would do the same in the same month in the same place. The *Titan* sinks, and more than half of the passengers die, just as with the *Titanic*. The number of people on board who die in the book and the number in the future accident are nearly identical. The similarities don't stop there. The fictional *Titan* and the real *Titanic* both had three propellers and two masts. Both had a capacity of three thousand people. Both hit the iceberg close to midnight. Did Robertson have a premonition? I mean, what are the odds?

In the 1500s, Nostradamus wrote:

B'tes farouches de faim fleuves tranner
Plus part du champ encore Hister sera,
En caige de fer le grand sera treisner,
Quand rien enfant de Germain observa.

This is often translated to:

Beasts wild with hunger will cross the rivers,
The greater part of the battle will be against Hister.
He will cause great men to be dragged in a cage of iron,
When the son of Germany obeys no law.

That's rather creepy, considering that it seems to describe a guy with a tiny mustache born about four hundred years later. Here is another prophecy:

Out of the deepest part of the west of Europe,
From poor people a young child shall be born,
Who with his tongue shall seduce many people,
His fame shall increase in the Eastern Kingdom.

Wow. Hister certainly sounds like Hitler, and that second quatrain seems to drive it home. Actually, many of Nostradamus's predictions are about a guy from Germania who wages a great war and dies mysteriously. What are the odds?

If any of this seems too amazing to be coincidence, too odd to be random, too similar to be chance, you are not so smart. Allow me to explain.

Say you go on a date, and the other person reveals he or she drives the same kind of car you do. It's a different color, but the same model. Well, that's sort of neat, but nothing amazing.

Let's say later on you learn your date's mom's name is the same as your mom's, and your mothers have the same birthday. Hold on a second. That's pretty cool. Maybe the hand of fate *is* pushing you toward the other person. Later still, you find out you both own the box set of *Monty Python's Flying Circus*, and you both grew up loving Rescue Rangers. You both love pizza, but hate rutabagas. This is meant to be, you think. You are made for each other.

But, take a step back. Now take another. How many people in the world own that model of car? You are both about the same age, so your mothers are too, and their names were probably common in their time. Since you and your date have similar backgrounds and grew up in the same decade, you probably share the same childhood TV shows. Everyone loves Monty Python. Everyone loves pizza. Many people hate rutabagas.

Looking at the factors from a distance, you can accept the reality of random chance. You are lulled by the signal. You forget about noise. With meaning, you overlook randomness, but meaning is a human construction. You have just committed the Texas sharpshooter fallacy.

The fallacy gets its name from imagining a cowboy shooting at a barn. Over time, the side of the barn becomes riddled with holes. In some places there are lots of them, in others there are few. If the cowboy later paints a bull's-eye over a spot where his bullet holes clustered together, it looks like he is pretty good with a gun. By painting a bull's-eye over a cluster of bullet holes, the cowboy places artificial order over natural random chance. If you have a human brain, you do this all of the time. Picking out clusters of coincidence is a predictable malfunction of normal human logic.

When you are dazzled by the idea of Nostradamus predicting Hitler, you ignore how he wrote almost one thousand ambiguous predictions, and most of them make no sense at all. He seems even less interesting when you find out Hister is the Latin name for the Danube River. When you marvel at the similarities between the *Titan* and the *Titanic*, you disregard that in the novel only thirteen people survived, and the ship sank right away, and the *Titan* had made many voyages, and it had sails. In the novel, one of the survivors fought a polar bear before being rescued. When you are befuddled by the Lincoln and Kennedy connections, you neglect to notice Kennedy was Catholic and Lincoln was born Baptist. Kennedy was killed with a rifle, Lincoln with a pistol. Kennedy was shot in Texas, Lincoln in Washington, D.C. Kennedy had lustrous auburn hair, while Lincoln wore a haberdasher's wet dream.

With all three examples there are thousands of differences, all of which you ignored, but when you draw the bull's-eye around the clusters, the similarities—whoa. If hindsight bias and confirmation bias had a baby, it would be the Texas sharpshooter fallacy.

When reality shows are filmed, the producers have hundreds of hours of footage. When they condense that footage into an hour, they paint a bull's-eye around a cluster of holes. They find a narrative in all the mundane moments, extracting the good bits and tossing aside the rest. This means they can create any orderly story they wish from their reserves of chaos. Was that one girl really a horrific bitch? Was that guy with the gelled hair and fake tan really that dumb? Unless you can pull back and see the entire barn, you'll never know.

The reach of the fallacy is far greater than reality shows, presidential trivia, and spooky coincidences. When you use the sharpshooter fallacy to determine cause from effect, it can harm people. One of the reasons scientists form a hypothesis and then try to disprove it with new research is to avoid the Texas sharpshooter fallacy. Epidemiologists are especially wary of it as they study the factors that lead to the spread of disease. If you look at a map of the United States with dots assigned to where cancer rates are highest, you will notice areas of clumping. It looks like you have a pretty good indication of where the groundwater must be poisoned, or where high-voltage power lines are bombarding people with damaging energy fields, or where cell phone towers are frying people's organs, or where nuclear bombs must have been tested. A map like that is a lot like the side of the sharpshooter's barn, and presuming there must be a cause for cancer clusters is the same as drawing bull's-eyes around them. More often than not, cancer clusters have no scary environmental cause. There are many agents at work. People who are related tend to live near one another. Old people tend to retire in the same areas. Eating, smoking, and exercise habits tend to be similar region to region. And, after all, one in three people will develop cancer in his or her lifetime. To accept that things like residential cancer clusters are often just coincidence is deeply unsatisfying. The powerlessness, the feeling you are defenseless to the whims of chance, can be assuaged by singling out an antagonist. Sometimes you need a bad guy, and the Texas sharpshooter fallacy is one way you can create one.

According to the Centers for Disease Control the number of autism cases among eight-year-olds increased 57 percent from 2002 to the 2006. Looking back over the last twenty years, the rate of autism has gone up 200 percent. Today, one in seventy male children has some form of autism spectrum disorder. It seemed absolutely nuts when those numbers were first released. Parents around the world panicked. Something must be causing autism numbers to rise, right? Early on, a bull's-eye was painted around vaccines because symptoms seemed to show up about the same time as kids were getting vaccinated. Once they had a target, a cluster, people failed to see all the other correlations. After years of research and millions of dollars, vaccines have been ruled out, but many refuse to accept the findings. Singling out vaccines while ignoring the millions of other factors is the same as noting the *Titan* hit an iceberg but omitting it had sails.

Lucky streaks at the casino, hot hands in basketball, a tornado sparing a church—these are all examples of humans finding meaning after the fact, after the odds are tallied and the numbers have moved on. You are ignoring the times you lost, the times the ball missed the basket, and all the homes the tornado blindly devoured.

In World War II, Londoners took notice when bombing raids consistently missed certain neighborhoods. People began to believe German spies lived in the spared buildings. They didn't. Analysis afterward by psychologists Daniel Kahneman and Amos Tversky showed the bombing strike patterns were random.

Anywhere people are searching for meaning, you will see the Texas sharpshooter fallacy. For many, the world loses luster when you accept the idea that random mutations can lead to eyeballs or random burn patterns on toast can look like a person's face.

If you were to shuffle a deck and draw out ten cards, the chances of the sequence you drew coming up are in the trillions, no matter what the cards are. If you drew out an ordered suit, it would be astonishing, but the chances are the same as any other set of ten cards. The meaning is a human construct.

Look outside. See that tree? The chances of it growing there on that spot, on this planet, circling this star, in this galaxy, among the billions of galaxies in the known universe, are so incredibly small it seems to have meaning, but that meaning is only a figment of your imagination. You are drawing a bull's-eye around a cluster on a vast barn. The odds of it being there are no less astronomical than the odds of it being in the patch of dirt beside it. The same is true if you looked out onto a desert and found a lizard, or into the sky and found a cloud, or into space and saw nothing but hydrogen atoms floating alone. There is a 100 percent chance something will be there, be anywhere, when you look; only the need for meaning changes how you feel about what you see.

To admit the messy slog of chaos, disorder, and random chance rules your life, rules the universe itself, is a painful conceit. You commit the Texas sharpshooter fallacy when you need a pattern to provide meaning, to console you, to lay blame. You mow your lawn, arrange your silverware, comb your hair. Whenever possible, you oppose the forces of entropy and thwart their relentless derangement. Your drive to do this is primal. You need order. Order makes it easier to be a person, to navigate this sloppy world. For ancient man, pattern recognition led to food and protected people from harm. You are able to read these words because your ancestors recognized patterns and changed their behavior to better acquire food and avoiding becoming it. Evolution has made us into beings looking for clusters where chance events have built up like sand into dunes.

Carl Sagan said in the vastness of space and the immensity of time it was a joy to share a planet and epoch with his wife. Even though he knew fate didn't put them together, it didn't take away the wonder he felt when he was with her.

You see patterns everywhere, but some of them are formed by chance and mean nothing. Against the noisy background of probability things are bound to line up from time to time for no reason at all. It's just how the math works out. Recognizing this is an important part of ignoring coincidences when they don't matter and realizing what has real meaning for you on this planet, in this epoch.

6

Procrastination

THE MISCONCEPTION: *You procrastinate because you are lazy and can't manage your time well.*

THE TRUTH: *Procrastination is fueled by weakness in the face of impulse and a failure to think about thinking.*

Netflix reveals something about your own behavior you should have noticed by now, something that keeps getting between you and the things you want to accomplish. If you have Netflix, especially if you stream it to your TV, you tend to gradually accumulate a cache of hundreds of films you think you'll watch one day.

Take a look at your queue. Why are there so damn many documentaries and dramatic epics collecting virtual dust in there? By now you could draw the cover art to *Dead Man Walking* from memory. Why do you keep passing over it?

Psychologists actually know the answer to this question, to why you keep adding movies you will never watch to your growing collection of future rentals, and it's the same reason you believe you will eventually do what's best for yourself in all the other parts of your life, but rarely do.

A study conducted in 1999 by Read, Loewenstein, and Kalyanaraman had people pick three movies out of a selection of twenty-four. Some were lowbrow, like *Sleepless in Seattle* or *Mrs. Doubtfire*. Some were highbrow, like *Schindler's List* or *The Piano*. In other words, it was a choice between movies that promised to be fun and forgettable and those that would be memorable but required more effort to absorb. After picking, the subjects had to watch one movie right away. They then had to watch another in two days and a third two days after that. Most people picked *Schindler's List* as one of their three. They knew it was a great movie because all of their friends said it was, and it had earned dozens of the highest awards. Most didn't, however, choose to watch it on the first day. Instead, people tended to pick lowbrow movies on the first day. Only 44 percent went for the heavier stuff first. The majority tended to pick comedies, like *The Mask,* or action flicks, like *Speed,* when they knew they had to watch their choice forthwith. Planning ahead, people picked highbrow movies 63 percent of the time for their second movie and 71 percent of the time for their third. When they ran the experiment again but told subjects they had to watch all three selections back-to-back, *Schindler's List* was thirteen times less likely to be chosen at all. The researchers had a hunch people would go for the junk food first, but plan healthy meals in the future.

Many studies over the years have shown you tend to have time-inconsistent preferences. When asked if you would rather have fruit or cake one week from now, you will usually say fruit. A week later, when the slice of German chocolate and the apple are offered, you are statistically more likely to go for the cake.

This is why your Netflix queue is full of great films you keep passing over for *Family Guy*. With Netflix, the choice of what to watch right now and what to watch later is like candy bars versus carrot sticks. When you are making plans, your better angels point to the nourishing choices, but in the moment you go for what tastes good.

This is sometimes called present bias—being unable to grasp that what you want will change over time, and what you want now isn't the same thing you will want later. Present bias explains why you buy lettuce and bananas only to throw them out later when you forget to eat them. This is why when you are a kid you wonder why adults don't own more toys. Present bias is why you've made the same resolution for the tenth year in a row, but this time you mean it. You are going to lose weight and forge a six-pack of abs so ripped you can deflect arrows.

You weigh yourself. You buy a workout DVD. You order a set of weights. One day you have the choice between going for a run or watching a movie, and you choose the movie. Another day you are out with friends and can choose a cheeseburger or a salad. You choose the cheeseburger. The slips become more frequent, but you keep saying you'll get around to it. You'll start again on Monday, which becomes a week from Monday. Your will succumbs to a death by a thousand cuts. By the time winter comes, it looks like you already know what your resolution will be the next year.

Procrastination manifests itself within every aspect of your life.

You wait until the last minute to buy Christmas presents. You put off seeing the dentist, or getting that thing checked out by the doctor, or filing your taxes. You forget to register to vote. You need to get an oil change. There is a pile of dishes getting higher in the kitchen. Shouldn't you wash clothes now so you don't have to waste a Sunday cleaning everything you own?

Perhaps the stakes are higher than choosing to play Angry Birds instead of doing sit-ups. You might have a deadline for a grant proposal, or a dissertation, or a book.

You'll get around to it. You'll start tomorrow. You'll take the time to learn a foreign language, to learn how to play an instrument. There's a growing list of books you will read one day.

Before you do though, maybe you should check your e-mail. You should head over to Facebook too, just to get it out of the way. A cup of coffee would probably get you going; it won't take long to go grab one. Maybe just a few episodes of that show you like.

You can try to fight it back. You can buy a daily planner and a to-do list application for your phone. You can write yourself notes and fill out schedules. You can become a productivity junkie surrounded by instruments to make life more efficient, but these tools alone will not help, because the problem isn't you are a bad manager of your time—you are a bad tactician in the war inside your brain.

Procrastination is such a pervasive element of the human experience there are more than 600 books for sale promising to snap you out of your bad habits, and this year alone 120 new books on the topic were published. Obviously this is a problem everyone admits to, so why is it so hard to defeat?

To explain, consider the power of marshmallows.

Walter Mischel conducted experiments at Stanford University throughout the late 1960s and early 1970s in which he and his researchers offered a bargain to children. The kids sat at a table in front of a bell and some treats. They could pick a pretzel, a cookie, or a giant marshmallow. They told the little boys and girls they could either eat the treat right away or wait a few minutes. If they waited, they would double their payoff and get two treats. If they couldn't wait, they had to ring the bell, after which the researcher would end the experiment.

Some made no attempt at self-control and just ate right away. Others stared intensely at the object of their desire until they gave in to temptation. Many writhed in agony, twisting their hands and feet while looking away. Some made silly noises. In the end, one third couldn't resist. What started as an experiment about delayed gratification has now, decades later, yielded a far more interesting set of revelations about metacognition—thinking about thinking.

Mischel has followed the lives of all his subjects through high school, college, and into adulthood, where they accumulated children, mortgages, and jobs. The revelation from this research is kids who were able to overcome their desire for short-term reward in favor of a better outcome later weren't smarter than the other kids, nor were they less gluttonous. They just had a better grasp of how to trick themselves into doing what was best for them. They watched the wall instead of looking at the food. They tapped their feet instead of smelling the confection. The wait was torture for all, but some knew it was going to be impossible to just sit there and stare at the delicious, gigantic marshmallow without giving in. The ones who were better at holding off their desire to snatch the marshmallow used that same power to squeeze more out of life. The ones who rang the bell quickly showed a higher incidence of behavioral problems. The ones who could hold out ended up with SAT scores that were on average more than two hundred points higher than scores for the ones who ate the marshmallow.

Thinking about thinking—this is the key. In the struggle between should versus want, some people have figured out something crucial: Want never goes away. Procrastination is all about choosing want over should because you don't have a plan for those times when you can expect to be tempted. You are really bad at predicting your future mental states. In addition, you are terrible at choosing between now and later. Later is a murky place where anything could go wrong.

If I were to offer you $50 now or $100 in a year, which would you take? Clearly, you'll take the $50 now. After all, who knows what could happen in a year, right? OK, so what if I instead offered you $50 in five years or $100 in six years? Nothing has changed other than adding a delay, but now it feels just as natural to wait for the $100. After all, you already have to wait a long time. A being of pure logic would think, *more is more,* and pick the higher amount every time, but you aren't a being of pure logic. Faced with two possible rewards, you are more likely to take the one that you can enjoy now over one you will enjoy later—even if the later reward is far greater. In the moment, rearranging the folders on your computer seems a lot more rewarding than some task due in a month which might cost you your job or your diploma, so you wait until the night before. If you considered which would be more valuable in a month—continuing to get your paycheck or having an immaculate desktop—you would pick the greater reward. The tendency to get more rational when you are forced to wait is called hyperbolic discounting, because your dismissal of the better payoff later diminishes over time and makes a nice slope on a graph.

Evolutionarily it makes sense to always go for the sure bet now; your ancestors didn't have to think about retirement or heart disease. Your brain evolved in a world where you probably wouldn't live to meet your grandchildren. The stupid monkey part of your brain wants to gobble up candy bars and go deeply into debt.

Hyperbolic discounting makes later an easy place to throw all the things you don't want to deal with, but you also overcommit to future plans for the same reason. You run out of time to get things done because you think in the future, that mysterious fantastical realm of possibilities, you'll have more free time than you do now.

One of the best ways to see how bad you are at coping with procrastination is to notice how you deal with deadlines. Let's imagine you are in a class where you must complete three research papers in three weeks, and the instructor is willing to allow you to set your own due dates. You can choose to turn in your papers once a week, or two in the first week and one in the second. You can turn them all in on the last day, or you can spread them out. You could even choose to turn in all three at the end of the first week and be done. It's up to you, but once you pick you have to stick with your choice. If you miss your deadlines, you get a big fat zero.

How would you pick? The most rational choice would be the last day for every paper. It gives you plenty of time to work hard on all three and turn in the best possible work. This seems like a wise choice, but you are not so smart.

The same choice was offered to a selection of students in a 2002 study conducted by Klaus Wertenbroch and Dan Ariely. They set up three classes, and each had three weeks to finish three papers. Class A had to turn in all three papers on the last day of class, Class B had to pick three different deadlines and stick to them, and Class C had to turn in one paper a week. Which class had the better grades? Class C, the one with three specific deadlines, did the best. Class B, which had to pick deadlines ahead of time but had complete freedom, did the second best, and the group whose only deadline was the last day, Class A, did the worst. Students who could pick any three deadlines tended to spread them out at about one week apart on their own. They knew they would procrastinate, so they set up zones in which they would be forced to perform. Still, overly optimistic outliers who either waited until the last minute or chose unrealistic goals pulled down the overall class grade. Students with no guidelines at all tended to put off their work until the last week for all three papers. The ones who had no choice and were forced to spread out their procrastination did the best because the outliers were eliminated. Those people who weren't honest with themselves about their own tendencies to put off their work or who were too confident didn't have a chance to fool themselves.

If you fail to believe you will procrastinate or become idealistic about how awesome you are at working hard and managing your time, you never develop a strategy for outmaneuvering your own weakness.

Procrastination is an impulse; it's buying candy at the checkout. Procrastination is also hyperbolic discounting, taking the sure thing in the present over the caliginous prospect someday far away. You must be adept at thinking about thinking to defeat yourself at procrastination. You must realize there is the you who sits there now reading this, and there is the you some time in the future who will be influenced by a different set of ideas and desires; a you for whom an alternate palette of brain functions will be available for painting reality.

The *now*-you may see the costs and rewards at stake when it comes time to choose studying for the test instead of going to the club, eating the salad instead of the cupcake, writing the article instead of playing the video game. The trick is to accept that the *now*-you will not be the person facing those choices, it will be the *future*-you—a person who can't be trusted. Future-you will give in, and then you'll go back to being now-you and feel weak and ashamed. Now-you must trick future-you into doing what is right for both parties. This is why food plans like Nutrisystem work for many people. Now-you commits to spending a lot of money on a giant box of food that future-you will have to deal with. People who get this concept use programs like Freedom, which disables Internet access on a computer for up to eight hours, a tool allowing now-you to make it impossible for future-you to sabotage your work.

Capable psychonauts who think about thinking, about states of mind, about set and setting, can get things done not because they have more willpower or drive, but because they know productivity is a game played against a childish primal human predilection for pleasure and novelty that can never be excised from the soul. Your effort is better spent outsmarting yourself than making empty promises through plugging dates into a calendar or setting deadlines for push-ups.

7

Normalcy Bias

THE MISCONCEPTION: *Your fight-or-flight instincts kick in and you panic when disaster strikes.*
THE TRUTH: *You often become abnormally calm and pretend everything is normal in a crisis.*

If you knew a horrific mile-wide force of nature was headed toward your home, what would you do? Would you call your loved ones? Would you head outside and look for the oncoming storm? Would you leap into a bathtub and cover yourself with a mattress?

No matter what you encounter in life, your first analysis of any situation is to see it in the context of what is normal for you and then compare and contrast the new information against what you know usually happens. Because of this, you have a tendency to interpret strange and alarming situations as if they were just part of business as usual.

For three days in 1999, a series of horrific tornadoes scrubbed clean the Oklahoma countryside. Among them was a monster force of nature later called the Bridge Creek–Moore F5. The F5 part of the name comes from the Enhanced Fujita Scale. It goes from EF1 to EF5 and measures the intensity of a twister. Less than 1 percent of tornadoes ever reach the top level. At 4, cars go airborne and whole houses are leveled. To reach level 5 on the Enhanced Fujita Scale, a tornado's winds must exceed 200 miles per hour. The winds in Bridge Creek–Moore reached 320. Warnings were issued thirteen minutes in advance, yet many people did nothing as the monster approached. They milled around and hoped the killer would spare them. They didn't attempt to run for safety. In the end, the beast destroyed 8,000 homes and killed 36 people. Many more would surely have perished if there had been no warning at all. For instance, a similar twister in 1925 killed 695. So, given there *was* a warning, why did some people not heed the call to action and seek shelter from the colossus?

The tendency to flounder in the face of danger is well understood and expected among tornado chasers and meteorologists. Tales of those who choose to ride out hurricanes and tornado-spewing storm clouds are common. Weather experts and emergency management workers know you can become enveloped in a blanket of calm when terror enters your heart. Psychologists refer to it as normalcy bias. First responders call it negative panic. This strange counterproductive tendency to forget self-preservation in the event of an emergency is often factored into fatality predictions in everything from ship sinkings to stadium evacuations. Disaster movies get it all wrong. When you and others are warned of danger, you don't evacuate immediately while screaming and flailing your arms.

In his book *Big Weather,* tornado chaser Mark Svenvold wrote about how contagious normalcy bias can be. He recalled how people often tried to convince him to chill out while fleeing from impending doom. He said even when tornado warnings were issued, people assumed it was someone else's problem. Stake-holding peers, he said, would try to shame him into denial so they could remain calm. They didn't want him deflating their attempts at feeling normal.

Normalcy bias flows into the brain no matter the scale of the problem. It will appear whether you have days and plenty of warning or are blindsided with only seconds between life and death.

Imagine you are in a Boeing 747 airplane as it touches down after a long flight. You hide a sigh of relief once the ground ceases to rush closer and you hear the landing gear chirp against the runway. You release the hand rests as the engines power down. You sense the bustle of four hundred people preparing to leave. The tedious process of taxiing to the terminal begins. You play back some of the moments on the giant plane, thinking how it was a pleasant flight with few bumps and nice people all around. You are already collecting your things and getting ready to remove your seat belt. You look out the window and try to make out something familiar in the fog. Without warning, shock waves of heat and pressure tear into your flesh. A terrible blast rattles your organs and tears at all corners of the plane. A noise like two trains colliding under your chin bursts eardrums up and down the aisles. An explosion tunnels through the spaces around you, filling every gap and crevice with streamers of flame surging down the aisles and over your head, under your feet. They recede just as quickly, leaving unbearable heat. Clumps of your hair crumple into ashes. Now all you hear is the crackle of fire.

Imagine you are sitting on this plane now. The top of the craft is gone and you can see the sky above you. Columns of flame are growing. Holes in the sides of the airliner lead to freedom. How would you react?

You probably think you would leap to your feet and yell, "Let's get the hell out of here!" If not this, then you might assume you would coil into a fetal position and freak out. Statistically, neither of these is likely. What you would probably do is far weirder.

In 1977, on an island in the Canaries called Tenerife, a series of mistakes led to two enormous 747 passenger planes colliding with each other as one attempted takeoff.

A Pan Am aircraft with 496 people on board was taxiing along the runway in dense fog when a Dutch KLM flight with 248 inside asked to be cleared for takeoff on the same airstrip. The fog was so thick the KLM crew couldn't see the other airplane, and both were invisible to the control tower. The crew misheard their instructions. Thinking they had just been given permission, they began to speed toward the other plane. Air traffic controllers tried to warn them, but radio interference garbled the messages. Too late, the captain of the KLM flight saw the other craft ahead of him. He pulled up hard, dragging the tail along the ground, but couldn't take flight. He screamed as half of the KLM aircraft smashed into the Pan Am at 160 miles per hour.

The KLM airplane bounced off the Pan Am jet, soared for five hundred feet, and then tumbled in a terrible jet fuel explosion. Everyone on board disintegrated. The fire was so intense it would burn until the next day.

Rescue crews spilled out onto the tarmac, but they didn't drive out to the Pan Am flight. Instead, they rushed to the flaming wreckage of the KLM plane. For twenty minutes, in the chaos, firefighters and emergency personnel thought they were dealing with only one problem and believed the flames peeking out from the fog in the distance were just more wreckage. The survivors on board the Pan Am flight would not be rescued. The engines were still running at full power because the pilot had attempted to turn at the last second, and the crew couldn't switch them off because the wires had been severed. The crash sheared away most of the top half of the 747. People lay in pieces from the impact. Flames spread through the carnage. A massive fire began to take over the plane. Smoke filled the fuselage. To live, people had to act quickly. They had to un-buckle, move through the chaos onto the intact wing, and then jump twenty feet onto wreckage. Escape was possible, but not all of the survivors would attempt it. Some bolted into action, unbuckled loved ones and strangers and pushed them out to safety. Others stayed put and were consumed. Soon after, the center fuel tank ex-ploded, killing all but the seventy people who had made their way outside.

According to Amanda Ripley's book, *The Unthinkable*, investi-gators later said the survivors of the initial impact had one minute before the fire took them. In that one minute, several dozen people who could have escaped failed to take action, failed to break free of paralysis.

Why did so many people flounder when seconds mattered?

Psychologist Daniel Johnson has rigorously studied this strange behavior. In his research he interviewed survivors of the Tenerife crash among many other disasters, including skyscraper fires and sinking ships, to better understand why some people flee when oth-ers do not.

In Johnson's interview with Paul and Floy Heck, both passen-gers on the Pan Am flight, they recalled not only their traveling companions sitting motionless as they hustled to find a way out, but dozens of others who also made no effort to stand as the Hecks raced past them.

In the first moments of the incident, right after the top of the plane was sliced open, Paul Heck looked over to his wife, Floy. She was motionless, frozen in place and unable to process what was happening. He screamed for her to follow him. They unbuckled, clasped hands, and he led her out of the plane as the smoke began to billow. Floy later realized she possibly could have saved those sitting in a stupor just by yelling for them to join her, but she too was in a daze, with no thoughts of escape as she blindly followed her husband. Years later, Floy Heck was interviewed by the *Orange County Register*. She told the reporter she remembered looking back just before leaping out of a gash in the wall. She saw her friend still in the seat next to where they had been sitting with her hands folded in her lap, her eyes glassed over. Her friend did not survive the fire.

In any perilous event, like a sinking ship or a towering inferno, a shooting rampage or a tornado, there is a chance you will become so overwhelmed by the perilous overflow of ambiguous information that you will do nothing at all. You will float away and leave a senseless statue in your place. You may even lie down. If no one comes to your aid, you will die.

John Leach, a psychologist at the University of Lancaster, also studies freezing under stress. He says about 75 percent of people find it impossible to reason during a catastrophic event or impending doom. On the edges, the 15 or so percent on either side of the bell curve react either with unimpaired, heightened awareness or blubbering, confused panic.

According to Johnson and Leach, the sort of people who survive are the sort of people who prepare for the worst and practice ahead of time. They've done the research, or built the shelter, or run the drills. They look for the exits and imagine what they will do. They were in a fire as a child or survived a typhoon. These people don't deliberate during calamity because they've already done the deliberation the other people around them are just now going through.

Normalcy bias is stalling during a crisis and pretending everything will continue to be as fine and predictable as it was before. Those who defeat it act when others don't. They move when others are considering whether or not they should.

As Johnson points out, the brain must go through a procedure before the body acts—cognition, perception, comprehension, decision, implementation, and *then* movement. There's no way to overclock this, but you can practice until these steps individually are no longer complex, and thus no longer take up valuable brain computation cycles. Johnson likens it to playing an instrument. If you've never played a C chord on a guitar, you have to think your way through it and awkwardly press down on the strings until you make a clumsy twang. With a few minutes of practice, you can strum without as much deliberation and create a more pleasant sound.

To be clear, normalcy bias isn't freezing at the first signs of danger like a rabbit who confronts a snake, which is a real behavior humans can succumb to. To suddenly stop moving and hope for the best is called fear bradycardia, and it is an automatic and involuntarily instinct. This is sometimes referred to as tonic immobility. Animals like gazelles will become motionless if they sense a predator is nearby in the hopes of tricking its motion-tracking abilities by blending into the background. Some animals go so far as to feign death in what is called thanatosis.

In 2005, researchers at the University of Rio de Janeiro were able to induce fear bradycardia in humans just by showing subjects photos of injured people. The participants' heart rates plummeted and their muscles stiffened immediately. To be sure, this sort of behavior happens in a disaster, but we are talking about something different with normalcy bias.

Much of your behavior is an attempt to lower anxiety. You know you aren't in any danger when everything is safe and expected. Normalcy bias is self-soothing through believing everything is just fine. If you can still engage in your normal habits, still see the world as if nothing bad is happening, then your anxiety stays put. Normalcy bias is a state of mind out of which you are attempting to make everything OK by believing it still is.

Normalcy bias is refusing to believe terrible events will include you even though you have every reason to think otherwise. The first thing you are likely to feel in the event of a disaster is the supreme need to feel safe and secure. When it becomes clear this is impossible, you drift into a daydream where it is.

Survivors of 9/11 say they remember gathering belongings before leaving offices and cubicles. They put on coats and called loved ones. They shut down their computers and had conversations. Even in their descent, most moved at a leisurely pace—no screaming or running. There was no need for anyone to say "Remain calm everyone," because they weren't freaking out. They were begging the world to return to normal by engaging in acts of normalcy.

To reduce the anxiety of impending doom, you first cling to what you know. You then mine others for information. You strike up dialogs with coworkers, friends, and family. You become glued to the television and the radio. You gather with others to trade what you know so far. Some believe this is what happened as the Bridge Creek–Moore F5 tornado approached, which caused some people not to seek shelter. All the tools of pattern recognition, all the routines you've become accustomed to are rendered useless in a horrific event. The emergency situation is too novel and ambiguous. You have a tendency to freeze not because panic has overwhelmed you but because normalcy has disappeared.

Ripley calls this moment when you freeze "reflexive incredulity." As your brain attempts to disseminate the data, your deepest desire is for everyone around you to assure you the bad thing isn't real. You wait for this to happen past the point when it becomes obvious it will not.

The holding pattern of normalcy bias continues until the ship lurches or the building shifts. You may remain placid until the tornado throws a car through your house or the hurricane snaps the power lines. If everyone else is milling around waiting for information, you will too.

Those who are deeply concerned with evacuation procedures—first responders, architects, stadium personnel, the travel industry—are aware of normalcy bias, and write about it in manuals and trade journals. In a 1985 paper published in the *International Journal of Mass Emergencies and Disasters,* sociologists Shunji Mikami and Ken'Ichi Ikeda at the University of Tokyo identified the steps you are likely to go through in a disaster. They said you have a tendency to first interpret the situation within the context of what you are familiar with and to greatly underestimate the severity. This is the moment, when seconds count, that normalcy bias costs lives. A predictable order of behaviors, they said, will then unfold. You will seek information from those you trust first and then move on to those nearby. Next, you'll try to contact your family if possible, and then you'll begin to prepare to evacuate or seek shelter. Finally, after all of this, you'll move. Mikami and Ikeda say you are more likely to dawdle if you fail to understand the seriousness of the situation and have never been exposed to advice about what to do or been in a similar circumstance. Even worse, you stall longer if you fall back on the old compare-and-contrast tendencies where you try to convince yourself the encroaching peril is not much different than what you are used to—normalcy bias.

They use a 1982 flood in Nagasaki as an example. Light flooding occurred there every year, and the residents assumed the heavy rainfall was part of a familiar routine. Soon, though, they realized the waters were getting higher and doing so faster than in years past. At 4:55 P.M., the government issued a flood warning. Still, some waited to see just how peculiar the flooding would be, how out of the ordinary. Only 13 percent of residents had evacuated by 9 P.M. In the end, 265 were killed.

When Hurricane Katrina bore down on my home in Mississippi, I remember going to the grocery store for food, water, and supplies and being shocked by the number of people who had only a few loaves of bread and couple of bottles of soda in their carts. I remember their frustration as they waited in line behind me with all my bottled water and canned goods. I told them, "Sorry, but you can never be too prepared." Their response? "I don't think it's going to be a big deal." I often wonder what those people did for the two weeks we were without electricity and the roads were impassable.

Normalcy bias is a proclivity you can't be rid of. Everyday life seems prosaic and mundane because you are wired to see it as such. If you weren't, you would never be able to handle the information overload. Think of moving into a new apartment or home, or buying a new car or cell phone. At first, you notice everything and spend hours adjusting settings or arranging furniture. After a while, you get used to the normalcy and let things go. You may even forget certain aspects of your new home until a visitor points them out to you and you rediscover them. You acclimate to your surroundings so you can notice when things go awry; otherwise life would be all noise and no signal.

Sometimes though, this habit of creating background static and then ignoring it gets in the way. Sometimes you see static when you shouldn't and yearn for normalcy when it cannot be found. Hurricanes and floods, for example, can be too big, slow, and abstract to startle you into action. You truly can't see them coming. The solution, according to Mikami, Ikeda, and other experts, is repetition on the part of those who can help, those who can see the danger better than you. If enough warnings are given and enough instructions are broadcast, then those things become the new normal, and you will spring into action.

Normalcy bias can be scaled up to larger events as well. Global climate change, peak oil, obesity epidemics, and stock market crashes are good examples of larger, more complex events in which people fail to act because it is difficult to imagine just how abnormal life could become if the predictions are true. Regular media overhyping and panic-building over issues like Y2K, swine flu, SARS, and the like help fuel normalcy bias on a global scale. Pundits on both sides of politics warn of crises that can be averted only by voting one way or the other. With so much crying wolf, it can be difficult to determine in the frenzied information landscape when to be alarmed, when it really is not a drill. The first instinct is to gauge how out of the norm the situation truly is and act only when the problem crosses a threshold past which it becomes impossible to ignore. Of course, this is often after it is too late to act.

8

Introspection

THE MISCONCEPTION: *You know why you like the things you like and feel the way you feel.*

THE TRUTH: *The origin of certain emotional states is unavailable to you, and when pressed to explain them, you will just make something up.*

Imagine a painting the world considers beautiful, something like *Starry Night* by Van Gogh. Now imagine you have to write an essay on why it is popular. Go ahead, think of a reasonable explanation. No, don't keep reading. Give it a shot. Explain why Van Gogh's work is great.

Is there a certain song you love, or a photograph? Perhaps there is a movie you keep returning to over the years, or a book. Go ahead and imagine one of those favorite things. Now, in one sentence, try to explain why you like it. Chances are, you will find it difficult to put into words, but if pressed you will probably be able to come up with something.

The problem is, according to research, your explanation is probably going to be total bullshit. Tim Wilson at the University of Virginia demonstrated this in 1990 with the Poster Test. He brought a group of students into a room and showed them a series of posters. The students were told they could take any one they wanted as a gift and keep it. He then brought in another group and told them the same thing, but this time they had to explain why they wanted the poster they each picked. Wilson then waited six months and asked the two groups what they thought of their choices. The first group, the ones who just got to grab a poster and leave, all loved their choice. The second group, the ones who had to write out why they were choosing one over the others, hated theirs. The first group, the grab-and-go people, usually picked a nice, fancy painting. The second group, the ones who had to explain their choice, usually picked an inspirational poster with a cat clinging to a rope.

According to Wilson, when you are faced with a decision in which you are forced to think about your rationale, you start to turn the volume in your emotional brain down and the volume in your logical brain up. You start creating a mental list of pros and cons that would never have been conjured up if you had gone with your gut. As Wilson noted in his research, "Forming preferences is akin to riding a bicycle; we can do it easily but cannot easily explain how."

Before Wilson's work, the general consensus was to see careful deliberation as good, but he showed how the act of introspection can sometimes lead you to make decisions that look good on virtual paper but leave you emotionally lacking. Wilson knew previous research at Kent State had shown that ruminations about your own depression tend to make you more depressed, but distraction leads to an improved mood. Sometimes, introspection is simply counterproductive. Research into introspection calls into question the entire industry of critical analysis of art—video games, music, film, poetry, literature—all of it. It also makes things like focus groups and market analysis seem less about the intrinsic quality of the things being judged and more about what the people doing the judging find to be plausible explanations of their own feelings. When you ask people why they do or do not like things, they must then translate something from a deep, emotional, primal part of their psyche into the language of the higher, logical, rational world of words and sentences and paragraphs. The problem here is those deeper recesses of the mind are perhaps inaccessible and unconscious. The things that are available to consciousness might not have much to do with your preferences. Later, when you attempt to justify your decisions or emotional attachments, you start worrying about what your explanation says about you as a person, further tainting the validity of your inner narrative.

In the Poster Test, most people truly preferred the nice painting to the inspirational cat, but they couldn't conjure up a rational explanation of why, at least not in a way that would make logical sense on paper. On the other hand, you can write all sorts of bullshit about a motivational poster. It has a stated and tangible purpose.

Wilson conducted another experiment in which people were shown two small photos of two different people and were asked which one was more attractive. They were then handed what they were told was a larger version of the photo they'd picked, but it was actually a picture of a completely different person. They were then asked why they'd chosen it. Each time, the person dutifully spun a yarn explaining his or her choice. The person had never seen the photo before, but that didn't make the task of explaining why he or she had preferred it in an imaginary past any more difficult.

Another of Wilson's experiments had subjects rate the quality of jam. He placed before them five varieties of jam which had previously been ranked by *Consumer Reports* as the first, eleventh, twenty-fourth, thirty-second, and forty-fourth best jams on the market. One group tasted and ranked how good they thought the jams were. The other group had to write out what they did and did not like about each one as they tasted it. As with the posters, the people who didn't have to explain themselves gravitated toward the same ones *Consumer Reports* said were best. The people forced to introspect rated the jams inconsistently and had varying preferences based on their explanations. Taste is difficult to quantify and put into words, so the explainers focused on other aspects like texture or color or viscosity. None of which in the end made much difference to the non-explainers.

Believing you understand your motivations and desires, your likes and dislikes, is called the introspection illusion. You believe you know yourself and why you are the way you are. You believe this knowledge tells you how you will act in all future situations. Research shows otherwise. Time after time, experiments show introspection is not the act of tapping into your innermost mental constructs but is instead a fabrication. You look at what you did, or how you felt, and you make up some sort of explanation that you can reasonably believe. If you have to tell others, you make up an explanation they can believe too. When it comes to explaining why you like the things you like, you are not so smart, and the very act of having to explain yourself can change your attitudes.

In this new era of Twitter and Facebook and blogs, just about everyone is broadcasting his or her love or hate of art. Just look at all the vitriol and praise being lobbed back and forth over *Avatar* or *Black Swan*. When *Titanic* earned its Oscars, some people were saying it might just be the greatest film ever made. Now it's considered good but schmaltzy, a well-made film but decidedly melodramatic. What will people think in a hundred years?

It would be wise to remember that many of the works we now consider classics were in their time critically panned. For instance, this is how one reviewer described *Moby Dick* in 1851:

> This is an ill-compounded mixture of romance and matter-of-fact. The idea of a connected and collected story has obviously visited and abandoned its writer again and again in the course of composition. The style of his tale is in places disfigured by mad (rather than bad) English; and its catastrophe is hastily, weakly, and obscurely managed. We have little more to say in reprobation or in recommendation of this absurd book. Mr. Melville has to thank himself only if his horrors and his heroics are flung aside by the general reader, as so much trash belonging to the worst school of Bedlam literature—since he seems not so much unable to learn as disdainful of learning the craft of an artist.
>
> —HENRY F. CHORLEY, IN *London Athenaeum*

This book is now considered one of a handful of great American novels and is held up as an example of the best pieces of literature ever written. Chances are, though, no one can truly explain why.

9

The Availability Heuristic

THE MISCONCEPTION: *With the advent of mass media, you understand how the world works based on statistics and facts culled from many examples.*

THE TRUTH: *You are far more likely to believe something is commonplace if you can find just one example of it, and you are far less likely to believe in something you've never seen or heard of before.*

Do more words begin with "r" or have "r" as the third letter?

Think about it for a second—rip, rat, revolver, reality, relinquish. If you are like most people, you think there are more that begin with "r"—but you're wrong. More words in the English language have the letter in the third position than in the first—car, bar, farce, market, dart. It is much easier to believe the first option because it takes more concentration to think of words with "r" in the third position. Try it.

If someone you know gets sick from taking a flu shot, you will be less likely to get one even if it is statistically safe. In fact, if you see a story on the news about someone dying from the flu shot, that one isolated case could be enough to keep you away from the vaccine forever. On the other hand, if you hear a news story about how eating sausage leads to anal cancer, you will be skeptical, because it has never happened to anyone you know, and sausage, after all, is delicious. The tendency to react more rapidly and to a greater degree when considering information you are familiar with is called the availability heuristic.

The human mind is generated by a brain that was formed under far different circumstances than the modern world offers up on a daily basis. Over the last few million years, much of our time was spent with fewer than 150 people, and what we knew about the world was based on examples from our daily lives. Mass media, statistical data, scientific findings—these things are not digested as easily as something you've seen with your own eyes. The old adage "I'll believe it when I see it" is the availability heuristic at work.

Politicians use this all the time. Whenever you hear a story that begins with "I met a mother of two in Michigan who lost her job because of a lack of funding for . . ." or something similar, the politician hopes the anecdote will sway your opinion. He or she is betting that the availability heuristic will influence you to assume that this one example is indicative of a much larger group of people.

It's simply easier to believe something if you are presented with examples than it is to accept something presented in numbers or abstract facts.

School shootings were considered to be a dangerous new phenomenon after Columbine. That event fundamentally changed the way kids are treated in American schools, and hundreds of books, seminars, and films have been produced in an attempt to understand the sudden epidemic. The truth, however, was that there hadn't been an increase in school shootings. According to research by Barry Glassner, author of *The Culture of Fear*, during the time when Columbine and other school shootings got major media attention, violence in schools was down over 30 percent. Kids were more likely to get shot in school before Columbine, but the media during that time hadn't given you many examples. A typical schoolkid is three times more likely to get hit by lightning than to be shot by a classmate, yet schools continue to guard against it as if it could happen at any second.

Amos Tverksy and Daniel Kahneman pinpointed the availability heuristic, in their 1973 research. Their subjects had to listen to a tape recording of names being said aloud that included nineteen famous men and twenty that the subjects had never heard before. They repeated the study with names of women as well. After they heard the names, subjects had to either recall as many names as they could or identify them from a word bank. About 66 percent of the people recalled famous people more often than the unfamiliar names, and 80 percent said the lists contained more famous names than non-famous. The word test about how often "r" is in the third position was Tversky and Kahneman's idea too. In both studies they showed the more available a bit of information is, the faster you process it. The faster you process it, the more you believe it and the less likely you become to consider other bits of info.

When you buy a lottery ticket, you imagine yourself winning like those people on television who get suddenly famous when their numbers are chosen, because people who don't win don't get interviewed. You are far more likely to die in a car crash on the way to buy the ticket than you are to win, but this information isn't as available. You don't think in statistics, you think in examples, in stories. When it comes to buying lottery tickets, fearing the West Nile virus, looking for child molesters, and so on, you use the availability heuristic first and the facts second. You decide the likelihood of a future event on how easily you can imagine it, and if you've been bombarded by reports or have filled your head with fears, those images will overshadow new information that might contradict your beliefs.

10

The Bystander Effect

THE MISCONCEPTION: *When someone is hurt, people rush to their aid.*

THE TRUTH: *The more people who witness a person in distress, the less likely it is that any one person will help.*

If your car were to break down and your cell phone had no service, where do you think you would have a better chance of getting help—a country road or a busy street? To be sure, more people will see you on a busy street. On the country road, you might have to wait a long time before someone comes by. So which one?

Studies show you have a better chance on the country road. Why?

Have you ever seen someone broken down on the side of the road and thought, "I could help them, but I'm sure someone will be along." Everyone thinks that. And no one stops. This is called the bystander effect.

In 1968, Eleanor Bradley fell and broke her leg in a busy department store. For forty minutes, people just stepped over and around her until one man finally stopped to see what was wrong. In 2000, a group of young men attacked sixty women at a Central Park parade in New York City. Thousands of people looked on. No one used a cell phone to call police. The culprit in both cases was the bystander effect. In a crowd, your inclination to rush to someone's aid fades, as if diluted by the potential of the group. Everyone thinks someone is going to eventually do something, but with everyone waiting together, no one does.

The most famous illustration of this phenomenon is the story of Kitty Genovese. According to a newspaper article in 1964, she was stabbed by an attacker at 3 A.M. in a parking lot in front of her New York City apartment complex. The attacker ran away when she screamed for help, but not one of the thirty-eight witnesses came to her rescue. The story goes on to say the attacker returned over and over for thirty minutes while people watched on from surrounding apartment windows as he stabbed her. The story has since been thoroughly debunked, a case of sensational reporting, but at the time it was written it led to intense interest in the phenomenon from psychologists. Social psychologists started studying the bystander effect soon after the story went viral, and they determined that the more people present when a person needs emergency help, the less likely it is any one of them will lend a hand.

In 1970, psychologists Bibb Latane and John Darley created an experiment in which they would drop pencils or coins. Sometimes they would be in a group, sometimes with one other person. They did this six thousand times. The results? They got help 20 percent of the time in a group, 40 percent of the time with one other person. They decided to up the stakes, and in their next experiment they had someone fill out a questionnaire. After a few minutes, smoke would start to fill the room, billowing in from a wall vent. They ran two versions of the experiment. In one, the person was alone; in the other, two other people were also filling out the questionnaire. When alone, people took about five seconds to get up and freak out. Within groups people took an average of 20 seconds to notice. When alone, the subject would go inspect the smoke and then leave the room to tell the experimenter he or she thought something was wrong. When in a group, people just sat there looking at one another until the smoke was so thick they couldn't see the questionnaire. Only three people in eight runs of the group experiment left the room, and they took an average of six minutes to get up.

The findings suggest the fear of embarrassment plays into group dynamics. You see the smoke, but you don't want to look like a fool, so you glance over at the other person to see what they are doing. The other person is thinking the same thing. Neither of you react, so neither of you becomes alarmed. The third person sees two people acting like everything is OK, so that third person is even less likely to freak out. Everyone is influencing every other person's perception of reality thanks to another behavior called the illusion of transparency. You tend to think other people can tell what you are thinking and feeling just by looking at you. You think the other people can tell you are really worried about the smoke, but they can't. They think the same thing. No one freaks out. This leads to pluralistic ignorance—a situation where everyone is thinking the same thing but believes he or she is the only person who thinks it. After the smoke-filled room experiment, all the participants reported they were freaking out on the inside, but since no one else seemed alarmed, they assumed it must just be their own anxiety.

The researchers decided to up the ante once more. This time, they had people fill out a questionnaire while the experimenter, a woman, shouted in the other room about how she had injured her leg. When alone, 70 percent of people left the room to check on her.

When in a group, 40 percent checked. If you were to walk along a bridge and see someone in the water screaming for help, you would feel a much greater urge to leap in and pull them to safety than you would if you were part of a crowd. When it's just you, all the responsibility to help is yours. The bystander effect gets stronger when you think the person who needs help is being harmed by someone that person knows. Lance Shotland and Margaret Straw showed in a 1978 experiment when people saw two actors, a man and a woman, pretending to physically fight, they often wouldn't intervene if the woman shouted, "I don't know why I ever married you!" People helped 65 percent of the time if she instead shouted, "I don't know you!" Many other studies have shown it takes only one person to help for others to join in. Whether it is to donate blood, assist someone in changing a tire, drop money into a performer's coffers, or stop a fight—people rush to help once they see another person leading by example.

One final, awesome example is the Good Samaritan experiment. Darley and Batson in 1973 got a group of Princeton Theological Seminary students together and told them to prepare a speech on the parable of the Good Samaritan from the Bible. The point of the parable is to stop and help people in need. In the Gospel of Luke, Jesus tells his disciples about a traveler who is beaten and robbed then left to die along a road. A priest and another man walk past him, but a Samaritan stops to help even though the man is Jewish and Samaritans weren't in the habit of helping out Jews. After filling out some questionnaires, with the story fresh in their minds, some groups were told they were late to give the speech in a nearby building. In other groups the subjects were told they had plenty of time. Along their path to the other building an actor was slumped over and groaning, pretending to be sick and in need of help. Of the seminary students who had plenty of time, about 60 percent stopped and helped. The ones in a rush? Ten percent helped, and some even stepped over the actor on their way.

So the takeaway here is to remember you are not so smart when it comes to helping people. In a crowded room, or a public street, you can expect people to freeze up and look around at one another.

Knowing that, you should always be the first person to break away from the pack and offer help—or attempt escape—because you can be certain no one else will.

The Dunning-Kruger Effect

THE MISCONCEPTION: *You can predict how well you would perform in any situation.*

THE TRUTH: *You are generally pretty bad at estimating your competence and the difficulty of complex tasks.*

Imagine you are very good at a particular game. Pick anything—chess, *Street Fighter*, poker—doesn't matter. You play this game with friends all the time, and you always win. You get so good at it, you start to think you could win a tournament. You get online and find where the next regional tournament is; you pay the entrance fee and get your ass handed to you in the first round. It turns out, you are not so smart. All this time, you thought you were among the best of the best, but you were really just an amateur. This is the Dunning-Kruger effect, and it's a basic element of human nature.

Think of all the YouTube stars over the last few years—the people poorly twirling weapons and singing off-key. These performances are terrible, and not in a self-aware, ironic way. No, they are genuinely awful, and you wonder why someone would put themselves on a worldwide stage in such an embarrassing way. The thing is, they don't imagine the worldwide audience as being more so-phisticated than the small audience of friends, family, and peers they usually stand before. As the philosopher Bertrand Russell once said, "In the modern world the stupid are cocksure while the intel-ligent are full of doubt."

The Dunning-Kruger effect is what makes *America's Got Talent* and *American Idol* possible. At the local karaoke bar you might be the best singer in the room. Up against the entire country? Not so much.

Have you ever wondered why people with advanced degrees in climate science or biology don't get online and debate global warm-ing or evolution? The less you know about a subject, the less you believe there is to know in total. Only once you have some experi-ence do you start to recognize the breadth and depth you have yet to plunder.

Of course, these are generalities. The economist Robin Hanson noted in 2008 that the Dunning-Kruger effect becomes a popular catchphrase near election time because it helps to paint opponents as being morons.

The actual research that coined the term was performed by Jus-tin Kruger and David Dunning in experiments at Cornell around 1999. They had students take humor and logic tests and then report how well they thought they had scored. Some people accurately predicted their own skill levels. Some knew they sucked at humor, and they were right. Others had a hunch they were better at telling jokes than most and had this belief confirmed. So sometimes people who are really good at something are well aware and can accurately predict their scores, but not always. Overall, the study showed you are not very good at estimating your own competence.

More recent studies have attempted to refute the absolute black-

and-white predictions of Dunning-Kruger—that the unskilled are the least aware of it. A study by Burson, Larrick, and Klayman in 2006 showed that "on easy tasks, where there is a positive bias, the best performers are also the most accurate in estimating their standing, but on difficult tasks, where there is a negative bias, the worst performers are the most accurate."

So the Dunning-Kruger effect isn't always influencing you to think that you are awesome when you are actually mediocre. It breaks down like this: The more skilled you are, the more practice you've put in, the more experience you have, the better you can compare yourself to others. As you strive to improve, you begin to better understand where you need work. You start to see the complexity and nuance; you discover masters of your craft and compare yourself to them and see where you are lacking. On the other hand, the less skilled you are, the less practice you've put in, and the fewer experiences you have, the worse you are at comparing yourself to others on certain tasks. Your peers don't call you out because they know as little as you do, or they don't want to hurt your feelings. Your narrow advantage over novices leads you to think you are the shit. Charles Darwin said it best: "Ignorance more frequently begets confidence than does knowledge." Whether it's playing guitar or writing short stories or telling jokes or taking photos—whatever— amateurs are far more likely to think they are experts than actual experts are. Education is as much about learning what you don't know as it is about adding to what you do.

The recent explosion of reality programming is a great example of the Dunning-Kruger effect. A whole industry of assholes is making a living off of making attractive yet untalented people believe they are actually genius auteurs. The bubble around reality stars is so thick, they may never escape it. At some point, the audience is in on the joke—yet the people in the center of the tragedy are often completely unaware.

As someone moves from novice to amateur to expert to master, the lines between each stage are difficult to recognize. The farther ahead you get, the longer it takes to progress. Yet the time it takes to go from novice to amateur feels rapid, and that's where the Dunning-Kruger effect strikes. You think the same amount of practice will move you from amateur to expert, but it won't.

Everyone experiences the Dunning-Kruger effect from time to time. Being honest with yourself and recognizing all your faults and weaknesses is not a pleasant way to live. Feeling inadequate or incompetent is paralyzing—you have to plow through those emotions to get out of bed. Seen along a spectrum, Dunning-Kruger is on the opposite end from depression with its crippling insecurity.

Don't let the Dunning-Kruger effect cast its shadow over you. If you want to be great at something, you have to practice, and then you have to sample the work of people who have been doing it for their whole lives. Compare and contrast and eat some humble pie.

12

Apophenia

THE MISCONCEPTION: *Some coincidences are so miraculous, they must have meaning.*

THE TRUTH: *Coincidences are a routine part of life, even the seemingly miraculous ones. Any meaning applied to them comes from your mind.*

Screenwriters and novelists have discovered over the years a number of tropes that you tend to understand without much explanation, plots that satisfy the mind of every viewer or reader.

Every story needs a strong protagonist with whom you can identify. If they are down on their luck or recently fell from grace, you see them as being approachable. If they are plucky and face great odds, again, you root for them without having to think about it. Early on, the protagonist will save someone without having to, and you start to like him or her. On the other side, you need a dastardly antagonist who harms someone for no reason, a person who ignores the rules and wants only to satisfy him- or herself no matter the cost. The hero or heroine leaves his or her normal world and enters into a new life full of adventure. Just when it seems as though the protagonist will fail, he or she overcomes whatever has been in the way, in order to defeat the antagonist, sometimes even saving the world in the process. When the hero or heroine returns to home, he or she has been changed for the better. If the story is a tragedy, the protagonist ends up worse off than when the story began.

Joseph Campbell made it his life's work to identify the common mythology in all humans, the stories you and everyone else know in your hearts. He called the outline above the hero's journey, and if you think about all the movies and books you've digested over the years, you will recognize almost every story is some variation of this tale. From folklore and theater, to modern cinema and video games, the hero's journey is a monomyth that plugs into your mind like a key into a lock.

You love to watch highly paid actors play professional make-believe because you naturally think in images and stories, in narratives that unfold with characters who fill up your world. Math, science, and logic are much harder to contemplate than social situations. You are keenly aware of what role you play and who is on the stage, the story of your life. Just as with television and film, your memory tends to delete the boring parts and focus on the highlights—the plot points.

A certain kind of story, a mystery, plays on a type of narrative you often believe to be unfolding in the real world. In a mystery like *The Da Vinci Code,* or in a television series like *Lost,* where mysterious happenings are at the center of the plot, clues pop up that turn out to be connected in some strange way. You can't help but be intrigued by the patterns slowly coalescing. It drives you crazy. You find yourself compelled to keep turning the page or popping in the next disc to see what happens, to see how everything connects in the end.

When you do this in the real world, it is called apophenia. Apophenia is an umbrella term that encompasses other phenomena, like the Texas sharpshooter fallacy and pareidolia. When you commit the Texas sharpshooter fallacy, you draw a circle around a series of random events and decide there is some meaning in the chaos that isn't really there. In pareidolia, you see shapes like clouds or tree limbs as people or faces. Apophenia is refusing to believe in clutter and noise, in coincidence and chance.

Apophenia most often appears in your life when you experience synchronicity. Small moments of synchronicity seem meaningful even when you know they can't be. If the date lines up in an interesting way, like say 8/9/10, people talk about it. You can't just ignore it when something that should be random sorts itself out and becomes orderly. The clock reads 11:11 P.M. The next time you look, it reads 12:12 A.M. A brief sense of wonder turns your head askew, and then you move on. Synchronicity may show up in bigger ways as well. If you had a dream about a terrible flood and then turned on the morning news to see a flood had washed away the homes of hundreds of people in a distant place, it would be hard not to feel a chill run down your spine.

Apophenia becomes an issue only when you decide coincidences and random sorting are more than the occasional signal rising from the noise. You might think deaths always come in threes when deaths are a constant part of life. You might find it amazing you share the same birthday as a dozen of your favorite celebrities, even though at any given time you share your birthday with about 16 million people. You might think the number 23 has some special power because it appears so often, when it doesn't appear any more than other numbers. Maybe you gamble all night, convinced you are seeing patterns in the cards or meaning in the wheels of the slot machine, yet the odds never change. You might see a person who wins the lottery three times in a row as having an extra helping of magical luck, but multiple lottery winners are actually rather common.

When you connect the dots in your life in a way that tells a story, and then you interpret the story to have a special meaning, this is true apophenia. Say you are crossing the street when a homeless man grabs your shirt and pulls you out of traffic just as a motorcycle goes screaming by. You offer to give him money in appreciation for saving your life, and he refuses. The next day you read in the newspaper about the rise in homelessness in your city. A week later, you are searching online for a new job and see a position is open for a social worker in a city you've always wanted to live in. You might think, in the story of your life, these are all scenes leading up to your destiny as a champion of the downtrodden. You quit your job, move far away, and pay it forward. In this way, you can see apophenia isn't always a bad thing. You need a sense of meaning to get out of bed, to push forward against the grain. Just remember that meaning comes only from within.

Your mind is preorganized to notice order, even when the order is defined by your culture and not your synapses. The ancient Greeks and Babylonians believed numbers held special sacred meanings, and they attached numerical values to all aspects of humanity. The early Christians were fond of doing the same, especially (cf. the number three and the Trinity). In all religions and cultures, certain numbers are occasionally promoted above the others as having special significance. Once this happens, apophenia causes people to notice them more than usual. In general, you prefer nice round numbers that correspond to the decimal system you've grown accustomed to using. When you have a choice, apophenia influences you to sort items into groups that have meaning, like ten, fifty, one hundred, and so on. As a society, currency notes are influenced by the same affection for pleasing numerals.

The law of truly large numbers is something skeptics like to point out when apophenia strikes. The law says in a large sample of occurrences, many coincidences will emerge. On a planet with close to 7 billion people, there is a lot of opportunity for flukes. When people notice coincidences, they remember them and tell others. Sometimes they make their way into the news. When coincidences don't happen, no one cares. You end up with an echo chamber of tales where stories of coincidence have no competition.

J. E. Littlewood, a mathematician at Cambridge University, wrote about the law of truly large numbers in his 1986 book, *Littlewood's Miscellany*. He said the average person is alert for about eight hours every day, and something happens to the average person about once a second. At this rate, you will experience 1 million events every thirty-five days. This means when you say the chances of something happening are one in a million, it also means about once a month. The monthly miracle is called Littlewood's Law.

More often than not, apophenia is the result of the most dependable of all delusions—the confirmation bias. You see what you want to see and ignore the rest. When what you want to see is something meaningful, you ignore all the things in the story of your life that are meaningless. Apophenia isn't just seeing order in chaos, it is believing you were destined to see it. It is believing miracles are so rare you should stand up and take notice when they occur, so you can decode their meaning. Mathematically speaking, though, there is a miracle happening every time you turn a page of this book.

13

Brand Loyalty

THE MISCONCEPTION: *You prefer the things you own over the things you don't because you made rational choices when you bought them.*

THE TRUTH: *You prefer the things you own because you rationalize your past choices to protect your sense of self.*

The Internet changed the way people argue.

Check any comment system, forum, or message board and you will find people going at it, debating why their chosen product is better than the other guy's.

Mac vs. PC, PS3 vs. Xbox 360, iPhone vs. Android—it goes on and on.

Usually, these arguments are between men, because men will defend their ego no matter how slight the insult. These are also usually about geeky things that cost lots of money, because these battles take place on the Internet, where tech-savvy people get rowdy, and the more expensive a purchase, the greater the loyalty to it.

In the world of Web site comment sections, rabid fans are often called fanboys. It is Internet slang for obsessive fandom. The term originated at a comic book convention in 1973 as the title of a fan-made magazine about Marvel comics, but in recent years it mutated into a soft insult that can be applied to anyone who goes out of his way to tell others about his love for . . . stuff. When someone writes a dozen paragraphs online defending his favorite thing or slandering a competitor, he is quickly branded as a fanboy. Fanboyism isn't anything new, it's just a component of branding, which is something marketers and advertisers have known about since Quaker Oats created a friendly logo to go on their burlap sacks.

There was, of course, no friendly Quaker family making the oats back in 1877. The company wanted people to associate the trustworthiness and honesty of Quakers with their product. It worked.

This was one of the first attempts to create brand loyalty—that nebulous emotional connection people have with certain companies, which turns them into defenders and advocates for corporations who don't give a shit.

In experiments at Baylor University where people were given Coke and Pepsi in unmarked cups and then hooked up to a brain scanner, the device clearly showed a certain number of them preferred Pepsi while tasting it. When those people were told they were drinking Pepsi, a fraction of them, the ones who had enjoyed Coke all their lives, did something unexpected. The scanner showed their brains scrambling the pleasure signals, dampening them. They then told the experimenter afterward they had preferred Coke in the taste tests.

They lied, but in their subjective experience of the situation, they didn't. They really did feel like they preferred Coke after it was all over, and they altered their memories to match their emotions. They had been branded somewhere in the past and were loyal to Coke. Even if they actually enjoyed Pepsi more, huge mental constructs prevented them from admitting it, even to themselves.

Add this sort of loyalty to something expensive, or a hobby that demands a large investment of time and money, and you get a fanboy. Fanboys defend their favorite stuff and ridicule the competition, ignoring facts if they contradict their emotional connection.

So what creates this emotional connection to stuff and the companies who make doodads?

Choice.

Those people who have no choice but to buy certain products, like toilet paper and gasoline, are called "hostages" by marketers and advertising agencies. Since they can't choose to own or not to own the product, they are far less likely to care if one version of toilet paper is better than another, or one gas station's fuel is made by Shell or Chevron.

On the other hand, if the product is unnecessary, like an iPad, there is a great chance the customer will become a fanboy because he had to choose to spend a big chunk of money on it. It's the choosing of one thing over another that leads to narratives about why you did it, which usually tie in to your self-image.

Branding builds on this by giving you the option to create the person you think you are through choosing to align yourself with the mystique of certain products.

Apple advertising, for instance, doesn't mention how good their computers are. Instead, they give you examples of the sort of people who purchase those computers. The idea is to encourage you to say, *Yeah, I'm not some stuffy, conservative nerd. I have taste and talent and took art classes in college.*

Are Apple computers better than Microsoft-based computers?

Is one better than the other when looked at empirically, based on data and analysis and testing and objective comparisons?

It doesn't matter, because those considerations come after a person has begun to see him- or herself as the sort of person who would own one. If you see yourself as the kind of person who owns Apple computers, or who drives hybrids, or who smokes Camels, you've been branded. And once a person is branded, that person will defend the brand by finding flaws in the alternative choice and pointing out benefits in his or her own.

There are a number of cognitive biases that converge to create this behavior.

The endowment effect pops up when you feel like the things you own are superior to the things you do not.

Psychologists demonstrate this by asking a group of people how much they think a water bottle is worth. The group will agree to an amount around $5, and then someone in the group will be given the bottle for free.

Then, after an hour, they ask the person how much they would be willing to sell the bottle back to the experimenter for. They usually ask for more money, like $8. Ownership adds special emotional value to things, even if those things were free.

Another bias is the sunk cost fallacy. This is when you've spent money on something you don't want to own or don't want to do and can't get it back. For instance, you might pay too much for some take-out food that really sucks, but you eat it anyway, or you sit through a movie even after you realize it's terrible.

Sunk cost can creep up on you too. Maybe you've been a subscriber to something for a long time and you realize it costs too much, but you don't end your subscription because of all the money you've invested in the service so far. Is Blockbuster better than Netflix, or TiVo better than a generic DVR? If you've spent a lot of money on subscription fees, you might be unwilling to switch to alternatives because you feel invested in the brand.

These biases feed into the big daddy of behaviors that are responsible for branding, fanboyism, and Internet arguments about why the thing you own is better than the thing the other guy owns—choice supportive bias.

It works like this: You have several options for, say, a new television. Before you make a choice, you tend to compare and contrast all the different qualities of all the televisions on the market. Which is better, Samsung or Sony, plasma or LCD, 1080p or 1080i—ugh, so many variables! You eventually settle on one option, and after you make your decision you then look back and rationalize your actions by believing your television was the best of all the televisions you could have picked.

In retail, this is a well-understood phenomenon, and to prevent buyer's remorse they try not to overwhelm you with choice. Studies show that if you have only a handful of options at the point of purchase, you will be less likely to fret about your decision afterward.

It's purely emotional, the moment you pick. People with brain damage to their emotional centers who have been rendered into Spock-like beings of pure logic find it impossible to decide things as simple as which brand of cereal to buy. They stand transfixed in the aisle, contemplating every element of their potential decision—the calories, the shapes, the net weight—everything. They can't pick because they have no emotional connection to anything.

To combat post-decisional dissonance, the feeling you have committed to one option when the other option may have been better, you make yourself feel justified in what you selected to lower the anxiety brought on by questioning yourself.

All of this forms a giant neurological cluster of associations, emotions, details of self-image, and biases around the things you own.

So the next time you get ready to launch into one hundred reasons why your cell phone or TV or car is better than someone else's, hesitate. Because you're not trying to change the other person's mind—you're trying to prop up your own.

14

The Argument from Authority

THE MISCONCEPTION: *You are more concerned with the validity of information than the person delivering it.*
THE TRUTH: *The status and credentials of an individual greatly influence your perception of that individual's message.*

It would be hard not to feel somewhat intimidated while sitting across from a professor with all his or her degrees and certificates staring back at you. Behind that huge desk, surrounded by books and ancient statues, inside an aging, hallowed building, the professor seems to channel the might and weight of all of academia.

When he or she opines on the history of civilization, you might be inclined to see the professor's point of view as more correct, more thoroughly meditated upon than that of your cousin who collects ketchup packets. You would be right. Indeed, it is more likely that a professor of history will know why the Roman Empire fell and what can be learned from it than your condiment-obsessed relative will know these things. Those who devote their lives to the study or practice of a given idea are worth listening to when it comes to the areas of their expertise, but this doesn't mean all their opinions are golden.

If the professor tells you how much he or she wishes the Spice Girls would reunite and play on campus, you would be committing logical fallacy if you decided you should maybe rethink your musical taste. When you see the opinions of some people as better than others on the merit of their status or training alone, you are arguing from authority.

Should you listen to a highly trained scuba diver's advice before plunging into the depths of the ocean? Yes. Should you believe that person when the diver talks about seeing a mermaid making love to a dolphin? No.

This book often brings up the consensus of scientists on certain behaviors as a way to prove how deluded you are. It is not a fallacy to trust the consensus of thousands of researchers on how to interpret the evidence provided by decades of studies. Science focuses on the facts, not the people who unearth them, but that doesn't mean large groups of people can't agree on something that is totally wrong.

Neurologist Walter Freeman won the 1949 Nobel Prize for Medicine in honor of his work—lobotomizing mentally ill people by jabbing a spike behind their eyeballs. Some reports say he performed this technique around 2,500 times, often without anesthesia. He took a practice that had previously required drilling into the skull and turned it into an outpatient procedure. At first, he used an ice pick, but eventually he developed short, thin metal spears he drove through the back of the eye socket with a mallet. The technique made formerly unruly mental patients calmer, as you might imagine severe brain damage would. It became a popular way to treat patients in mental facilities, and Freeman drove a van he called the lobotomobile around the country to teach the technique wherever he could. Somewhere close to twenty thousand people were lobotomized in this way before science corrected itself. Freeman was criticized by many in his heyday, but for two decades his work continued, and it earned him the highest accolade possible. Even the sister of President John F. Kennedy was lobotomized. Today, the ice-pick lobotomy is condemned by medicine as a barbaric and naive approach to dealing with mental illness.

The rise and fall of the ice-pick lobotomy had a lot to do with the argument from authority. Freeman and others had jumped the gun on the scientific evidence. Without all the facts in place, they used psychosurgery because it gave them the results they were looking for. Hospitals welcomed Dr. Freeman; his authority went unquestioned as, one after another, he pulled aside patients who needed help and turned them into zombies. Just two decades later, the science caught up to Freeman and revealed that what he was doing was unnecessary from a medical standpoint and horrific from a moral one. His license to practice was revoked, and he died an outcast. The same community who lauded him in one era rejected him in another.

This sort of turnover in science is common, although it happens less today than in years past when so little was understood about these sorts of influences. Like most modern professions, science guards against the argument from authority by working against it, questioning every nugget of new info so as to avoid what happened in neurology throughout the 1940s. Still, the argument does play a role. Whether in churches or legislatures, botany or business, those who are held in high regard can cause a lot of damage when no one is willing to question their authority.

You naturally look to those in power as having something special you lack, a spark of something you would like to see inside yourself. This is why people sometimes subscribe to the beliefs of celebrities who endorse exotic religions or denounce sound medicines.

If you feel more inclined to believe something is true because it comes from a person with prestige, you are letting the argument from authority spin your head. If something is controversial, it usually means there are many experts who disagree. You would be wise to come to your own conclusions based on the evidence, not the people delivering it. On the other hand, if there is widespread consensus, you can relax your skepticism. Just don't relax it completely.

If a celebrity basketball player tells you to buy a particular brand of batteries, ask yourself if the basketball player seems like an expert on electrochemical energy storage units before you take the player's word.

15

The Argument from Ignorance

THE MISCONCEPTION: *When you can't explain something, you focus on what you can prove.*
THE TRUTH: *When you are unsure of something, you are more likely to accept strange explanations.*

There is a pleasant sense of wonder that can fill your heart when you take in the natural world and realize how much you don't know.

How does the mighty oak spring from a lowly acorn? How does a river carve out a vast canyon? How could the universe begin from a microscopic dot and explode into all the matter and energy you see today? How can you be thinking about calling someone right as they dial your number and tell you they were thinking of you too?

It is easy to succumb to mystical thinking when you compare what you know for sure to the vast expanse of things yet unsolved. If you aren't up-to-date on the latest scientific research, you may put concepts like tiny seeds becoming giant plants in the realm of the unknown. You've probably met people like this, who see things like magnets and Stonehenge as unsolvable mysteries. People in awe of such things see them as magical and miraculous, or perhaps believe the explanation is beyond modern human comprehension. The emotions roused when you are humbled by the splendor of nature and the ingenuity of ancient people are nice. It feels good to ponder the mysterious.

The only problem with these emotions is science has explained much of the world both outside and inside your head. This is a bummer for fans of *Unsolved Mysteries* or *Ripley's Believe it or Not* or *In Search Of*. More recently, *Ghost Hunters* and *The Unexplained* have earned big ratings by showcasing the spooky stuff science has ruined.

Outside of science, mystical New Age props like crystals and dowsing rods play on your tendency toward pattern recognition. You look for cause and effect, but when the cause is unclear you commit a logical fallacy by thinking all the possible causes are equal.

That strange feeling you get when you walk into an old house—could it be a haunting? Are those strange creaks and bumps attempts at communication from the spirit realm? The strange lights in the sky, are they aliens preparing to probe unsuspecting farm families? Did those tracks in the forest come from a friendly, misunderstood Sasquatch?

Most of what gets filed under the realm of the paranormal is the result of people committing the argument-from-ignorance fallacy, or *argumentum ad ignorantiam* if you prefer the Latin logic terminology. Put simply, this is when you decide something is true or false because you can't find evidence to the contrary. You don't know what the truth is, so you assume any explanation is as good as another. Maybe those lights were alien spacecraft, maybe not. You don't know, so you think the likelihood they were intergalactic visitors is roughly the same as those lights being from a helicopter far away.

You can't disprove something you don't know anything about, and the argument-from-ignorance fallacy can make you feel as though something is possible because you can't prove otherwise. You know this book is in your hands right now, but when you leave the room you can't be sure it does not come to life and eat your dust bunnies for sustenance. Despite this, you don't feel inclined to lock away this book at night just in case it builds up enough strength to devour your face. You not being able to disprove this book secretly hungers for flesh does not improve the odds it does. The same holds true for leprechauns and unicorns, chupacabra and the Loch Ness Monster. These things aren't more likely just because you can't prove they don't exist.

Lack of proof neither confirms nor denies a proposition. Is there life on other planets? We can't say yes or no just because it hasn't been discovered yet. No matter how you feel about the question, you would be incorrect to assume the lack of evidence proves your assumption. At the same time, you can't just live your life so open-minded you never accept proof. Was Michael Jackson a time traveler sent from the future to teach the world to moonwalk? You can't exactly prove this is false, but there is enough evidence to the contrary to assume he was a singer born in 1958, not a time lord from 3022.

Some people think the Holocaust didn't happen, or human beings never walked on the moon, but there is plenty of evidence for both. People who refuse to believe such things claim they need more evidence before they can change their minds, but no amount of evidence will satisfy them. Any shred of doubt allows them to argue from ignorance.

16

The Straw Man Fallacy

THE MISCONCEPTION: *When you argue, you try to stick to the facts.*

THE TRUTH: *In any argument, anger will tempt you to reframe your opponent's position.*

When you are losing an argument, you often use a variety of deceptive techniques to bolster your opinion. You aren't trying to be sneaky, but the human mind tends to follow predictable patterns when you get angry with other people and do battle with words.

One of the most reliable and sturdy logical fallacies is the straw man, and even though its probability of appearing is high, you often don't notice when you are using it or being beat over the head with it.

It works like this: When you get into an argument about either something personal or something more public and abstract, you sometimes resort to constructing a character who you find easier to refute, argue, and disagree with, or you create a position the other person isn't even suggesting or defending. This is a straw man.

It happens so often, professional debaters and science advocates are trained to look for the straw man fallacy both in themselves and opponents when asserting their opinions or shooting down the claims of others. The straw man fallacy takes the facts and assertions of your opponent and replaces them with an artificial argument you feel more comfortable dealing with.

The straw man fallacy follows a familiar pattern. You first build the straw man, then you attack it, then you point out how easy it was to defeat it, and then you come to a conclusion.

For instance, say you are arguing about whether or not people should be allowed to own pet chickens. You think chickens are hideous creatures, thanks to an unfortunate incident in childhood when you were attacked by a bloodthirsty hen at a petting zoo, and since then you have made it your life's mission to keep poultry away from children. Your opponent wants the city ordinances to be changed so he can breed fancy varieties of chickens who look like sea anemones and sell them to pet stores.

You say, "If we allow people to breed chickens in their backyards, soon they'll be in the streets and on the subway. Eventually, people will be taking their chickens to work with them and including them in Christmas cards with the rest of the family. In a world like that, what will happen to the poultry industry? No one will want to eat something that could be their pet. I don't think I want to live in a world like that, would you? So, no, we shouldn't allow this ordinance to pass."

In creating a fantasy scenario where the world goes mad if the other person's argument were to win, you have constructed a straw man. It is easy to see the downsides of and hard to defend, but it also isn't what the other person was suggesting. Now the other person has to clarify his or her argument by assuring everyone he or she has no desire to see restaurant chains close because of this proposal. The other person now must argue against the feathery doomsday you've invented instead of just pointing out the reasonable ways people could be allowed to raise a few domesticated fowl.

Within any debate over a controversial topic, you will see straw men tossed out by both sides. Sometimes people morph the straw man into a warning about a slippery slope where allowing one side to win would put humanity on a course of destruction. Any time someone begins an attack with "So you're saying we should all just . . ." or "Everyone knows . . . ," you can bet a straw man is coming. When you start or someone else starts to imagine a future hellscape thanks to the ideas of the opposition becoming reality, there is a straw man in the room. Straw men can also be born out of ignorance. If someone says, "Scientists tell us we all come from monkeys, and that's why I homeschool," this person is using a straw man, because science doesn't say we all come from monkeys.

Pay attention the next time you disagree with someone, and see if you start or the other person starts to construct a man out of straw. Keep in mind whoever does it is using a logical fallacy, and even if that person succeeds, he or she didn't really win.

17

The Ad Hominem Fallacy

THE MISCONCEPTION: *If you can't trust someone, you should ignore that person's claims.*

THE TRUTH: *What someone says and why they say it should be judged separately.*

Sometimes an argument can get so heated you start calling the other person names. You attack the other person instead of the position that person has taken. It is easier to disagree with someone you see as nasty or ignorant. Calling someone a bigot, or an idiot, or an asshole feels good, but it does not prove you right or that person wrong.

This makes sense, but you don't always notice when you are doing it. When you assume someone is incorrect based on who that person is or what group he or she belongs to, you have committed the ad hominem fallacy. *Ad hominem* is Latin for "to the person," which is where you sometimes take the argument when things get out of hand.

Imagine you are part of jury in the case of a man who is accused of stealing a car. The prosecutor might bring up the past of the defendant to show he's committed crimes before, or have people from his past claim he is a liar. Once the seed is planted—this guy is a liar and a thief—it might sway your opinion of the argument at hand. No matter what the man says, somewhere in your head you will doubt it because you don't trust liars. If the guy on trial told you the sky was blue and bread was edible, you would have no problem believing it. The fallacy disappears. Only his argument about something you are still unsure of is affected. If he tells you he didn't steal the car, the lawyer's ad hominem attack may cause you to ignore the evidence and commit a logical fallacy.

What if a prominent scientist is caught falsifying his research? Do you now see everything that scientist has ever discovered as bunk? What if all the research leading up to the unethical act was properly peer-reviewed and scrutinized? The tendency to label the scientist as a shifty and unprincipled person is hard to shake. The logical misstep is to assume all the scientist's work is false because of who he or she is, the label you have placed on this person. You might do the same with a journalist who gets too many facts wrong. You think if this journalist made up one story, then all the writer's other stories are probably made up too. You would be right to feel skeptical, but jumping to a conclusion based on how you feel about the journalist as an individual would be a mistake.

Perhaps someone criticizes your driving and you respond with "You have no room to talk. You are the worst driver in the world." There it is again. You are dismissing the other person's argument by attacking the person instead of the claim.

Just calling someone a name is not a fallacy. You must discount the person's position based on your impression of his or her character before you get into trouble. If you refuse to listen to the financial advice of a drug addict because the addict wastes money on pills, now you're cooking with fallacies. If a smoker tells you he or she thinks it should be legal to smoke in restaurants, you can't wave your hand in the air and dismiss that opinion just because the person offering it has a personal stake in the matter. Maybe the smoker has a point, maybe not, but the fact that he or she is a smoker shouldn't confuse your thinking.

A political attack ad might say something like "Don't vote for Susan Smith because she practiced voodoo in college." Just because someone is a practicing voodoo priestess doesn't mean she can't balance a budget. Political opponents also hope you will commit the ad hominem fallacy when they point out who their opponent hangs out with or who they have done business with in the past. Guilt by association is often the ad hominem fallacy at work. If someone hangs out with crooks or crazies, maybe that person is a criminal or a lunatic. A politician's policies and the people he or she barbecues with are separate issues.

However, this is not to say that if you see a man in a banana suit playing a flute and carrying a sign that reads THE END IS NEAR! you should race home to kiss your family good-bye. Avoiding the ad hominem fallacy does not mean you have to trust everything you hear equally. Still, you can't be logically certain the banana man is wrong. Maybe the end *is* near, but you should make up your mind based on the evidence he can bring to the table. If his opinion is based on the chatter of pigeons, you can probably ignore it.

The ad hominem fallacy can also work in reverse. You might assume someone is trustworthy because they speak well, or have a respectable job. It is hard to believe an astronaut would put on a diaper and drive across the country to kill the wife of her lover, but it did happen once. The inverse ad hominem fallacy would steer you into delusion if you were on the jury in the astronaut's trial and refused to believe the evidence because of your respect for space explorers.

You tend to see people as characters and look for consistency in their behavior. This is usually a good thing, as it helps you sort out whom you can trust. Wondering whether or not someone can be trusted and wondering whether or not someone is telling the truth are two different things. Judging character has been such a useful tool for so long in the evolutionary history of human beings it can overshadow your logic. You might be a great judge of character, but you need to be a great judge of evidence to avoid delusion.

18

The Just-World Fallacy

THE MISCONCEPTION: *People who are losing at the game of life must have done something to deserve it.*
THE TRUTH: *The beneficiaries of good fortune often do nothing to earn it, and bad people often get away with their actions without consequences.*

A woman goes out to a club wearing stilettos and a miniskirt with no underwear. She gets pretty drunk and stumbles home in the wrong direction. She ends up lost in a bad neighborhood. She gets raped.

Is she to blame in some way? Was this her fault? Was she asking for it?

People often say yes to all three in studies asking similar questions after presenting similar scenarios. When you hear about a situation you hope never happens to you, you tend to blame the victim, not because you are a terrible person but because you want to believe you are smart enough to avoid the same fate. You inflate whatever amount of responsibility the victim may bear into something bigger, something you would never do. The truth, though, is rape is rarely something predicated on bad behavior on the part of the victim. Usually, the rapist is someone familiar, and it doesn't matter what the victim was wearing or doing beforehand. The rapist is always to blame, but most awareness campaigns are targeted at women, not men. The message boils downs to "Don't do something that might get you raped."

It is common in fiction for the bad guys to lose and the good guys to win. This is how you would like to see the world—just and fair. In psychology, the tendency to believe that this is how the real world works is called the just-world fallacy.

More specifically, this is the tendency to react to horrible misfortune, like homelessness or drug addiction, by believing the people stuck in these situations must have done something to deserve it. The key word there is "deserve." This is not an observation that bad choices may lead to bad outcomes. The just-world fallacy helps you to build a false sense of security. You want to feel in control, so you assume as long as you avoid bad behavior, you won't be harmed. You feel safer when you believe those who engage in bad behavior end up on the street, or pregnant, or addicted, or raped.

In a 1966 study by Melvin Lerner and Carolyn Simmons, seventy-two women watched a woman solve problems and get electric shocks when she messed up. The woman was actually pretending, but the women watching didn't know this. When asked to describe the woman getting shocked, many of the observers devalued her. They berated her character and her appearance. They said she deserved it.

Lerner also taught a class on society and medicine, and he noticed many students thought the poor were just lazy people who wanted a handout. So he conducted another study where he had two men solve puzzles. At the end, one of them was randomly awarded a large sum of money. The observers were told the reward was completely random. Still, when asked later to evaluate the two men, people said the one who got the award was smarter, more talented, better at solving puzzles, and more productive. A giant amount of research has been done since Lerner's studies, and most psychologists have come to the same conclusion: You want the world to be fair, so you pretend it is.

The just-world fallacy is probably built into the human mind. No matter how liberal or conservative you are, some notion of it pulls on your emotional reaction to hearing about the suffering of others. In a study published in 2010 by Robert Thornberg and Sven Knutsen at Linkoping University in Sweden, researchers asked teenagers to explain what causes bullying in school. While most students said the bullies were power-hungry and cruel, 42 percent blamed the victim for being an easy target. Ask yourself: When you saw people bullying others in school, did you think the victims should stand up for themselves? Did you think the ones being harassed and teased should learn how to dress, how to act more confident, how to hide their nerdishness? In movies about bullies, the main character always has to learn how to stand up and fight back. The bullies get theirs only when the victim takes responsibility. The research says that while you know bullies are the bad guys, you accept it as unchangeable. The world is full of bad guys. The victims, however, have the power to end their own torment. In the same study, 21 percent of the students blamed themselves—the audience. Fewer still said the culprit was society or human nature. The world, most thought, was just and fair, only the people in it—victims and bullies—were to blame when bad things happened.

You've heard that what goes around comes around, or maybe you've seen a person get what was coming to them and thought,

"That's karma for you." These are shades of the just-world fallacy. It sucks to think the world isn't fair. A world with the righteous on one side of the scale and evil on the other—that seems to make sense. You want to believe those who work hard and sacrifice get ahead and those who are lazy and cheat do not. This, of course, is not always true. Success is often greatly influenced by when you were born, where you grew up, the socioeconomic status of your family, and random chance. All the hard work in the world can't change those initial factors. Accepting this does not mean those born poor should just give up. After all, not taking action guarantees not getting results. In a just world, this would be the only rule, no matter what the initial conditions of your struggle were. The real world is more complicated. People can and do escape, but this doesn't mean those who haven't aren't trying their damnedest to claw out of bad situations. If you look to the downtrodden and wonder why they can't pull themselves out of poverty and get a nice job like you, you are committing the just-world fallacy. You are ignoring the unearned blessings of your station.

It is infuriating when cheats and con artists get ahead in the world while firemen and policemen put in long hours for little pay. Deep down, you want to believe hard work and virtue will lead to success, and evil and manipulation will lead to ruin, so you go ahead and edit the world to match those expectations. Yet, in reality, evil often prospers and never pays the price.

The psychologist Jonathan Haidt says many people who don't consciously believe in karma still believe deep down in some version of it, calling it whatever seems appropriate in their own culture. They see systems like welfare or affirmative action as disrupting the balance of the natural world. Slackers, they think, would get what they deserve if the government kept their noses out of it. Their bad karma would come around to crush them, but unnatural forces prevent it. Meanwhile, since these people play by the rules, pay taxes, and sacrifice hours of life for overtime pay, they assume it has to be for a reason. Their pursuit of the good life can't be futile. The rich, they think, must deserve what they have. One day all the good karma they are generating will lift them even higher up in the social hierarchy to join the others who have what they deserve. The just-world fallacy tells them fairness is built into the system, and so they rage when the system artificially unbalances karmic justice.

Why do we think this way?

Psychologists are unsure. Some say it is a need to be able to predict the outcome of your own behavior, or to feel secure in your past decisions. More research is needed. To be sure, you would like to live in a world where people in white hats bring people in black hats to justice, but you don't.

Don't let this discourage you, though. You can accept that life is unfair and still relish it. You aren't in total control of your life, but there is a nice big chunk of your life over which you have complete authority—beat that part to a pulp. Just remember the unfair nature of the world, the randomness of birthright, means people often suffer adversity and enjoy opulence through no effort of their own. If you think the world is just and fair, people who need help may never get it. Realize that even though we are all responsible for our actions, the blame for evil acts rests on the perpetrator and never the victim. No one deserves to be raped or bullied, robbed or murdered. To make the world more just and fair, you have to make it harder for evil to thrive, and you can't do this just by reducing the number of its potential targets.

19

The Public Goods Game

THE MISCONCEPTION: *We could create a system with no regulations where everyone would contribute to the good of society, everyone would benefit, and everyone would be happy.*

THE TRUTH: *Without some form of regulation, slackers and cheaters will crash economic systems because people don't want to feel like suckers.*

Before you hear about the public goods game, you need to understand the tragedy of the commons. The idea comes from a 1968 essay by geologist Garrett Hardin that suggested you aren't very good at sharing.

Imagine a giant lake filled with fish. You and three others are the only people who know about it. You all agree to take just as many fish from the lake as you need to eat. As long as everyone takes just what he or she needs, the lake will stay full of fish.

One day, you happen to notice one of the others has started taking more than he or she needs and is selling the extra fish in a nearby town. Eventually that person has a better fishing rod than you.

What do you do?

If you start overfishing too, you will also be able to get a better rod, maybe even a boat. Maybe you could partner up against the cheater. Maybe everyone will just start taking as many fish as desired. Maybe you could just tell the world about the lake. All of these scenarios will probably lead to the ruin of the common good. If you do nothing, the lake will still be able to support you and the other two, but the cheater wins. Anger over unfair situations is something you can't help but feel.

In situations like the imaginary lake above, in an effort not to fall behind, everyone loses. A big holiday meal, for example, can become a zero-sum game if everyone piles a plate, but if everyone takes only what he or she needs, everyone wins. The tragedy of taking from a common good is over time the common good will be depleted out of just a tiny amount of greed. One misguided exploiter can crash the system. Greed is contagious.

So what about a public good, a thing which everyone contributes to instead of takes from? It seems the same is true. Cheaters can ruin the system, not by themselves, but because the infectious nature of their gluttony is spread as people catch on to being shortchanged. Unfortunately, research into human behavior shows you are not so smart when it comes to contributing to the public good.

The public goods game works like this:

A group of people sits around a table, and each person is given a few dollars. The group is told they can put as much money as they want in the community pot. An experimenter then doubles the pot, and everyone then gets an equal portion back.

If it's ten people and everyone gets $2, and everyone puts in that money, the pot would be $20. It gets doubled to $40 and divided by ten. Everyone gets back $4. The game proceeds in rounds, and you would think everyone would just put the maximum amount in the pot each time—but they don't. Someone usually gets the gist of the game and realizes that one can put in very little, or nothing at all, and start making more money than everyone else.

If everyone but you puts in $2, the pot would be $18. It gets doubled to $36 and everyone gets back $3.60—including you, the one who put nothing in at all.

In experiments where this game is played so everyone can see who puts in a fair share, the pot tends to grow for a while and then it starts to shrink as people test the water by withholding funds. The behavior spreads, because no one wants to be a chump, and eventually the economy grinds to a halt. If people are allowed the option of punishing cheaters, the cheating stops, and everyone wins. If instead of punishment, people are given the choice to reward good players, the economy again crashes after a few rounds.

The crazy thing about this game is how illogical it is to stop contributing just because someone in the group is free riding. If everyone else is still being a good citizen of the game, everyone will still win. The old emotional brain kicks in, however, when you see cheating. It's an innate response that served your ancestors well. You know deep down that cheaters must be punished because it takes only one cheater to make the economy sputter out. You would rather lose the game than help someone who isn't helping you.

This game is sometimes used to illustrate how regulation is necessary to keep any sort of nonprofit public good alive. Streetlights would never get put along dark roads, and bridges would collapse if people weren't forced to pay taxes. Purely logical creatures could be trusted to figure out life isn't a zero-sum game, but you are not a purely logical creature. You will cheat if you think the system is cheating you.

The urge to help others and discourage cheating is something that helped primates like you survive in small groups for millions of years, but when the system becomes gigantic and abstract like the budget for a nation or the welfare system for an entire state, it becomes difficult to make sense of the world through those old evolutionary behaviors.

The tragedy of the commons can be used to make a case for private property in order to encourage you to take care of your piece of the world, but you might think not everyone is going to buy a fuel-efficient car and recycle plastic, so why should you?

The public goods game suggests regulation through punishment discourages slackers.

It isn't you don't want to help; you just don't want to help a cheater or do more work than a slacker—even if your not helping leads to ruining the game for you and everyone else.

20

The Ultimatum Game

THE MISCONCEPTION: *You choose to accept or refuse an offer based on logic.*

THE TRUTH: *When it comes to making a deal, you base your decision on your status.*

Imagine you win $1 million in the lottery, but there's a catch.

This is a new experimental lottery in which the state says you must share your winnings with a stranger. You get to decide how the money is split, but the other person can reject your offer. If the other person rejects it, you both get nothing. You get only one chance, and the two of you will never see each other again. How much do you offer?

Right about now the very thing that most makes you human has been activated. What separates you most from the rest of the animals is your complex social reasoning skills. Millions of variables are interplaying in your head, and you are running as many simulations as you can conjure to predict the future. You are imagining what the other person will do based on all your instincts and experiences.

You now have ten seconds to decide.

Oh no. What to do?

The most logical thing to do would be to offer the stranger a small sum. How about $1,000? After all, if that person refuses, he or she gets nothing. Unfortunately for you, people don't approach a situation like this with logic. When fairness is at stake, emotions take over. Somewhere deep in your brain, you can predict this, and like most people, you will offer the other person something closer to half.

When this experiment is performed with real money and real people in the lab, most offers less than 20 percent of the total amount are rejected. In this scenario, the bare minimum you would have to offer is $200,000—even though you are the one who won the money.

Give this problem to a computer, and it will take anything above zero. Something is better than nothing to a purely logical mind. Give this problem to a human, and you must deal with 3 million years of evolution.

In the wild, we lived in small groups—usually fewer than 150 people. It was vitally important to understand where you ranked in such a group. Survival depended on your relationships and your standing. Reputation and status are more important than money to primates. People with lots of money gain high status, but if you were in the middle of a zombie apocalypse, the money would suddenly become paper again. Your status would quickly be determined by other factors.

In the lottery situation, the money you offer to the other person is interpreted as your estimation of his or her status in the social hierarchy. If the other person accepts less than 20 percent, he or she will feel inferior and disrespected. The person will lose status in the eyes of others. No matter how large or small the amount, in experiments with real people, offering less than 20 percent ensures that both parties lose. You know this instinctively, and most people offer around half of their prize when the ultimatum game is played in a laboratory. When you know the other party could exact revenge on you for being unfair, it encourages the sort of altruism that allowed your ancestors to escape into civilization.

This effect is even greater if the person making the final decision has low serotonin levels. If a person feels sad and unwanted, he or she will demand more money before accepting. That person's default settings give him or her a sense of lower status, and thus the person is unwilling to lower it even further by accepting an unfair offer.

When experimenters change the rules so the person making the offer gets to keep his or her share no matter what, just about everyone tries to screw the other person by offering around 10 percent.

This situation comes up in life all the time. You decide when to ask for a raise, or make a move in the bar, or get up on stage and sing, based on your perceived status within a group. If it is low, you won't risk further damage. If it is high, you expect better treatment.

The promise of revenge is one way human beings ensure fairness, and you are precisely tuned to expect it. Your perceived status is part of the unconscious equation you work out when accepting, refusing, and making offers with other people. You are not so smart, so you are willing to get nothing if it ensures fair treatment in the future and a more secure place on the social ladder.

21

Subjective Validation

THE MISCONCEPTION: *You are skeptical of generalities.*

THE TRUTH: *You are prone to believing vague statements and predictions are true, especially if they are positive and address you personally.*

Based on the data I've collected from the comments, e-mails, and other browsing information generated by the You Are Not So Smart blog, all cross-referenced with demographics information prepared in marketing studies for the placement of this book on shelves around the world, I have a pretty good idea of who you are.

Here are my findings:

You have a need for other people to like and admire you, and yet you tend to be critical of yourself. While you have some personality weaknesses, you are generally able to compensate for them. You have considerable unused capacity that you have not turned to your advantage. Disciplined and self-controlled on the outside, you tend to be worried and insecure on the inside. At times you have serious doubts as to whether you have made the right decision or done the right thing. You prefer a certain amount of change and variety and become dissatisfied when hemmed in by restrictions and limitations. You also pride yourself on being an independent thinker and do not accept others' statements without satisfactory proof. But you have found it unwise to be too frank in revealing yourself to others. At times you are extroverted, affable, and sociable, while at other times you are introverted, wary, and reserved. Some of your aspirations tend to be rather unrealistic.

Does this sound accurate? Does it describe you?

It should. It describes everyone.

All the above statements came from a 1948 experiment by Bertram R. Forer. He gave his students a personality test and told them each one had been personally assessed, but then gave everyone the same analysis.

He asked his students to look over the statements and rate them for accuracy. On average, they rated the bogus analysis as 85 percent correct—as if it had been personally prepared to describe each one of them. The block of text above was actually a mishmash of lines from horoscopes collected by Forer for the experiment.

The tendency to believe vague statements designed to appeal to just about anyone is called the Forer effect, and psychologists point to this phenomenon to explain why people fall for pseudoscience like biorhythms, iridology, and phrenology, or mysticism like astrology, numerology, and tarot cards. The Forer effect is part of a larger phenomenon psychologists refer to as subjective validation, which is a fancy way of saying you are far more vulnerable to suggestion when the subject of the conversation is you.

Since you are always in your own head, thoughts about what it means to be you take up a lot of mental space. With some cultural variations, most people are keen on being individuals, unique and special persons whose hopes and dreams and fears and doubts are all their own. If you have the means, you personalize everything: your license plate, your ring tone, your computer's desktop wallpaper, your bedroom's walls.

Everything around you says something about your personality. Cultivating an incomparable self either through consumption or creation is not something you take lightly. Yet somewhere between nature and nurture, we are all far more similar than we think. Genetically, you and your friends are almost identical. Those genes create the brain that generates the mind from which your thoughts spring. Thus, genetically, your mental life is as similar to everyone else's as the feet in your shoes. Culturally, we differ. Our varying experiences in our varying environments shape us. Still, deep below, we are the same, and the failure to notice this can be exploited.

If a statement is ambiguous *and* you think it addresses you directly, you will boil away the ambiguity by finding ways to match the information up with your own traits. You think back to all the time spent figuring out who you are, dividing your qualities from the qualities of others, and apply the same logic.

Here's an excerpt from a real horoscope at horoscopes.com: "At some point during the day, you might have the feeling that you aren't working hard enough to keep the forward motion going, and you might feel panic rise. This could prove a good motivating factor, but you don't need to push yourself harder than you're going now. You're on a roll and it's likely to continue. Just pace yourself."

Now here's another one from the same source on the same day but for a different sign: "Don't be too hard on yourself if you're dragging a little toward the end of the day. You'll be able to re-charge your batteries before tomorrow. In the evening, relax at home with a good book."

Seen straight on, horoscopes describe the sort of things we all experience, but pluck one from the bunch, turn it ever so slightly, and you will see it matching all the details of your life. If you believe you live under a sign, and the movement of the planets can divine your future, a general statement becomes specific.

It is this hope that gives subjective validation its power. If you want the psychic to be real, or the sacred stones to forecast the un-known, you will find a way to believe them even when they falter. When you need something to be true, you will look for patterns; you connect the dots like the stars of a constellation. Your brain abhors disorder. You see faces in clouds and demons in bonfires. Those who claim the powers of divination hijack these natural hu-man tendencies. They know they can depend on you to use subjec-tive validation in the moment and confirmation bias afterward.

The psychologist Ray Hyman has spent most of his life studying the art of deception. Before he entered the halls of science, he worked as a magician and then moved on to mentalism after dis-covering he could make more money reading palms than perform-ing card tricks. The crazy thing about Hyman's career as a palm reader is, like many psychics, over time he began to believe he actu-ally did have psychic powers. The people who came to him were so satisfied, so bowled over, he thought he must have a real gift. Sub-jective validation cuts both ways.

Hyman was using a technique called cold reading, where you start with the wide-angle lens of generalities and watch the other person for cues so you can constrict the focus down to what seems like a powerful insight into the other person's soul. It works because people tend to ignore the little misses and focus on the hits. As he worked his way through college, another mentalist, Stanley Jaks, took Hyman aside and saved him from delusion by asking him to try something new—tell people the opposite of what he believed their palms revealed. The result? They were just as flabbergasted by his abilities, if not more so. Cold reading was powerful, but tossing it aside, he was still able to amaze. Hyman realized what he said didn't matter as long as his presentation was good. The other person was doing all the work, tricking him- or herself, seeing the general as the specific just like in the Forer effect.

Mediums and palm readers, those who speak for the dead or see into the beyond for cash, depend on subjective validation. Remember, your capacity to fool yourself is greater than the abilities of any conjurer, and conjurers come in many guises. You are a creature impelled to hope. As you attempt to make sense of the world, you focus on what falls into place and neglect that which doesn't fit, and there is so much in life that does not fit.

When you see a set of horoscopes, read all of them. When someone claims he or she can see into your heart, realize that all of our hearts are much the same.

22

Cult Indoctrination

THE MISCONCEPTION: *You are too smart to join a cult.*

THE TRUTH: *Cults are populated by people just like you.*

Cults are a side effect of natural human tendencies. You have an innate desire to belong to a group and to hang out with interesting people. If you have ever admired someone you have never actually met—like a musician—you've experienced the seed of the cult phenomenon.

The word "cult" is slippery, because seen from far away, many organizations, institutions, and religions could be seen as cults. The line between groups and cults is blurry. The fuzzy line is why you are far more likely to end up in a cult than you think.

The research on cults suggests you don't usually join for any particular reason; you just sort of fall into them the way you fall into any social group. After all, when did you join your circle of friends? Your group of close friends has likely changed a great deal over the years, but have you made many active choices concerning who you hang out with other than avoiding the ones who are a pain in the ass?

The sorts of people who join cults are not all insecure or emotionally weak. You'd like to think that you are not the sort of person who could be beguiled by a charismatic leader with a clear vision—but you are not so smart. According to psychologist David Myers, cults form around sparkly, interesting individuals—Jim Jones, David Koresh, L. Ron Hubbard, Charles Manson—but people don't usually follow the leader, they follow the ideals the leader proclaims to be serving. These leaders seem to have things figured out, and you want to figure those things out too. Gandhi, Che Guevara, Terence McKenna, and Socrates are all great thinkers who seemed to have access to secrets, insights into something bigger. Naturally, people followed them, hoping to gain their mojo through osmosis. Were their followers in a cult? See, that's where the definition falls apart. This is why you are susceptible to this sort of behavior.

As a primate, you are keenly aware of group dynamics. You are hardwired to want to hang out with people and associate yourself with groups. Your survival has depended on it for millions of years. In addition, you don't evaluate your behavior and choices and feelings in order to understand who you are. Instead, you have an idealistic vision of yourself, a character you've dreamed up in your mind, and you are always trying to become this character. You seek out groups to affiliate with to better solidify who you are in the story you tell yourself—the story explaining why you do the things you do.

Myers says cults start with a charismatic individual. Maybe this person believes he is special in some way, or maybe he is just naturally interesting. People start hanging out with him, and a spontaneous group forms with the charismatic person becoming an authority figure. If this person has an agenda, or a goal, or enemies he wants eliminated, he will cultivate the goodwill of his fans into action. If he has difficult goals to reach, he will try to expand his group with recruitment or proselytizing, often hiding his true intentions so as not to scare away potential members. Some leaders know what they are doing, but some just serve their instincts and accidentally form cults around themselves before they realize what they've done. How these people wield their power over others ultimately determines how history will label them. Those who abuse their power and take advantage of their followers, like Jim Jones and Charles Manson, form what you traditionally consider a cult. Others, like Mohandas Ghandi, who convinced thousands to follow him on foot for 241 miles as he walked to the sea to protest a tax on salt, aren't seen as cult leaders. Any group with a charismatic leader has the potential to break away and form a subculture. Some make the world a better place. Others convince people to kill themselves.

If you have ever called yourself a fan of anyone—a musician, a director, a writer, a politician, a technological genius, a scientist— you are experiencing the first stage of cult indoctrination. If you were to meet the person you most admire and be offered the chance to hang out with him or her on a regular basis—would you? You would. What happens next would depend on a chaotic series of variables; sometimes the result is a cult, and sometimes those cults live on beyond their leaders. There is no agent behind it, no person deciding to form or join a cult. Cults aren't designed. They form as a result of normal human tendencies going awry.

23

Groupthink

THE MISCONCEPTION: *Problems are easier to solve when a group of people get together to discuss solutions.*
THE TRUTH: *The desire to reach consensus and avoid confrontation hinders progress.*

When a group of people come together to make a decision, every demon in the psychological bestiary will be summoned.

Conformity, rationalization, stereotyping, delusions of grandeur—they all come out to play, and no one is willing to fight them back into hell because it might lead to abandoning the plan or a nasty argument. Groups survive by maintaining harmony. When everyone is happy and all egos are free from harm it tends to increase productivity. This is true whether you are hunting buffalo or selling televisions. Team spirit, morale, group cohesion—these are golden principles long held high by managers, commanders, chieftains, and kings. You know instinctively that dissent leads to chaos, so you avoid it.

This is all well and good until you find yourself in a group your brain isn't equipped to deal with—like at work. The same mind that was formed to deal with group survival around predators and prey doesn't fare so well when dealing with bosses and fiscal projections. No matter what sort of job you have, from time to time everyone has to get together and come up with a plan. Sometimes you do this in small groups, sometimes as an entire company. If your group includes a person who can hire or fire, groupthink comes into play.

With a boss hanging around, you get nervous. You start observing the other members of the group in an attempt to figure out what the consensus opinion is. Meanwhile, you are simultaneously weighing the consequences of disagreeing. The problem is, every other person in the group is doing the same thing, and if everyone decides it would be a bad idea to risk losing friends or a job, a false consensus will be reached and no one will do anything about it.

Often, after these sorts of meetings, two people will talk in private and agree they think a mistake is being made. Why didn't they just say so in the meeting?

Psychologist Irving Janis mapped out this behavior through research after reading about the U.S. decision to invade southern Cuba—the Bay of Pigs. In 1961, President John F. Kennedy tried to overthrow Fidel Castro with a force of 1,400 exiles. They weren't professional soldiers. There weren't many of them. Cuba knew they were coming. They were slaughtered. This led to Cuba getting friendly with the USSR and almost led to nuclear apocalypse. John F. Kennedy and his advisers were brilliant people with all the data in front of them who had gotten together and planned something incredibly stupid. After it was over, they couldn't explain why they did it. Janis wanted to get to the bottom of it, and his research led to the scientific categorization of groupthink, a term coined earlier by William H. White in *Fortune* magazine.

It turns out, for any plan to work, every team needs at least one asshole who doesn't give a shit if he or she gets fired or exiled or excommunicated. For a group to make good decisions, they must allow dissent and convince everyone they are free to speak their mind without risk of punishment.

It seems like common sense, but you will rationalize consensus unless you know how to avoid it. How many times have you settled on a bar or restaurant no one really wanted to go to? How many times have you given advice to someone that you knew wasn't really your honest opinion?

The recent housing market collapse, the failure to prevent the attack at Pearl Harbor, the sinking of the *Titanic*, the invasion of Iraq—all of these can be attributed to situations in which groupthink led to awful decisions.

True groupthink depends on three conditions—a group of people who like one another, isolation, and a deadline for a crucial decision.

As a primate, you are quick to form groups and then feel as if you should defend those groups from the ill wishes of other groups. When groups get together to make a decision, an illusion of invulnerability can emerge in which everyone feels secure in the cohesion. You begin to rationalize other people's ideas and don't reconsider your own. You want to defend the group's cohesion from all harm, so you suppress doubts, you don't argue, you don't offer alternatives—and since everyone is doing this, the leader of the group falsely assumes everyone is in agreement.

Research says the situation can be avoided if the boss is not allowed to express his or her expectations, thus preventing the boss's opinion from automatically becoming the opinion of others. In addition, if the group breaks into pairs every once in a while to discuss the issue at hand, a manageable level of dissent can be fostered.

Even better, allow outsiders to offer their opinions periodically during the process, to keep people's objectivity afloat. Finally, assign one person the role of asshole and charge that person with the responsibility of finding fault in the plan. Before you come to a consensus, allow a cooling off period so emotions can return to normal.

The research shows that groups of friends who allow members to disagree and still be friends are more likely to come to better decisions. So the next time you are in a group of people trying to reach consensus, be the asshole. Every group needs one, and it might as well be you.

24

Supernormal Releasers

THE MISCONCEPTION: *Men who have sex with RealDolls are insane, and women who marry eighty-year-old billionaires are gold diggers.*

THE TRUTH: *The RealDoll and rich old sugar daddies are both supernormal releasers.*

The Australian jewel beetle has sex with beer bottles.

The beetles are a light chocolate color with dimples all down their back and dark black legs and heads that peek out from underneath their carapaces. Their bodies are big and long instead of round, and they resemble cicadas more than they do ladybugs.

The male Australian jewel beetle is hardwired to like certain aspects about the female jewel beetle. They like females to be big, brown, and shiny. The bottles they make love to are bigger, browner, and shinier than any female could ever hope to be. In Australia, a certain type of bottle called stubbies overstimulates male jewel beetles. In a trash heap filled with bottles, you will often see every single stubby covered in male jewel beetles trying to get it on. The stubbies are what evolutionary psychologists call supernormal releasers. They are superstimuli, better than the real thing. The beetles will mate with these bottles even while being devoured by ants.

This sort of behavior is common across the animal kingdom. Anything that directly affects your survival can become a super-stimulus if exaggerated enough. Birds can become confused by eggs from other, parasitic birds who hijack their nests. The eggs look like theirs, but are much bigger, so they sit atop them even though they belong to another. There are orchids that have powerful scents like a female wasp's or a bee queen's, and males mate with the flower, getting covered in pollen in the process. Back when people lived in the wild, where high-calorie food was scarce, your ancestors developed an intense desire to gobble up as much animal fat as they could when they were lucky enough to find it. Now you can't stop eating french fries and cheeseburgers.

If you associate something with survival, but find an example of that thing that is more perfect than anything your ancestors could have ever dreamed of—it will overstimulate you.

When it comes to mate selection, the genders are usually divided into two camps. One has to carry the offspring and reproduce less often; the other can reproduce many times over without much risk. In this scenario, supernormal releasers either exaggerate the fertility and health of the egg carriers, or the status and resources of the sperm carriers.

For human ladies, a tux on a man who owns a private jet and three homes in Italy creates a powerful set of supernormal releasers. Most women wouldn't hook up with a man who looks like the Crypt Keeper, but if he owns a publishing empire or a fortune equivalent to the gross domestic product of a European nation, some will. For human guys, symmetry, big breasts, wide hips, narrow waists, lustrous hair, and voluptuous lips add up to a powerful supernormal releaser. Most men wouldn't have sex with a plastic corpse, but the strength of RealDoll sales over the years shows some will. Both of these examples are the human equivalent of those sexy beer bottles.

Psychologist David Buss has spent his career studying the preferences of men and women when it comes to selecting a mate both for short-term flings and long-term relationships. In his book *The Evolution of Desire,* he points to one crucial aspect which seems to be held above all others when men are making a snap judgment about physical attraction—the hip-to-waist ratio. In many studies around the world, no matter what cultural significance is placed on body type, a ratio in which the waist is about 70 percent the width of the hips is always preferred. According to Buss, a hip-to-waist ratio of .67 to .80 correlates to health, reproductive and otherwise. Women with this ratio truly are healthier, and this is something men know unconsciously. Psychologist Devendra Singh's 1993 study of *Playboy* centerfolds showed although the women in the magazine had become thinner over the years, their average hip-to-waist ratio remained a constant .70.

The strange thing about this natural tendency for men to prefer small waists and big hips is how a superstimulus with physically impossible features produces even more attraction. Psychologist Kerri Johnson's research into hip-to-waist ratios in 2005 showed both men and women used this metric to determine the gender of silhouettes. Her eye-tracking computer programs clearly showed both sexes first looked at the face and then moved around the hip area to see the telltale signs of gender. Her research also showed when men were asked to rate attractiveness they were drawn to a .70 waist. But they were drawn to waists of .60 and .50 even more.

A waist this small would make it impossible for a woman to bear children. So the superstimuli weren't telling the man this was an incredibly fertile and healthy woman; they were just a shortcut, a heuristic. Men's brains were telling them small waists and big hips were good. Since waists so small the woman wouldn't be able to bear children were unlikely in nature, there was no adjustment built into the heuristic to not be attracted to super-tiny waists.

Johnson also had men and women walk on a treadmill and told half of the subjects she was measuring their efficiency. She told the other half she was measuring how sexually attractive they were. When told they were being judged for sexiness, the women unconsciously swooshed their hips from side to side, which made it appear to observers as if their hip-to-waist ratio had magically been reduced. This is how superstimuli boggle your mind. Your mental shortcuts aren't prepared to deal with exaggerations. Barbie dolls, anime characters, and ancient fertility statues are impossible versions of women, but both sexes unconsciously know about the magic of the hip-to-waist ratio and the power of superstimuli.

Men are easy to manipulate thanks to having fewer metrics by which they judge potential mates, and thus advertising has long been preying on their tendencies. Women will buy products in an attempt to become the impossible goal. Men will buy products in an attempt to mate with the impossible goal. Sexy and sexist advertising can kill two birds with one stone. Advertisers use genetic freaks with abnormal symmetry, lit by professionals, altered by makeup artists, and finished off with Photoshop until they are nothing more than realistic cartoons—just like a RealDoll.

For women, a superstimulus has to have more than just a rocking body and a good hip-to-waist ratio. Women have more to lose when they make a bad decision, so they have evolved a more complex and particular set of metrics by which potential mates are judged. David Buss says those include, but are not limited to, economic capacity, social status, ambition, stability, intelligence, commitment, and height. Any one of these guides for reproductive success in both a short-term or long-term mate can become a superstimulus, but for a man to be a supernormal releaser he would need to possess several. A tall, rich doctor who is both kind and faithful is far more attractive than a short waiter who lives with his parents and is quick to anger, no matter how sculpted his chest is.

Don't leave this subject thinking you are above all of this. Even if you don't act on your impulses, you still feel them. Eventually, something will overtake you, even if it's as small as a sandwich with two pieces of fried chicken for a bun instead of bread. A study at Rutgers University in 2003 showed the average size of what most Americans considered a fair portion of food had increased significantly in twenty years. A glass of orange juice is now 40 percent larger. A bowl of cornflakes is 20 percent bigger. Plates in restaurants have grown by 25 percent in size. The influence of superstimuli has changed what people think is a generous helping, but no one noticed until recently.

Remember, you take mental shortcuts whenever possible to determine when something is awesome. When a stimulus goes from good to great, it does not mean it truly is better than the normal version. If the normal version is something that had to be created, had to be fabricated into something illusory, there is a good chance you'll have to fight your natural tendencies to be overwhelmed by superstimuli. Australian jewel beetles are doomed to lust for beer bottles in garbage heaps because they can't overcome their desires. You can.

25

The Affect Heuristic

THE MISCONCEPTION: *You calculate what is risky or rewarding and always choose to maximize gains while minimizing losses.*

THE TRUTH: *You depend on emotions to tell you if something is good or bad, greatly overestimate rewards, and tend to stick to your first impressions.*

Suppose I offered you the chance to earn some fast cash just by picking red jelly beans out of a bowl.

I give you two options, a giant bowl with hundreds of red beans mixed in with hundreds of others, or a small bowl containing fifty mixed beans with a higher ratio of red beans than the larger bowl. The bowls are even labeled with your odds of winning. The big one says 7 percent; the small one says 10 percent. Each time you pull out a red one, I'll give you $1. Which bowl do you pick?

In a 1994 study Veronika Denes-Raj and Seymour Epstein published in the *Journal of Personality and Social Psychology,* they discovered that people picked the big bowl over the little bowl, even though the red ratio was higher in the smaller bowl. When asked why, they said they just felt like their chances were better because there were more red beans in the big bowl despite knowing the true odds were against them.

The tendency to make poor decisions and ignore odds in favor of your gut feelings is called the affect heuristic. It is always getting between you and your best interests, and it starts when you make a snap judgment about something new.

The first time you meet someone, billions of microthoughts ricochet through the chemical and electrical conduits in your cranium. You begin making judgments about the person's character before you realize it. You may notice a handshake that is strong and vigorous, that the person's posture is forward and sturdy, that his or her smile is perfect and warm. You take all these features and multiply them by how the person is dressed, divide by the way the person smells, and factor age into a huge equation that forms a first impression in your unconscious. This person is good. Let's get to know this person.

What if you meet someone who keeps making racist remarks, has a swastika tattooed on one wrist, and smells like mushroom gravy? Before you can turn your emotions into thoughts, you are increasing the distance between you and that person's funk.

Common sense says first impressions fade as you get to know someone, but first impressions matter more than you realize. Research shows the first impression you have about a person, or anything else, tends to linger. A study in 1997 by Wilkielman, Zajonc, and Shwartz created first impressions in subjects with images of smiles and frowns. The people in the study saw a photo of either a happy or a sad face flash briefly on a screen and then were shown an unfamiliar Chinese character and asked to say whether or not they liked it. People tended to say they liked the characters that followed the smiles over the ones that followed frowns, but later on when they saw the same characters with the expressions preceding them reversed, they didn't change their answers. Their first impression remained.

You boil down your initial judgment of just about everything in life to "this is good" or "this is bad" and then put the burden of proof on future experience to show you otherwise. You might like someone early on but learn of severe faults over time. You wait for your first impression to be chiseled away instead of promptly changing your opinion of that person's character. Maybe the person dresses well and waxes poetic on the virtues of good hygiene but gets touchy-feely and hits on every person of the opposite sex who's around for more than four minutes. Maybe the person beats his or her children but spends weekends at a nursing home teaching the elderly how to use computers. How much evidence would you need to move a new acquaintance from one category to the other?

The affect heuristic is one way you rapidly come to a conclusion about new information. You use it to drop data into two broad categories—good and bad—and then you choose to avoid or seek out what you have judged. The affect heuristic is the Holy Grail of cognitive biases in advertising and politics. When you can associate your product or candidate with positive things or your competitors and opponents with negative things, you win. If you build up enough associations, your product can become eponymous with the category it occupies. Facial tissues become Kleenex. Pain medicine becomes Aspirin. Bandages become Band-Aids.

There is debate among psychologists on just how powerful and trustworthy snap decisions are, but there is no doubt they play a large role in who you are and how you interpret your senses. When first impressions linger and influence how you feel about second, third, and fourth impressions, you are being befuddled by the affect heuristic.

Much of the machinery of the mind takes place behind closed doors in corridors of the unconscious, and these ruminations are part of a give-and-take with the conscious mind. Psychologists sometimes divide the mind into parts that correspond with the evolution of the brain. This is an oversimplification, but it is useful to see in the various parts the story of how your brain evolved from the simple versions carried around by insects and fish. It helps to make sense of how the mind is formed if you see the brain layered like an archaeological dig that is stratified with the oldest artifacts underneath the more recent. The oldest parts lie mostly in the hind-brain. These structures, among others, are concerned with your survival and help regulate all those things you don't have to think about, like breathing and balancing on one foot. The mid-brain structures were shaped by your primate ancestors and grant you emotions and social awareness. The top layer, the most recently evolved, reasons and calculates. The frontal lobes and neocortex act as executive offices of the mind, taking suggestions from all other structures and formulating plans of action.

Your rational, mathematical, reasonable, and methodical mind is slow and plodding. It takes notes and uses tools. Your irrational, emotional, instinctive mind is lightning-fast. When you decide to change your own oil, or install a new dishwasher, you depend on processing, on instructions and measurements, but less on emotions. You depend on snap judgments, on feelings that can't be described with equations, when you decide where to go to lunch or what movie to rent. The conscious mind is still making choices, but the unconscious mind is providing feelings and influence. A great deal of your life is contemplated by the emotional brain, which means in social situations and matters of life and death your thoughts and behaviors are inspired by automatic and unconscious triggers, suggestions from a shadowy place that is difficult to access and explain. There are many books on the topic, but for our purposes just keep in mind how powerful an influence your mood is on the decision-making regions of your mind. You can see the mind as divided into automatic, emotional, and rational spheres of thought. Let's reduce this to two, the conscious you and the unconscious you.

Unconscious-you has a lot in common with mice. A mouse eats about 15 percent of its body weight in food every day. A 180-pound man would have to eat more than a pound of food an hour to match such a cranked-up metabolism. These tiny, frenetic creatures are curious but cautious, and like any animal in the wild, mice base most of their behavior on the tug-of-war between risk and reward. Since a mouse needs to eat all the time, it is constantly faced with situations where it must weigh the danger of foraging against its hunger for calories. The mouse has a primitive brain, so it can't base its choices on reason, on a careful analysis of economic benefits versus systemic losses. It feels its way through life with the rodent equivalent of intuition. When it faces a novel situation, it decides whether or not to proceed without using the same kind of logic you are able to summon. Otherwise, mousetraps would be useless. Go back far enough and you share a common ancestor with the mouse, and those unconscious abilities to recognize risk and reward evolved into the versions you and the mouse both still use. The recognition of risk isn't something you determine with imaginary spreadsheets and slide rules of the mind. While blueprints and diagrams require careful planning, identifying risk comes from the gut, or, more accurately, it comes from the emotion-generating structures in your brain. A simple assessment of a situation as either good or bad kept your ancestors out of the mouths of predators and away from the business end of a spear most of the time, but when the problem is too complicated—like a mousetrap to a foraging rodent—you can really screw things up.

When you return to a place where snakes slither underfoot and food grows on bushes, your attention collapses to what is within reach. Your risk instincts serve you well when you are back in the same conditions your brain was evolved to deal with, like if you're lost in the woods while hiking or hunting. In any circumstance where the only concerns are those of immediate risk and reward, the software handed down through your genes can get you pretty far. Fast-forward to typical human life today, and now your ancient mind must deal with a world mostly out of reach. Loans and retirement plans, heart disease and elections are far less tangible than the growling of your belly and the creatures that slink through the night. Your risk-avoidance systems are great when the situation is concrete but are pretty crappy when dealing with abstraction.

Antoine Becharo and Hanna Demasio in 1997 published a study in the journal *Science* that is often cited as a great demonstration of the unconscious you. They hypothesized your reasoning "is preceded by a nonconscious biasing step that uses neural systems other than those that support declarative knowledge." In other words, you are problem-solving before you are aware of it.

In the study, participants played a card game without any idea of what the rules were. They knew only they would earn money when they won and lose money when they lost. To play, they drew cards one at a time off the top of four separate decks until the psychologists said they were finished. The first two decks paid handsomely but were loaded with losing cards that took a lot of money away from the subjects. The other two decks paid meagerly, but the losing card's fees were small. Over time, the people playing would shift from the high-reward but high-risk decks to the low-reward, low-risk ones. The powers of pattern recognition shaped their behavior toward the best choices without their knowing exactly what they were doing. As fascinating as this is, the study goes further. The participants were hooked up to sensors that measured the moisture levels of their skin, a facet of the human body automatically and unconsciously mind-controlled by the sympathetic nervous system. Those levels began to spike as the people reached for the high-risk decks well before they stopped picking those cards. The unconscious was noticing the risks and placing warnings in the suggestion box about how to proceed long before the decision-making conscious mind was able to act. Questioned later, about a third of the subjects were unable to explain why they decided to stick to the safe cards.

Decisions about risk and reward begin with the unconscious you. Unconscious-you notices things are either bad or good, dangerous or safe, before conscious-you can put those feelings into words. Good things reward you, bad things harm you. When you are determining if something is good, you are saying it is worth the risk of obtaining it. Would you sleep overnight with a poisonous snake loose in your apartment? The risk of being bitten in your sleep greatly outweighs the reward of sleeping in your own bed, so probably not. Would you fly to Las Vegas for a vacation? The risk of dying in a plane crash is worth the reward of seeing Penn & Teller and gambling in the desert, so you buy a ticket and deal with the turbulence.

These calculations aren't done on a blackboard in your mind; they are derived from consultation with gut feelings, emotional twinges rising like the tips of icebergs from the inky depths of your unconscious. Your species, all species, have been making decisions from the gut for far longer than from careful contemplation, so the influence of these mental machinations is great.

In 1982, a patient known to neuroscience as Elliot developed a brain tumor in his orbitofrontal cortex. Although it wrecked his life, it gave to science an unprecedented look into how important emotion is to decision making. Before the tumor, Elliot was a successful accountant with a home, a wife, and savings in the bank. After the tumor, he became unable to make snap decisions and would instead become transfixed when asked to choose something as simple as which shirt to wear in the morning. His emotional brain became unable to communicate with his rational brain after his tumor was removed. When researchers hooked him up to the same sort of skin conductance measurement devices used in the card game stud, he registered no emotional response to photos of mangled bodies or other images normal people instantly recoil from. To him, the images were neither good nor bad. He became a being of pure rational thought, seeing every bit of information flowing into his mind with cold logic. Elliot could no longer make simple choices because he had no emotions. If he had to pick something to eat from a menu, he would endlessly pore over all the variables as if the secrets of the universe were unfolding before him. Texture, size, shape, calories, flavor, the history of his diet, the price—all of these variables and hundreds more would be subdivided into more variables and then weighed against one another in an endless cycle of computation. Without emotion, it became incredibly difficult to settle on any one option. He became a robot without hate, love, or yearning. He eventually divorced, lost his job, money, house, and everything else from his former life except the love of his parents, who took him in.

The affect heuristic, therefore, is often a good thing. You need it to see danger and pick a place to eat after a concert. The problems arise when you must evaluate large numbers or percentages, when you must see connections and abstractions. This is why politicians who bring out charts and graphs tend to fail, and those who use anecdotes tend to win. Stories make sense on an emotional level, so anything that conjures fear, empathy, or pride will trump confusing statistics. It causes you to buy a security system for your house but neglect to purchase radon detectors. It makes you carry pepper spray while you clog your arteries with burritos. It installs metal detectors in schools but leaves french fries on the menu. It creates vegetarian smokers. Well-known, primal dangers are easy to see, easy to guard against, even when greater dangers loom. The affect heuristic speaks to your basic sensibilities about risk and reward while neglecting the big picture and the dangers of complex systems that require study and deeper understanding.

In 2000, Melissa L. Funicane, Ali Alhakami, Paul Slovic, and Stephen M. Johnson had subjects rate both how risky and how beneficial they felt natural gas, food preservatives, and nuclear power plants were on a scale of one to ten. The subjects were divided into groups where some people read only about the risks while others read about the benefits, and then each had to come up with revised ratings. As you might expect, people who read about the benefits later rated the technologies as being even more beneficial to society than they did at first. The weird part? They rated the risks as being lower. The gap widened. The same was true for the other group who rated the dangers as being more risky than they had in the first questionnaire and the benefits as less appealing. They were even more likely to widen the gap when given a short time limit to give an answer. Logically, risks and benefits are two different things and must be judged separately, but you don't judge things logically. The more something seems to benefit you, the less risky it seems overall. When you see something as good, the bad qualities are played down. When you see something as risky, the harder it becomes to notice the benefits. The affect heuristic is stronger still when something is familiar or speaks to the primal brain.

The feeling you get in your gut telling you yes or no, good or bad is greatly influenced by the affect heuristic. Keep this in mind when you notice fearful language and imagery coming from any source with an agenda. Remember your tendency to rush to judgment and stick with first impressions when someone is obviously playing up the positive side of an issue or begins to use euphemistic language. You are always looking for risks and rewards, but when you want to believe something is good you will unconsciously turn down the volume on the bad qualities, and vice versa. Any familiar danger will overshadow new threats, and first impressions are difficult to change.

26

Dunbar's Number

THE MISCONCEPTION: *There is a Rolodex in your mind with the names and faces of everyone you've ever known.*

THE TRUTH: *You can maintain relationships and keep up with only around 150 people at once.*

Think of a cup completely filled with water. You try to add one drop to this cup, and one drop spills out. You try to pour a cup of water into it, and a cup of water spills out. This is called a zero-sum system. To add anything to it you must remove an equal proportion.

The bank of names and faces and relationships in your mind, the one you use to keep up with who is a friend, who is a foe, and who is a potential mate—this bank is a zero-sum system too. The reason for this doesn't really have to do with how much space you have to keep the information, it has to do with how much energy you have on tap to devote to worrying about your place in your social world.

In other primates, social relationships are maintained by grooming—picking bugs off of one another. You don't go to a *Mad*

Men party and dig around in your friend's hair while watching the show. But getting together for any reason is still a grooming behavior. You hang out, work on projects, and talk on the phone to keep connected. Visiting friends just to shoot the shit is the human equivalent of picking ticks off of one another's backs. As technology has allowed you to be farther and farther apart yet still keep in touch with loved ones, your grooming behavior has remained constant. In fact, most of your innate gregariousness works as it always has by adapting to the norms of the era. In modern life, human relationships are no longer separated geographically. You can probably start with any one person alive and play six degrees of separation to get to any other person. Modern humans are deeply interconnected.

But you can't keep up with all those people and their connections, not in a real social way—you are not so smart. The truth is, out of this cluster of humans you can reliably manage to keep up with only around 150 people. More specifically, it's between 150 and 230. Giant cities full of other humans, Internet social networks with hundreds of people sharing status updates, corporations with branches around the world—your brain is incapable of handling the multitude of human contacts populating these examples. All those personalities and quirks, the history of your interactions with each, it becomes a giant file of social information that takes constant maintenance. Psychology has shown us the brain is not like a hard drive, so the problem with too many relationships isn't a space issue. The problem is more about the economic limits of your mental human relations department.

Why is this?

The neocortex of primates is the part of the brain responsible for keeping up with others. We can't be certain of what forces shaped the size of this part of the brain, but for each primate the size of the cortex correlates with the size of the average social group. Apes live in small groups; humans live in big ones. Robin Dunbar, the anthropologist who first presented this concept, figures the size of the average group is directly correlated with how efficiently the members can socially groom one another. Dunbar says that efficiency is predicted by how large the primate's neocortex is. According to Dunbar, the larger the group, the more time must be spent by each member to maintain social cohesion. Each person must do some grooming with each other person and then also keep up with who is friends with whom, who has a beef, and what each other's relative status is compared to his or hers and others'. The complexity builds exponentially with each new member. If someone you know moves away, you start to groom that person less and less, until you start to touch base once a year, or maybe lose touch for years. It takes far more effort to stay connected once a friend escapes your direct contact. That effort takes away from the time you can spend with other friends. Your brain was shaped in a world where this time also took away from other efforts—like hunting, gathering, and building shelter. There is a maximum amount of time and effort you can spend—it is a zero-sum system.

Since efficiency is the predictor of group size, you have an advantage over apes and monkeys in the form of language. Social grooming through language is more efficient than grooming through picking lice and fleas, Dunbar says. The preset amount of effort afforded you by your neocortex sets the limit on group size. To add more people to a group would ruin the cohesion. An unbalanced group fails. A balanced group succeeds.

This upper limit shaped the way humans have organized throughout history.

Sure enough, all the sciences that study tribes, bands, and villages have approximated ancient groups usually maxed out around 150 people. This is the approximate upper limit to how many people you can trust and count on for favors, whom you can call up and have a conversation with. Once you go over 150 people, Dunbar says about 42 percent of the group's time would have to be spent worrying about one another's relationships. It would take a lot of pressure from the environment for it to be worth growing a group to that level. Once people started coming up with ways to maintain larger groups, like armies, cities, and nations, humans started subdividing those groups. Dunbar's number explains why big groups are made of smaller, more manageable groups like companies, platoons, and squads—or branches, divisions, departments, and committees. No human institution can efficiently function above 150 members without hierarchies, ranks, roles, and divisions.

In the wild, it takes a lot of work to get a group of 150 people to cooperate and pursue a common goal. In modern life, you depend on institutional structure. As Malcolm Gladwell pointed out in his book *The Tipping Point,* if a company grows beyond 150 people, productivity sharply declines until the company divides its outlying entities into smaller groups. You function better in a cluster—that way everyone in that cluster is connected to one another and only certain individuals connect your cluster to other clusters.

Dunbar's number isn't fixed. It can be increased or decreased depending on the environment and tools you have available. You most likely have a much smaller group of friends than 150 people, but when you are incentivized to connect to more people than you would naturally associate with—like at your job or in a school—150 is the point where your neocortex cries uncle. With better tools—like telephones, Facebook, e-mail, *World of Warcraft* guilds, and so on—you become slightly more efficient at maintaining relationships, so the number can be larger, but not much larger. Dunbar's most recent research suggests even power-users of Facebook with 1,000 or more friends still communicate regularly with only around 150 people, and of that 150 they strongly communicate with a group of less than 20.

The social Web is revolutionizing the way institutions operate, and the way people communicate, but in the end it might not have much of an effect on the core social group you depend on for true friendship. You can maintain a giant number of weak ties to people on Facebook, Twitter, and whatever comes next, much like you can in a giant company. Strong ties, however, require constant grooming. People who use the number of friends they have on Facebook as a metric of their social standing are fooling themselves. You can share videos of fainting goats with hundreds of acquaintances and thousands of followers, but you can trust a secret only with a handful of true friends.

27

Selling Out

THE MISCONCEPTION: *Both consumerism and capitalism are sustained by corporations and advertising.*

THE TRUTH: *Both consumerism and capitalism are driven by competition among consumers for status.*

Beatniks, hippies, punk rockers, grunge rats, metal heads, goth kids, hipsters—see a pattern forming here?

Whether you lived through Freedom Summer or *Jem and the Holograms,* somewhere in your youth you started to realize who was in control, and you rebelled. You needed to self-actualize, to find your own way, and you sought out something real, something with meaning. You waved your hand at popular music, popular movies, and popular television. You dug deeper and disparaged all those mindless sheeple who gobbled up pop culture.

Yet you still listened to music and bought shirts and went to see movies. Someone was appealing to you despite your dissent. If you think you can buy your way to individuality, well, you are not so smart.

Since the 1940s, when capitalism and marketing married psychology and public relations, the Man has been getting much better and more efficient at offering you something to purchase no matter your taste.

Think about an archetypal punk rocker with chains and spikes, gaudy pants and a leather jacket. Yeah, he bought all of those clothes. Someone is making money off of his revolt. That's the paradox of consumer rebellion—everything is part of the system. We all sell out, because we all buy things. Every niche opened by rebellion against the mainstream is immediately filled by entrepreneurs who figure out how to make a buck off those who are trying to avoid what the majority of people are buying.

In the late 1990s and early 2000s, there were many stabs at trying to thwart this through artistic filmmaking—*Fight Club*, *American Beauty*, *Fast Food Nation*, *The Corporation*, etc. The creators of these works may have had the best intentions, but their work still became a product designed for profit. Their cries against consumption were consumed.

Michael Moore, Noam Chomsky, Kurt Cobain, Andy Kaufman—they may have been solely concerned with creating art or illustrating academic principles, but once their output fell into the marketplace, it found its audience, and that audience made them wealthy.

Joseph Heath and Andrew Potter, both philosophers, wrote a book about this in 2004 called *The Rebel Sell*. It's available in the United States as *Nation of Rebels*. The central theme of the book is you can't rage against the machine through rebellious consumption.

Here's the conventional thinking most countercultures are founded upon:

All the interconnected institutions in the marketplace need everyone to conform in order to sell the most products to the most people. The media, through press releases, advertising, entertainment, and so on, works to bring everyone into homogeneity by altering desires. To escape consumerism and conformity, you must turn your back and ignore the mainstream culture. The shackles will then fall away, the machines will grind to a halt, the filters will dissolve, and you will see the world for what it really is. The illusory nature of existence will end and we will all, finally, be *real*.

The problem, say Heath and Potter, is the system doesn't give a shit about conformity. In fact, it loves diversity and needs people like hipsters and music snobs so it can thrive.

For example, say there is this awesome band no one knows about except you and a few others. They don't have a record contract or an album. They just go out there and play, and they are great. You tell everyone about them as they build a decent fan base. They make an album that sells enough copies to allow them to quit their day jobs. That album gets them more gigs and more fans. Soon they have a huge fan base and get a record contract and get on the radio and play on *The Tonight Show*. Now they've sold out. So you hate them. You abandon the band and go looking for someone more authentic, and it all starts over again. This is the pump by which artists rise from the depths into the mainstream. It never stops, and over time it gets faster and more efficient.

Unknown bands are a special sort of commodity. Living in a loft in a dodgy part of town, wearing clothes from the thrift store, watching the independent film no one has heard of—these provide a special social status that can't be bought as easily as the things offered to the mainstream.

In the 1960s, it took months before someone figured out they could sell tie-dyed shirts and bell bottoms to anyone who wanted to rebel. In the 1990s, it took weeks to start selling flannel shirts and

Doc Martens to people in the Deep South. Now people are hired by corporations to go to bars and clubs and observe what the counterculture is into and have it on the shelves in the mall stores right as it becomes popular.

The counterculture, the indie fans, and the underground stars—they are the driving force behind capitalism. They are the engine.

This brings us to the point: Competition among consumers is the turbine of capitalism.

Everyone who lives above the poverty line but isn't wealthy pretty much has no choice but to work for a living doing something that rewards them with survival tokens. Working as a telemarketer, for example, allows you to have food, clothing, and shelter, but doesn't put you directly in charge of creating, growing, or killing those things you need for sustenance. Instead, you trade in tokens for those things. As a result, you have a lot of free time and some leftover tokens.

Back before mass production, people were often defined by their work, by their output. The things they owned usually either were things they hand made or were things other people made by hand. There was a weight, an infusion of soul, in everything a person owned, used, and lived in.

Today everyone is a consumer and has to pick from the same selection of goods as everyone else; and because of this people now define their personalities by how good their taste is, or how clever, or how obscure, or how ironic their choices are.

As Christian Lander, author of *Stuff White People Like*, pointed out in an interview with NPR, you compete with your peers by one-upping them. You attain status by having better taste in movies and music, by owning more authentic furniture and clothing. There are

100 million versions of every item or intellectual property you can own, so you reveal your unique character through how you consume.

Having a dissenting opinion on movies, music, or clothes, or owning clever or obscure possessions, is the way middle-class people fight one another for status. They can't out-consume one another because they can't afford it, but they can out-taste one another.

Since everything is mass-produced, and often for a mass audience, finding and consuming things that appeal to your desire for authenticity is what moves these items and artists and services and goods up from the bottom to the top—where they can be mass-consumed.

Hipsters, then, are the direct result of this cycle of indie, authentic, obscure, ironic, clever consumerism. Which, in itself, is ironic—but not like a trucker hat or Pabst Blue Ribbon. It is ironic in the sense the very act of trying to run counter to the culture is what creates the next wave of culture people will in turn attempt to counter.

I think "sell out" is yelled by those who, when they were selling, didn't have anything anyone wanted to buy.

—Patton Oswalt

Wait long enough, and what was once mainstream will fall into obscurity. When that happens, it will become valuable again to those looking for authenticity or irony or cleverness. The value, then, is not intrinsic. The thing itself doesn't have as much value as the perception of how it was obtained or why it is possessed. Once enough people join in, like with oversized glasses frames or slap bracelets, the status gained from owning the item or being a fan of the band is lost, and the search begins again.

You would compete like this no matter how society was constructed. Competition for status is built into the human experience at the biological level. Poor people compete with resources. The middle class competes with selection. The wealthy compete with possessions.

You sold out long ago in one way or another. The specifics of who you sell to and how much you make—those are only details.

28

Self-Serving Bias

THE MISCONCEPTION: *You evaluate yourself based on past successes and defeats.*

THE TRUTH: *You excuse your failures and see yourself as more successful, more intelligent, and more skilled than you are.*

In the early days of psychology there was a prevailing belief among scientists. They thought just about everyone had low self-esteem, inferiority complexes, and a cluster of self-loathing neuroses. Those old beliefs are still reverberating in the public consciousness, but they were mostly wrong. The research conducted over the last fifty years has revealed the complete opposite to be true. Day to day, you think you are awesome, or at least far more awesome than you are.

This is good. Self-esteem is mostly self-delusion, but it serves a purpose. You are biologically driven to think highly of yourself in order to avoid stagnation. If you were to stop and truly examine your faults and failures, you would become paralyzed by fear and doubt. Despite this, from time to time in your life, your personal hype machine sputters to a stop. You get depressed and anxious.

You question yourself and your abilities. Usually, it passes as your psychological immune system fights off the negative attitudes. In some places, like the modern United States, this hype machine is reinforced by a culture of exceptionalism.

This tendency to see yourself as above average is also bad. If you never see how much you are screwing up your life, mistreating your friends, and being a complete douche bag, you can destroy yourself without realizing how bad things have become.

In the 1990s, there was a lot of research aimed at discovering just how deluded people were when it came to failure and success. The findings of these studies showed you tend to accept credit when you succeed, but blame bad luck, unfair rules, difficult instructors, bad bosses, cheaters, and so on when you fail. When you are doing well, you think you are to blame. When you are doing badly, you think the world is to blame. This behavior can be observed in board games and senate races, group projects and final exams. When things are going your way, you attribute everything to your amazing skills, but once the tide turns, you look for external factors that prevented your genius from shining through. This gets even weirder when you let some time pass. All the dumb things you did when you were younger, all those poor decisions, you see them as being made by your former self. According to research conducted by Anne Wilson and Michael Ross in 2001, you see the person you used to be as a foolish bumbler with poor taste but your current self as a badass who is worthy of at least three times the praise.

This sort of thinking also spreads to the way you compare yourself to others. The last thirty years' worth of research shows just about all of us think we are more competent than our coworkers, more ethical than our friends, friendlier than the general public, more intelligent than our peers, more attractive than the average person, less prejudiced than people in our region, younger-looking than people the same age, better drivers than most people we know, better children than our siblings, and that we will live longer than the average lifespan. (As you just read that list, maybe you said to yourself, "No, I don't think I'm better than everyone." So you think you're more honest with yourself than the average person? You are not so smart.) No one, it seems, believes he or she is part of the population contributing to the statistics generating averages. You don't believe you are an average person, but you do believe everyone else is. This tendency, which springs from self-serving bias, is called the illusory superiority effect.

You are incredibly egocentric, just like everyone else. Your world is subjective by default, so it follows that most of your thoughts and behaviors are born of a subjective analysis of your personal world. The things affecting your daily life are always more significant than something happening far away or in the head of another person. When it comes to judging your abilities or your status, this egocentricity makes it difficult to see yourself as a number, an average. You find the idea repellent and search for a way to see yourself as unique. In 1999, Justin Kruger at the New York University Stern School of Business showed illusory superiority was more likely to manifest in the minds of subjects when they were told ahead of time a certain task was easy. When they rated their abilities after being primed to think the task was considered simple, people said they performed better than average. When he then told people they were about to perform a task that was difficult, they rated their performance as being below average even when it wasn't. No matter the actual difficulty, just telling people ahead of time how hard the undertaking would be changed how they saw themselves in comparison to an imagined average. To defeat feelings of inadequacy, you first have to imagine a task as being simple and easy. If you can manage to do that, illusory superiority takes over.

The self-serving bias and illusory superiority aren't limited to thoughts about performance. You also use these mental constructs to perceive how you stand in relationships and social situations. In 1993, Ezra Zuckerman and John Jost at Stanford University asked undergraduates at the University of Chicago to assess their popularity relative to their peers. They took those estimates and compared them with what others reported. They were building on the work of Abraham Tesser, who created self-evaluation maintenance theory in 1988. According to his research, you pay close attention to the successes and failures of friends more than you do to those of strangers. You compare yourself to those who are close to you in order to judge your own worth. In other words, you know Barack Obama and Johnny Depp are successful, but you don't use them as a standard for your own life to the degree you do coworkers, fellow students, or friends you've known since high school. Zuckerman and Jost had students list the number of people they considered friends and then asked if the subjects believed they had more friends than did their peers and more friends than the average student. Thirty-five percent of the students said they had more friends than the typical student, and 23 percent said they had fewer. This better-than-average feeling was enhanced when considering their peers—41 percent said they had more friendships than did the people they considered to be their friends. Only 16 percent said they had fewer. On average, everyone you know thinks they are more popular than you, and you think you are more popular than them.

Sure, some of your faults are just too obvious, even to you, but you compensate for those by inflating what you like most about you.

When you compare your skills, accomplishments, and friendships with those of others, you tend to accentuate the positive and eliminate the negative. You are a liar by default, and you lie most to yourself. If you fail, you forget it. If you win, you tell everyone. When it comes to being honest with yourself and those you love, you are not so smart. But self-serving bias keeps you going when the hype machine runs low on fuel.

29

The Spotlight Effect

THE MISCONCEPTION: *When you are around others, you feel as if everyone is noticing every aspect of your appearance and behavior.*

THE TRUTH: *People devote little attention to you unless prompted to.*

You spill a drink at a party. You get a mustard stain on your shirt. Your forehead is breaking out on the day you have to do a presentation. Oh no. What will people think? Chances are, they won't think anything. Most people won't notice at all, and if they do, they'll probably disregard and forget your imperfections and faux pas within seconds.

You lose some weight, buy a new pair of pants, and strut through doors expecting some sort of acknowledgment. Perhaps you get a new haircut, or buy a new watch. You spend an extra fifteen minutes in front of the mirror expecting the world to notice. You spend so much time thinking about your own body, your own thoughts and behaviors, you begin to think other people must be noticing too. The research says they aren't, at least not nearly as much as you are.

When in a group or public setting, you think every little nuance of your behavior is under scrutiny by everyone else. The effect is even worse if you must stand on a stage or go out with someone for the first time. You can't help but be the center of your universe, and you find it difficult to gauge just how much other people are paying attention since you are paying attention to you all the time. When you start to imagine yourself in the audience, you believe every little misstep is amplified. You are not so smart when it comes to dealing with crowds because you are too egocentric. Fortunately, everyone else is just as egocentric, and they are just as convinced that they are being scrutinized.

The spotlight effect was studied at Cornell in 1996 by Thomas Gilovich, who researched the degree to which people believe their actions and appearance are noticed by others. He had college students put on T-shirts featuring the smiling face of Barry Manilow and then knock on the door to a classroom where other subjects were filling out a questionnaire. When you are late to a class or to work, or walk into a crowded theater or nightclub, you feel as if all eyes are on you, judging and criticizing. These students had to shed their normal clothes for a shirt with a giant Barry Manilow head beaming back out into the world, so Gilovich hypothesized they would feel an especially strong version of the spotlight effect when they had to walk into the classroom. Each person did this, and then walked over and spoke with the researcher for a moment. The researcher then pulled up a chair and told the embarrassed subject to sit down, but right as they did they were told to stand back up and were then led out for a debriefing. They asked the subjects to estimate how many people noticed their shirt. The people wearing the embarrassing attire figured about half of the people in the room saw it and noticed how awful it was. When the researchers then asked the people in the classroom to describe the subject, about 25 percent recalled seeing Manilow. In a situation designed to draw attention, only a quarter of the observers noticed the odd clothing choice, not half. Gilovich repeated the experiment, but this time allowed the students to pick a "cool" shirt depicting Jerry Seinfeld, Bob Marley, or Martin Luther King Jr. In this run, the estimates were the same. They thought about half the class saw their awesome shirt. Less than 10 percent did. This suggests the spotlight effect is strong for both positive and negative images of yourself, but the real world is far less likely to give a shit when you are trying to look cool. Gilovich has repeated his work on crowded New York streets, and although people felt as if a giant spotlight was shining down illuminating their tiny place in the world and all eyes were upon them, in reality, most people didn't notice them at all.

The spotlight effect leads you to believe everyone notices when you drive around town in a new, expensive car. They don't. After all, the last time you saw an awesome car, do you remember who was driving it? Do you even remember the last time you saw an awesome car? This feeling extends into other situations as well. For instance, if you are playing *Rock Band* or singing karaoke or doing anything where you feel your actions are being monitored by others, you tend to believe every up and down of your performance is being cataloged and critiqued. Not so.

You will apologize or make fun of yourself in an attempt to soften the blows, but it doesn't matter. In 2001, Gilovich had subjects play a competitive video game and rate how much attention they thought their teammates and opponents were paying to their performance. He found people paid lots of attention to how they themselves were doing, but almost no attention to others. While playing, they felt like everyone else was keeping up with how good they were at the game.

Research shows people believe others see their contributions to conversation as being memorable, but they aren't. You think everyone noticed when you stumbled in your speech, but they didn't. Well, unless you drew attention to it by over-apologizing.

The next time you get a pimple on your forehead, or buy a new pair of shoes, or Tweet about how boring your day is, don't expect anyone to notice. You are not so smart or special.

30

The Third Person Effect

THE MISCONCEPTION: *You believe your opinions and decisions are based on experience and facts, while those who disagree with you are falling for the lies and propaganda of sources you don't trust.*

THE TRUTH: *Everyone believes the people they disagree with are gullible, and everyone thinks they are far less susceptible to persuasion than they truly are.*

I can see right through that politician's lies. People are such sheep. People are so stupid. People will believe anything. I prefer to lead, not follow.

Have you ever thought like this? Would it blow your mind to know everyone thinks this?

If we all think we aren't gullible and can't be swayed by advertising, political rhetoric, or charismatic con artists, then some of us must be deluding ourselves. Sometimes that's you.

A great many messages among the countless ones bombarding you every day are considered dangerous because they might sway other people or fester in their minds until they act out on the suggestions coming out of all manner of sources, from violent video games to late-night pundit programming. For every outlet of information, there are some who see it as dangerous not because it affects them, but because it might affect the thoughts and opinions of an imaginary third party. This sense of alarm about the impact of speech not on yourself but on others is called the third person effect.

As a modern human, you are bombarded with media messages, but you see yourself as less affected than others. Somehow you have been inoculated against the persuaders, you think, so you have nothing to worry about. You can't count on everyone else to be as strong as you are, so if you are like most people, there are some voices you think should be quiet. You might even go so far as to think some messages should be censored—not for you, for them.

Who is them? It changes with the zeitgeist. It might be children, or high school kids, or college students. It might be liberals or conservatives. It might be the elderly, the middle-class, the super-rich. Whatever groups you don't belong to become the groups who you think will be bowled over by messages you don't agree with.

Studies from the beginning of psychology up until today have revealed many ways in which people truly are affected by hidden persuasion. As you learned in the chapters on priming and the affect heuristic, just about anything you see or hear will in some way influence your later behavior. You tend to accept this as true for everyone but yourself.

Richard M. Perloff in 1993 and Bryant Paul in 2000 reviewed all the studies since researcher W. Phillips Davison first coined the term "third person effect" in 1983. Davison noticed some people saw certain messages in the media as a call to action, not because of what was being said, but because of who might hear it. He pointed to the third person effect as the source of outrage from religious leaders over "heretical propaganda" and the ire of political rulers over some speech out of a "fear of dissent." Furthermore, Davison saw such censorship as arising out of a belief that some messages might harm "more impressionable minds." Perloff and Paul found that the third person effect is magnified when you already have a negative opinion of the source, or if you personally think the message is about something you aren't interested in. In all, their meta-analysis showed the majority of people believe they aren't like the majority of people.

You don't want to believe you can be persuaded, and one way of maintaining this belief is to assume that all the persuasion flying through the air must be landing on other targets. Otherwise how could it be successful? Those advertisements for cheeseburgers are for fatties with no self-control, you think, until you are ravenous and are forced to choose between one fast-food place and another. Those alcohol billboards are for trendy hipsters, you assume, until you are at the office Christmas party and the guy at the open bar asks you what you want. Public service announcements about texting while driving are for people who don't live the kind of life you do, you think, until you find yourself feeling a twinge of shame when you reach for the phone to respond to an e-mail while waiting for the light to turn green.

When you watch your preferred news channel or read your favorite newspaper or blog, you tend to believe you are an independent thinker. You may disagree with people on the issues, but you see yourself as having an open mind, as a person who looks at the facts and reaches conclusions after rational objective analysis. On the other side of the television, networks and producers design programming based on statistics and ratings, on demographic analysis that cuts through the third person effect so you can keep on believing you aren't the kind of person who watches the shows you watch. You tend to think you are not like the people who live in your town, go to your school, work at your business, and so on. You are unique. You dance to the beat of a different drummer. You fail to realize just by living in your town, attending your school, and working at your job, you *are* the kind of person who would do those things. If you weren't, you would be doing something else. You might say, "Well, I have to be here. I have no choice," but you ignore how many of your peers are probably using the same excuse.

The third person effect isn't limited to advertising or politics. For just about every topic listed in this book there are many people who will read or hear about it and think these delusions and biases affect other people all the time, but not themselves.

The third person effect is a version of the self-serving bias. You excuse your failures and see yourself as more successful, more intelligent, and more skilled than you are. Research into the self-serving bias shows subjects tend to rate themselves as more skilled than their coworkers, better drivers than the average person, more attractive than people their age, and likely to live longer than the people they grew up with. It follows, then, that most people would believe they were less gullible than the majority. But remember, you can't be in the minority of every category.

When the third person effect leads you to condone censorship, take a step back and imagine the sort of messages people on the other side might think are brainwashing you, and then ask yourself if those messages should be censored too.

31

Catharsis

THE MISCONCEPTION: *Venting your anger is an effective way to reduce stress and prevent lashing out at friends and family.*

THE TRUTH: *Venting increases aggressive behavior over time.*

Let it out.

Left inside you, the anger will fester and spread, grow like a tumor, boil up until you punch holes in the wall or slam your car door so hard the windows shatter.

Those dark thoughts shouldn't be tamped down inside your heart where they can condense and strengthen, where they form a concentrated stockpile of negativity that could reach critical mass at any moment.

Go get yourself one of those squishy balls and work it over with death grips. Use both hands and choke the imaginary life out of it. Head to the gym and assault a punching bag. Shoot some people in a video game. Scream into a pillow.

Feel better? Sure you do. Venting feels great.

The problem is, it accomplishes little else. Actually, it makes matters worse and primes your future behavior by fogging your mind.

The concept of catharsis goes back at least as far as Aristotle and Greek drama. The word itself comes from from the Greek *kathairein,* "to purify" and "to clean." Releasing pent-up energy, or fluids, was Aristotle's counterargument to Plato, who felt poetry and drama filled people up with silliness and made them unbalanced. Aristotle thought it went the other way, and by watching people go muck through a tragedy or rise to a victory, you in the audience could vicariously release your tears or feel the rush of testosterone. You balanced out your heart by purging those emotions. It seems to make sense, and that's why the meme grafted itself to so much of human thought well before the great philosophers.

Releasing sexual tension feels good. Throwing up when you are sick feels good. Finally getting to a restroom feels good. Be it an exorcism or a laxative, the idea is the same: Get the bad stuff out and you'll return to normal. Balancing the humors—choleric, melancholic, phlegmatic, and sanguine—was the basis of medicine from Hippocrates up to the Old West, and the way you balanced out often meant draining something.

Fast-forward to Sigmund Freud.

Throughout the late 1800s and early 1900s, Freud was a superstar of science and pop culture, and his work influenced everything from politics and advertising to business and art. The turn of the century, nineteenth to twentieth, was an interesting time to be a scientist devoted to the mind, because there weren't many tools available. It was sort of like being an astronomer before the invention of telescopes. The rising stars in psychology made names for themselves by constructing elaborate theories of how the mind was organized and where your thoughts came from. Since the mind was completely unobservable, these theorists didn't have much data to fall back on, and so their personal philosophies and conjectures tended to fill in the gaps. Thanks to Freud, catharsis theory and psychotherapy became part of psychology. Mental wellness, he reasoned, could be achieved by filtering away impurities in your mind through the siphon of a therapist. He believed your psyche was poisoned by repressed fears and desires, unresolved arguments, and unhealed wounds. The mind formed phobias and obsessions around these bits of mental detritus. You needed to rummage around in there, open up some windows, and let some fresh air and sunlight in.

The hydraulic model of anger is just what it sounds like—anger builds up inside the mind until you let off some steam. If you don't let off this steam, the boiler will burst. It sounds reasonable. You may even look back on your life and remember times when you went batshit, punched a wall or broke a plate, and it made things better. But you are not so smart.

In the 1990s, psychologist Brad Bushman at Iowa State decided to study whether or not venting actually worked. At the time, self-help books were all the rage, and the prevailing advice when it came to dealing with stress and anger was to punch inanimate objects and scream into pillows. Bushman, like many psychologists before him, felt this might be bad advice.

In one of Bushman's studies he divided 180 students into three groups. One group read a neutral article. One read an article about a fake study that said venting anger was effective. The third group read about a fake study that said venting was pointless. He then had the students write essays for or against abortion, a subject about which they probably had strong feelings. He told them the essays would be graded by fellow students, but they weren't. When the students got their essays back, half were told their essays were superb. The other half had this scrawled across the paper: "This is one of the worst essays I have ever read!" Bushman then asked the subjects to pick an activity like playing a game, watching some comedy, reading a story, or punching a bag. The results? The people who read the article that said venting worked, and who later got angry, were far more likely to ask to punch the bag than those who got angry in the other groups. In all the groups, the people who got praised tended to pick nonaggressive activities.

So belief in catharsis makes you more likely to seek it out. Bushman decided to take this a step further and let the angry people seek revenge. He wanted to see if engaging in cathartic behavior would extinguish the anger, if it would be emancipated from the mind. The second study was basically the same, except this time when subjects got back their papers with "This is one of the worst essays I have ever read!" they were divided into two groups. The people in both groups were told they were going to have to compete against the person who graded their essay. One group first had to punch a bag, and the other group had to sit and wait for two minutes. After the punching and waiting, the competition began. The game was simple: Press a button as fast as you can. If you lose, you get blasted with a horrible noise. When you win, your opponent gets blasted. The students could set the volume the other person had to endure, a setting between zero and ten, with ten being 105 decibels. Can you predict what they discovered? On average, the punching bag group set the volume as high as 8.5. The time-out group set it to 2.47. The people who got angry didn't release their anger on the punching bag—their anger was sustained by it. The group that cooled off lost their desire for vengeance. In subsequent studies where the subjects chose how much hot sauce the other person had to eat, the punching bag group piled it on. The cooled off group did not. When the punching bag group later did word puzzles where they had to fill in the blanks to words like ch_ _e, they were more likely to pick ch<u>o</u>ke instead of ch<u>a</u>se.

Bushman has been doing this research for a while, and it keeps turning up the same results. If you think catharsis is good, you are more likely to seek it out when you get pissed. When you vent, you stay angry and are more likely to keep doing aggressive things so you can keep venting. It's druglike, because there are brain chemicals and other behavioral reinforcements at work. If you get accustomed to blowing off steam, you become dependent on it. The more effective approach is to just stop. Take your anger off of the stove.

Bushman's work also debunks the idea of redirecting your anger into exercise or something similar. He says it will only maintain your state or increase your arousal level, and afterward you may be even more aggressive than if you had cooled off. Still, cooling off is not the same thing as not dealing with your anger at all. Bushman suggests you delay your response, relax or distract yourself with an activity totally incompatible with aggression.

If you get into an argument, or someone cuts you off in traffic, or you get called an awful name, venting will not dissipate the negative energy. It will, however, feel great. That's the thing. Catharsis will make you feel good, but it's an emotional hamster wheel. The emotion that led you to catharsis will still be there afterward, and if the catharsis made you feel good, you'll seek that emotion out again in the future.

32

The Misinformation Effect

THE MISCONCEPTION: *Memories are played back like recordings.*

THE TRUTH: *Memories are constructed anew each time from whatever information is currently available, which makes them highly permeable to influences from the present.*

One night your friend tells a story about the time the both of you watched *Cool Hand Luke* and decided to try and eat as many hard-boiled eggs as you could stomach, but you got sick after five and swore never to eat them again. You are both laughing and clinking your glasses at the folly of your youth, when another friend blows your mind by saying, "No, that was me. You weren't even there."

Your mind reels as the pages of your own comic book flip by. You search the panels for scenes that could confirm or deny whether you have lost your mind, but you can't find conclusive evidence for either person's account. Who ate those eggs?

Maybe it's not this extreme, but every once in a while someone tells a story that conflicts with your recollection. The person embellishes with details that slipped past your mental fact-checkers.

When you notice, as above, it is a truly unsettling experience because normally you are oblivious to your faulty reconstruction of memory. Not only is your memory easily altered by the influence of others, you also smooth over the incongruences, rearrange time lines, and invent scenarios, but rarely notice you're doing this until you see yourself in a video, or hear another person's version of the events. You tend to see your memories as a continuous, consistent movie, yet if you think of the last film you saw, how much of it can you recall? Could you sit back, close your eyes, and recall in perfect detail every scene, every line of dialog? Of course not, so why do you assume you can do the same for the movie of your life?

Take out a piece of paper and get ready to write. Really do it; it will be fun.

OK.

Now, read the following list of words out loud one time, and then try to write as many of them as you can remember on the paper without looking back. When you think you have them all down on paper, come back to the book.

Go:

door, glass, pane, shade, ledge, sill, house, open, curtain, frame, view, breeze, sash, screen, shutter

Now, take a look at the list. How did you do? Did you write down all the words? Did you write the word "window" down? If this test is presented properly, 85 percent of people taking it will remember seeing "window" in the list, but it isn't there. If you did, you just gave yourself a false memory thanks to the misinformation effect.

In 1974, Elizabeth Loftus at the University of Washington conducted a study in which people watched films of car crashes. She then asked the participants to estimate how fast the cars were going, but she divided the people into groups and asked the question differently for each. These were the questions:

- About how fast were the cars going when they *smashed* into each other?
- About how fast were the cars going when they *collided* into each other?
- About how fast were the cars going when they *bumped* into each other?
- About how fast were the cars going when they *hit* each other?
- About how fast were the cars going when they *contacted* each other?

The people's answers in miles per hour averaged like this:

- Smashed—40.8
- Collided—39.3
- Bumped—38.1
- Hit—34.0
- Contacted—31.8

Just by changing the wording, the memories of the subjects were altered. The car crashes were replayed in the participants' minds, but this time the word "smashed" necessitated the new version of the memory include cars that were going fast enough to validate the adjective.

Loftus raised the ante by asking the same people if they remembered broken glass in the film. There was no broken glass, but sure enough the people who were given the word "smashed" in their question were twice as likely to remember seeing it.

Since then, hundreds of experiments into the misinformation effect have been conducted, and people have been convinced of all sorts of things. Screwdrivers become wrenches, white men become black men, and experiences involving other people get traded back and forth. In one study, Loftus convinced people they were once lost in a shopping mall as a child. She had subjects read four essays provided by family members, but the one about getting lost as a kid was fake. A quarter of the subjects incorporated the fake story into their memory and even provided details about the fictional event that were not included in the narrative. Loftus even convinced people they shook hands with Bugs Bunny, who isn't a Disney character, when they visited Disney World as a kid, just by showing them a fake advertisement where a child was doing the same. She altered the food preferences of subjects in one experiment where she lied to people, telling them they had reported becoming sick from eating certain things as a child. A few weeks later, when offered those same foods, those people avoided them. In other experiments, she implanted memories of surviving drowning and fending off animal attacks—none of them real, all of them accepted into the autobiography of the subjects without resistance.

Loftus has made it her life's work to showcase the unreliability of memory. She has rallied against eyewitness testimony and suspect lineups for decades now, and she also has criticized psychologists who say they can dredge up repressed memories from childhood. For instance, in one of her experiments she had subjects watch a pretend crime and then select the culprit out of a lineup. The police told the subjects the perpetrator was one of the people standing before them, but it was a trick. None of them were the real suspect, yet 78 percent of the people still identified one of the innocent people as the person who they saw committing the crime. Memory just doesn't work like that, Loftus says, but despite this, many of our institutions and societal norms persist as though it does.

There are many explanations as to why this is happening, but the effect is well established and predictable. Scientists generally agree memories aren't recorded like videos or stored like data on a hard drive. They are constructed and assembled on the spot as if with Legos from a bucket in your brain. Neurologist Oliver Sacks wrote in *The Island of the Colorblind* about a patient who became colorblind after a brain injury. Not only could he not see certain colors, he couldn't imagine them or remember them. Memories of cars and dresses and carnivals were suddenly drained, washed down. Even though this patient's memories were first imprinted when he could see color, they now could be conjured up only with the faculties of his current imagination. Each time you build a memory, you make it from scratch, and if much time has passed you stand a good chance of getting the details wrong. With a little influence, you might get big ones wrong.

In 2001, Henry L. Roediger III, Michelle L. Meade, and Erik T. Bergman at Washington University had students list ten items they would expect to see in a typical kitchen, toolbox, bathroom, and other common areas in most homes. Think about it yourself. What ten items would you expect to find in a modern kitchen? This idea, this imaginary place, is a schema. You have schemas for just about everything—pirates, football, microscopes—images and related ideas that orbit the archetypes for objects, scenarios, rooms, and so on. Those archetypes form over time as you see examples in life or in stories from other people. You also have schemas for places you've never been, like the bottom of the ocean or ancient Rome.

For instance, when you imagine the ancient Romans, do you see chariots and marble statues with bone-white columns stretching overhead? You probably do, because this is how ancient Rome is always depicted in movies and television. Would it surprise you to know those columns and sculptures were painted with a rainbow of colors that would be gaudy by today's aesthetic standards? They were. Your schema is fast, but inaccurate. Schemas function as heuristics; the less you have to think about these concepts the faster you can process thoughts that involve them. When a schema leads to a stereotype, a prejudice, or a cognitive bias, you trade an acceptable level of inaccuracy for more speed.

Back to the experiment. After the psychologists had the students list items they'd expect to find in various household locations, they brought in actors posing as a new batch of students and paired them up with the students who'd just made their lists. Together, the subjects and the confederates looked at slides depicting the familiar locations and were asked to pay close attention to what they saw so they could remember it later on. To clear their mental palates, the subjects did some math problems before moving on to the last part of the experiment. The students then returned with their partners and together recalled out loud what they remembered in the scenes, but the confederates included items that weren't in the pictures. The kitchen scene, for example, didn't feature a toaster or oven mitts, but both were falsely recalled by the actors. After the ruse, the subjects were handed a sheet of paper and asked to list all the things they could remember.

As you've deduced by now, the subjects were easily implanted with false memories for items they expected to be in the scenes.

They listed items that were never shown but had been suggested by their partners. Their schemas for kitchens already included toasters and oven mitts, so when the actors said they saw those things, it was no problem for their minds to go ahead and add them to the memory. If their partners had instead said they remembered seeing a toilet bowl in the kitchen, it would have been harder to accept.

In 1932, psychologist Charles Bartlett presented a folktale from American Indian culture to subjects and then asked them to retell the story back to him every few months for a year. Over time, the story become less like the original and more like a story that sounded as though it came from the culture of the person recalling it.

In the original story, two men from Egulac are hunting seals along a river when they hear what they believe are war cries. They hide until a canoe with five men approaches. The men ask them to join them in a battle. One man agrees; the other goes home. After this, the story gets confusing because in the battle someone hears someone else say the men are ghosts. The man who traveled with the warriors is hit, but it isn't clear what hits him or who. When he gets home, he tells his people what happened, saying he fought with ghosts. In the morning, something black comes out of his mouth, and he dies.

The story is not only strange, but written in an unusual way that makes it difficult to understand. Over time, the subjects reshaped it to make sense to them. Their versions became shorter, more linear, and many details were left out that didn't make sense in the first place. The ghosts became the enemy, or became the allies, but usually became a central feature of the tale. Many people interpreted them to be the undead, even though in the tale the word "ghost" identifies the name of the clan. The dying man is tended to. The seal hunters become fishermen. The river becomes a sea. The black substance becomes his soul escaping or a blood clot. After a year or so, the stories started to include new characters, totems, and ideas never present in the original, like the journey as a pilgrimage, or the death as a sacrifice.

Memory is imperfect, but also constantly changing. Not only do you filter your past through your present, but your memory is easily infected by social contagion. You incorporate the memories of others into your own head all the time. Studies suggest your memory is permeable, malleable, and evolving. It isn't fixed and permanent, but more like a dream that pulls in information about what you are thinking about during the day and adds new details to the narrative. If you suppose it could have happened, you are far less likely to question yourself as to whether it did.

The shocking part of these studies is how easily memory gets tainted, how only a few iterations of an idea can rewrite your autobiography. Even stranger is how as memories change, your confidence in them grows stronger. Considering the relentless bombardment to your thoughts and emotions coming from friends, family, and all media: How much of what you recall is accurate? How much of the patchwork is yours alone? What about the stories handed down through time or across a dinner table; what is the ratio of fiction to fact? Considering the misinformation effect not only requires you to be skeptical of eyewitness testimony and your own history, but it also means you can be more forgiving when someone is certain of something that is later revealed to be embellished or even complete fiction.

Consider the previous exercise when you falsely saw curtains in the list of things around a window. It took almost no effort to implant the memory because you were the one doing the implanting. Recognize the control you have over—wait, was it curtains?

33

Conformity

THE MISCONCEPTION: *You are a strong individual who doesn't conform unless forced to.*

THE TRUTH: *It takes little more than an authority figure or social pressure to get you to obey, because conformity is a survival instinct.*

On April 4, 2004, a man calling himself Officer Scott called a McDonald's in Mount Washington, Kentucky. He told the assistant manager, Donna Jean Summers, who answered the phone, there had been a report of theft and that Louise Ogborn was the suspect.

Ogborn, eighteen, worked at the McDonald's in question, and the man on the other line told Donna Jean Summers to take her into the restaurant's office, lock the door, and strip her naked while another assistant manager watched. He then asked her to describe the naked teenager to him. This went on for more than an hour, until Summers told Officer Scott she had to return to the counter and continue her duties. He asked her if her fiancé could take over, and so she called him to the store. He arrived shortly after, took the phone, and then started following instructions. Officer Scott told him to tell Ogborn to dance, do jumping jacks, and stand on furniture in the room. He did. She did. Then, Officer Scott's requests became more sexual. He told Summer's fiancé to make Ogborn sit in his lap and kiss him so he could smell her breath. When she resisted, Officer Scott told him to spank her naked bottom, which he did. More than three hours into the ordeal, Officer Scott eventually convinced Summers's fiancé to force Ogborn to perform oral sex while he listened. He then asked for another man to take over, and when a maintenance worker was called in to take the phone, he asked what was going on. He was shocked and skeptical. Officer Scott hung up.

The call was one of more than seventy made over the course of four years by one man pretending to be a police officer. He called fast-food restaurants in thirty-two states and convinced people to shame themselves and others, sometimes in private, sometimes in front of customers. With each call he claimed to be working with the parent corporation, and sometimes he said he worked for the bosses of the individual franchises. He always claimed a crime had been committed. Often, he said investigators and other police officers were on their way. The employees dutifully did as he asked, disrobing, posing, and embarrassing themselves for his amusement. Police eventually captured David Stewart, a Florida prison security guard who had in his possession a calling card that was traced back to several fast-food restaurants, including one that had been hoaxed. Stewart went to court in 2006 but was acquitted. The jury said there wasn't enough evidence to convict him. There were no more hoax phone calls after the trial.

What could have made so many people follow the commands of a person they had never met and from who they had no proof of his being a police officer?

If I were to hand you a card with a single line on it, and then hand you another card with an identical line drawn near two others, one longer and one shorter, do you think you could match up the original to the copy? Could you tell which line in a group of three was the same length as the one on the first card?

You could. Just about anyone would be able to match up lines of equal length in just a few seconds. Now, what if you were part of a group trying to come to a consensus, and the majority of the people said a line that was clearly shorter than the original was the one that matched? How would you react?

In 1951, psychologist Solomon Asch used to perform an experiment where he would get a group of people together and show them cards like the ones described above. He would then ask the group the same sort of questions. Without coercion, about 2 percent of people answered incorrectly. In the next run of the experiment, Asch added actors to the group who all agreed to incorrectly answer his questions. If he asked which line was the same, or longer, or shorter, or whatever, they would force one hapless subject to be alone in disagreement.

You probably think you would go against the grain and shake your head in disbelief. You think you might say to yourself, "How could these people be so stupid?" Well, I hate to break it to you, but the research says you would eventually break. In Asch's experiments, 75 percent of the subjects caved in on at least one question. They looked at the lines, knew the answer everyone else was agreeing to was wrong, and went with it anyway. Not only did they conform without being pressured, but when questioned later they seemed oblivious to their own conformity. When the experimenter told them they had made an error, they came up with excuses as to why they made mistakes instead of blaming the others. Intelligent people just like you caved in, went with the group, and then seemed confused as to why.

Asch messed around with the conditions of the experiment, trying it with varying numbers of actors and unwitting subjects. He found one or two people had little effect, but three or more was all he needed to get a small percentage of people to start conforming. The percentage of people who conformed grew proportionally with the number of people who joined in consensus against them. Once the entire group other than the subject was replaced with actors, only 25 percent of his subjects answered every question correctly.

Most people, especially those in Western cultures, like to see themselves as individuals, as people who march to a different beat. You are probably the same sort of person. You value your individuality and see yourself as a nonconformist with unique taste, but ask yourself: How far does this nonconformity go? Do you live in an igloo made of boar tusks in the Arizona desert while refusing to drink the public water supply? Do you speak a language you and your sister created as children and lick strangers on the face during the closing credits of dollar-theater matinees? When other people applaud, do you clap your feet together and boo? To truly refuse to conform to the norms of your culture and the laws of the land would be a daunting exercise in futility. You may not agree with the zeitgeist, but you know conformity is part of the game of life. Chances are, you pick your battles and let a lot of things slide. If you travel to a foreign country, you look to others as guides on how to behave. When you visit someone else's home, you do as that person does. In a college classroom you sit quietly and take notes. If you join a gym or start a new job, the first thing you do is look for clues as to how to behave. You shave your legs or your face. You wear deodorant. You conform.

As psychologist Noam Shpancer explains on his blog, "We are often not even aware when we are conforming. It is our home base, our default mode." Shpancer says you conform because social acceptance is built into your brain. To thrive, you know you need allies. You get a better picture of the world when you can receive information from multiple sources. You need friends because outcasts are cut off from valuable resources. So when you are around others, you look for cues as to how to behave, and you use the information offered by your peers to make better decisions. When everyone you know tells you about an awesome app for your phone or a book you should read, it sways you. If all of your friends tell you to avoid a certain part of town or a brand of cheese, you take their advice. Conformity is a survival mechanism.

The most famous conformity experiment was performed by Stanley Milgram in 1963. He had people sit in a room and take commands from a scientist in a lab coat. He told them they would be teaching word pairs to another subject in the next room, and each time their partner got an answer wrong they were to give them an electric shock. A control panel on a complicated-looking contraption clearly indicated the power of the shock. Switches along a single row were labeled with increasing voltages and a description. At the low end it read "slight shock." In the middle the switch was labeled "intense shock." At the end of the scale the switch read "XXX," which implied death. The man in the lab coat would prompt the subject pressing the buttons to shock the partner in the next room. With each shock, screams emanated from next door. After the screams, the scientist in the lab coat asked the subject to increase the voltage. The screams would get louder, and eventually subjects could hear the guy in the other room pleading for his life and asking the psychologist to end the experiment. Most subjects asked if they could stop. They didn't want to shock the poor man in the next room, but the scientist would urge them to continue, telling them not to worry. The scientist said things like "You have no other choice; you must go on" or "The experiment requires that you continue." To everyone's surprise, 65 percent of people could be prompted to go all the way to right below the "XXX." In reality, there were no shocks, and the other person was just an actor pretending to be in pain. Milgram's experiment has been repeated many times with many variations. The percentage of people who go all the way can be dropped to zero just by removing the authority figure, or it can be raised into the 90 percentile range by having someone else give the test while the subject has only to deliver the shocks. Again, with Milgram's experiment there was no reward or punishment involved—just simple conformity.

Milgram showed when you can see your actions as part of just following orders, especially from an authority figure, there is a 65 percent chance you will go to the brink of murder. Add the risk of punishment, or your own harm, and chances of conformity increase. Milgram's work was a response to the Holocaust. He wondered if an entire nation could have its moral compass smashed, or if conformity and obedience to authority were more likely the root of so much compliance to commit unspeakable evil. Milgram concluded his subjects, and probably millions of others, saw themselves as instruments instead of people. When they became extensions of the person doing the terrible act, their own will was put aside where it could remain clean of sin. Conformity, therefore, can be manufactured when the person looking for compliance convinces others they are tools instead of human beings.

The restaurant employees hoaxed by Officer Scott would later say this was what happened to them. Officer Scott's demands started small and bumped up incrementally, just like Milgram's shocks. By the time it was uncomfortable, the situation had grown in power. They feared retribution if they didn't follow new orders, and once they had crossed the line into territory their morality couldn't condone, they phased out of their own personality and into the role of an instrument of the law.

Be aware: Your desire to conform is strong and unconscious. Sometimes, like at a family dinner, the desire to keep everyone happy and to adhere to social conventions is a good thing. It keeps you close and connected to the norms that make it easier to work together in the modern world. But also beware of the other side— the dark places that conformity can lead to. Never be afraid to question authority when your actions could harm yourself or others. Even in simple situations, like the next time you see a line of people waiting to get into a classroom or a movie or a restaurant, feel free to break norms—go check the door and look inside.

34

Extinction Burst

THE MISCONCEPTION: *If you stop engaging in a bad habit, the habit will gradually diminish until it disappears from your life.*

THE TRUTH: *Any time you quit something cold turkey, your brain will make a last-ditch effort to return you to your habit.*

You've been there.

You get serious about losing weight and start to watch every calorie. You read labels, stock up on fruits and vegetables, hit the gym. Everything is going fine. You feel great. You feel like a champion. You think, "This is easy." One day you give in to temptation and eat some candy, or a doughnut, or a cheeseburger. Maybe you buy a bag of chips. You order the fettuccine alfredo. That afternoon, you decide not only will you eat whatever you want, but to celebrate the occasion you will eat a pint of ice cream. The diet ends in a catastrophic binge.

What the hell? How did your smooth transition from comfort food to human Dumpster happen? You just experienced an extinction burst.

Once you become accustomed to reward, you get really upset when you can't have it. Food, of course, is a powerful reward. It keeps you alive. Your brain didn't evolve in an environment where there was an abundance of food, so whenever you find a high-calorie, high-fat, high-sodium source, your natural inclination is to eat a lot of it and then go back to it over and over again. If you take away a reward like that, your brain throws a tantrum.

Extinction bursts are a component of extinction, one of the principles of conditioning. Conditioning is among the most basic factors shaping the way any organism—including you—reacts to the world. If you get rewarded by your actions, you are more likely to continue them. If punished, you are more likely to stop. Over time, you begin to predict reward and punishment by linking longer and longer series of events to their eventual outcomes.

If you want some chicken nuggets, you know you can't just snap your fingers and have them appear. You must engage in a long sequence of actions—acquire language, acquire money, acquire a car, acquire clothes, acquire fuel, learn to drive, learn to use money, learn where nuggets are sold, drive to the nuggets, use language, exchange money, etc. This string of behaviors could be sliced up into smaller and smaller components if we wanted to really dig down into the conditioning you have endured in order to be able to get nuggets in your mouth. Just driving the car from point A to point B is a complex performance that becomes automatic after hundreds of hours of practice. Millions of tiny behaviors, each one a single step in a process, add up to a single operation you have learned will pay off in reward. Think of rats in a maze, learning a complicated series of steps—turn left two times, turn right once, turn left, right, left, get cheese. Even microorganisms can be conditioned to react to stimuli and predict outcomes.

For a while in psychology, conditioning was the cat's pajamas. In the 1960s and '70s, Burrhus Frederic Skinner became a scientist celebrity by scaring the shit out of America with an invention called the operant conditioning chamber—the Skinner Box. The box is an enclosure with a combination of levers, food dispensers, an electric floor, lights, and loudspeakers. Scientists place animals in the box and either reward them or punish them to either encourage or discourage their behavior. Rats, for example, can be taught to push a lever when a green light appears to get a food pellet. Skinner demonstrated how he could teach a pigeon to spin in circles at his command by offering food only when it turned in one direction. Gradually, he withheld the food until the pigeon had turned a little farther and farther, until he had it going round and round. He could even get the pigeon to distinguish between the words "peck" and "turn" and get the pigeon to perform the corresponding behavior just by showing it a sign. Yes, in a sense, he taught a bird to read.

Skinner discovered you could get pigeons and rats to do complicated tasks by slowly building up chains of behaviors through handing out pellets of food. For example, if you want to teach a squirrel to water ski, you just need to start small and work your way up. Other researchers added punishment to the routines and discovered it too could be used like the pellets to encourage and discourage behavior. Skinner became convinced conditioning was the root of all behavior, and he didn't believe rational thinking had anything to do with your personal life. He considered introspection to be a "collateral product" of conditioning.

Some psychologists and philosophers still hold to the idea you are nothing but a sophisticated automaton, like a spider or a fish. You have no freedom, no free will. Your brain is made of atoms and molecules that must obey the laws of physics and chemistry, so some say your mind is thereby locked into service to the rules of the universe. Everything you have thought, felt, and done in your life was the natural mathematical aftermath of the Big Bang. To this wing of psychology, you are the same as an insect, just with a more complex nervous system responding to stimuli with a wider array of denser behavioral routines that only appear to give rise to consciousness. You may take comfort in knowing this is a hotly contested idea, one that goes back to the Greek philosophers who imagined the unconscious as wild horses pulling a chariot helmed by your upper-level reasoning. Whether or not you have free will, conditioning is real, and its impact can't be ignored.

There are two kinds of conditioning—classical and operant. In classical conditioning, something that normally doesn't have any influence becomes a trigger for a response. If you are taking a shower and someone flushes the toilet, which then causes the water to become a scalding torrent, you become conditioned to recoil in terror the next time you hear the toilet flush while lathering up. That's *classical* conditioning. Something neutral—the toilet flushing—becomes charged with meaning and expectation. You have no control over it. You recoil from the water without ever thinking, "I should recoil from this water else I get scalded." If you have ever been sick after eating or drinking something you love, you will avoid it in the future. The smell of it, or even the thought of it, can make you ill. For me, it's tequila. Ugh, gross. Classical conditioning keeps you alive. You learn quickly to avoid that which may harm you and seek out that which makes you happy, just like an amoeba.

The sort of complex behavior Skinner produced in animals was the result of *operant* conditioning. Operant conditioning changes your desires. Your inclinations become greater through reinforcement, or diminish through punishment. You go to work, you get paid. You turn on the air-conditioning and stop sweating. You don't run the red light, you don't get a ticket. You pay the rent, you don't get evicted. It's all operant conditioning, punishment and reward.

This finally brings us back to the third factor—extinction. When you expect a reward or a punishment and nothing happens, your conditioned response starts to fade away. If you stop feeding your cat, he will stop hanging around the food bowl and meowing. His behavior will go extinct. If you were to keep going to work and not get paid, eventually you would stop. This is when the extinction burst happens, right as the behavior is breathing its final breath. You wouldn't just not go to work anymore. You would probably storm into the boss's office and demand an explanation. If you got nowhere after gesticulating wildly and screaming, you might scoop your arm across his desk and leave in handcuffs.

Just before you give up on a long-practiced routine, you freak out. It's a final desperate attempt by the oldest parts of your brain to keep getting rewarded. You lock your keys in your apartment, but your roommate is asleep. You ring the doorbell and knock, but your roommate doesn't come. You ring the doorbell over and over and over. You start pounding on the door. If your computer freezes up, you don't just walk away, you start clicking all over the place and maybe go so far as to bang your fists on the keyboard. If a child doesn't get any candy at the checkout line, he or she may throw a giant tantrum because in the past such behavior has gotten candy. These are all extinction bursts—a temporary increase in an old behavior, a plea from the recesses of your psyche.

So back to that diet. You eliminate a reward from your life: awesome and delicious high-calorie foods. Right as you are ready to give the reward up forever, an extinction burst threatens to demolish your willpower. You become like a two-year-old in a conniption fit, and like the child, if you give in to the demands, the behavior will be strengthened. Compulsive overeating is a frenzied state of mind, food addiction under pressure until it bursts.

To give up overeating, or smoking, or gambling, or *World of Warcraft,* or any bad habit that was formed through conditioning, you must be prepared to weather the secret weapon of your unconscious—the extinction burst. Become your own Supernanny, your own Dog Whisperer. Look for alternative rewards and positive reinforcement. Set goals, and when you achieve them, shower yourself with garlands of your choosing. Don't freak out when it turns out to be difficult. Habits form because you are not so smart, and they cease under the same conditions.

35

Social Loafing

THE MISCONCEPTION: *When you are joined by others in a task, you work harder and become more accomplished.*
THE TRUTH: *Once part of a group, you tend to put in less effort because you know your work will be pooled together with others'.*

When you want to accomplish something big, something that will require a lot of time and effort like a start-up business or a short film, your instincts might tell you the more people you can afford to hire the better the work will be and the faster you will reach your goals. The truth though is when you join the efforts of others toward a common goal, everyone has a tendency to loaf more than if each was working alone. If you know you aren't being judged as an individual, your instinct is to fade into the background.

To prove this, psychologist Alan Ingham ruined tug-of-war forever. In 1974, he had people put on a blindfold and grab a rope. The rope was attached to a rather medieval-looking contraption that simulated the resistance of an opposing team. The subjects were told many other people were also holding the rope on their side, and he measured their effort. Then, he told them they would be pulling alone, and again he measured. They were alone both times, but when they thought they were in a group, they pulled 18 percent less strenuously on average.

This version of social loafing is sometimes called the Ringelmann effect after French engineer Maximilien Ringelmann, who discovered in 1913 that if he had people get together in groups to pull on a strain gauge, their combined efforts would tally up to be less than the sum of their individual strength measurements on the same instrument. Together, Ingham and Ringelmann's work introduced social loafing to psychology: You put in less effort when in a group than you would if working alone on the same project.

When the lead singer at the concert asks you to scream as loud as you can, and then he asks again, going, "I can't hear you! You can do better than that!" have you ever noticed that the second time is always louder? Why wasn't everyone yelling at the top of their lungs the first time? Some really cool scientists actually tested this in 1979. Bibb Latane, Kipling Williams, and Stephen Harkins at Ohio State University had people shout as loud as they could in a group and then alone, or vice-versa. Sure enough, the overall loudness of a small group of people was less than any one of them by themselves. You can even chart this on a graph. The more people you add, the less effort any one person does. It arches away like a perfect ski slope. You do this all the time, but you don't do it on purpose— well, except when you just mouth the words to the song everyone else is singing. In all of these experiments, the trick was to keep people from realizing what was going on. As long as you think you are part of a group, you unconsciously put in less effort. No one realizes it, and no one admits to it.

This behavior is more likely to show up when the task at hand is simple. With complex tasks, it is usually easy to tell who isn't pulling their weight. Once you know your laziness can be seen, you try harder. You do this because of another behavior called evaluation apprehension, which is just a fancy way of saying you care more when you know you are being singled out. Your anxiety levels decrease when you know your effort will be pooled with others'. You relax. You coast.

Sports scientists over the years have informed coaches of this behavior, so now most major teams isolate each player when they're trying to evaluate them, going so far as to film them individually with a different camera so the player won't fall prey to social loafing. This phenomenon has been observed in every possible situation involving group effort. Communal farms always produce less than individually owned farms. Factories where people do repetitive tasks with no supervision are less productive than ones where each person has an individual quota to reach.

Be aware, most organizations know all about social loafing these days; somewhere up the chain a psychologist has ratted you out. So it's likely, especially if you work for a corporation, that your output is being monitored in some way and you are being told about it so you'll work harder. They know when it comes to group effort, you are not so smart.

36

The Illusion of Transparency

THE MISCONCEPTION: *When your emotions run high, people can look at you and tell what you are thinking and feeling.*

THE TRUTH: *Your subjective experience is not observable, and you overestimate how much you telegraph your inner thoughts and emotions.*

You stand in front of your public speaking class with your notes centered on the lectern, your stomach performing gymnastics. You sat through all the other speeches, tapping the floor, transferring nervous energy into the tiles through a restless foot, periodically wiping your sweaty hands off on your pants. Each time the speaker concluded and the class applauded, you clapped along with everyone else, and as it subsided you realized how loud your heart was thumping when a fresh silence settled. Finally, the instructor called your name, and your eyes cranked open. You felt as if you had eaten a spoonful of sawdust as you walked up to the blackboard, planting each foot carefully so as not to stumble. As you begin to speak the lines you've rehearsed, you search the faces of your classmates.

"Why is he smiling? What is she scribbling? Is that a frown?"

"Oh no," you think, "they can see how nervous I am.

"I must look like an idiot. I'm bombing, aren't I? This is horrible. Please let a meteor hit this classroom before I have to say another word."

"I'm sorry," you say to the audience. "Let me start over."

Now it's even worse. What kind of moron apologizes in the middle of a speech? Your voice quavers. Flop sweat gathers behind your neck. You become certain your skin must be glowing red and everyone in the room is holding back laughter. Except, they aren't. They are just bored. Your anxiety is peaking, and it feels like waves of emotional energy must be radiating from your head in some sort of despair halo, but there is nothing to see on the outside other than your facial expressions and flushed skin. To get information out of one head and into another, it has to be transmitted through some sort of communication. Faces, sounds, gestures, words like the ones you are reading now—we must depend on these clunky tools because no matter how strong an emotion or how powerful an idea, it never seems as intense or potent to the world outside your mind as it does to the one within. This is the illusion of transparency.

You know what you are feeling and thinking, and you tend to believe those thoughts and emotions are leaking out of your pores, visible to the world, perceivable to the outside. You overestimate how obvious what you truly think must be and fail to recognize that other people are in their own little bubble, thinking the same thing about their inner worlds. When you try to imagine what other people are thinking, you have no choice but to start from inside your noggin. In there, among your inescapable self, you think your thoughts and feelings must be evident. Sure, when people are paying attention, they can read you to an extent, but you grossly over-estimate how much so.

You can test the illusion of transparency using a method created by Elizabeth Newton.

Pick a song everyone knows, like your national anthem, and have someone else sit across from you. Now tap out the song with your fingertips. After a verse or two, ask the other person what you were tapping. In your mind, you can hear every note, every instrument. In their mind, they can hear your fingers tapping. Pause here and try it out. I'll wait.

OK. I'm going to assume you've been tapping. How did you do? Did they figure out what you were trying to play? Probably not. In Newton's study, the tappers predicted the listeners would be able to guess the tune half of the time, but the listeners correctly guessed about 3 percent of the songs.

The huge discrepancy between what you think people will understand and what they really do has probably led to all sorts of mistakes in text messages and e-mails. If you are like me, you often have to back up and restate your case, or answer questions about your tone, or reword everything and try sending it again.

On the Internet, people often include "/s" at the end of a statement to indicate sarcasm (it's a programming joke, essentially meaning "conclude sarcasm"). It was so hard to communicate tone online we had to create a new punctuation mark. Getting an idea out of one head and into another is difficult, and much can be lost in the information transfer. An insight that slams into you like an avalanche won't have the same impact coming out of your mouth or fingertips.

In 1998, Thomas Gilovich, Victoria Medvec, and Kenneth Savitsky published their research on the illusion of transparency. They reasoned your subjective experience, or phenomenology, was so potent you would have a hard time seeing beyond it when you were in a heightened emotional state. Their hypothesis was based on the spotlight effect—the belief everyone is looking right at you, judging your actions and appearance, when in reality you disappear into the background most of the time. Gilovich, Medvec, and Savitsky figured the effect was so powerful it made you feel as if the imaginary spotlight could penetrate your gestures, words, and expressions and reveal your private world as well. They had Cornell students divide into groups. An audience would listen as individuals read questions from index cards and then answered them out loud. They either lied or told the truth based on what the card said to do on a label only they could see. Audience members were told they would get prizes based on how many liars they detected. Liars would say something like "I have met David Letterman." They then had to guess how many people could tell they had lied, while the audience tried to figure out who out of the five were fibbing. The results? Half of the liars thought they had been caught, but only a quarter were—they strongly overestimated their transparency. In subsequent experiments the variables were shuffled around and the lies presented in other ways; the results were nearly identical.

Studies in the 1980s showed you are confident in your ability to see through liars, yet you are actually terrible at it. On the other side, you think your own lies will be easy to detect. Gilovich, Medvec, and Savitsky moved on to another experiment. They sat students down in front of a video camera and a row of fifteen cups filled with red liquid. They asked to students to hide their expressions as they tasted the beverages, because five of the drinks were going to be rat nasty. They then had ten people watch the tape and asked the students who did the tasting to estimate how many of the observers would be able to tell when they had imbibed something gross. About a third of the observers could tell when people were disgusted, or at least they said they could and guessed well. The people doing the tasting predicted about half would be able to see through their attempts to hide revulsion. The illusion of transparency jacked up the powers of observation they imagined in their judges.

Pushing ahead, the researchers tried another experiment based on the research of Miller and McFarland on the bystander effect (the more people who witness an emergency, the less likely any one person will leap into action). Once again, their research showed when people were in a situation in which they felt concerned and alarmed, they assumed it was written all over their faces, when in reality it wasn't. So no one acted. In turn, they thought if other people were freaking out, they would be able to see it. In 2003, Kenneth Savitsky and Thomas Gilovich conducted a study to determine if they could short-circuit the illusion of transparency. They had people give public speeches on the spot and then rate how nervous they thought they looked to their audience. Sure enough, they said they looked like a wreck, but the onlookers didn't notice it. Still, in this experiment some people got stuck in a feedback loop. They thought they appeared nervous, so they started to try and compensate, and then they thought the compensation was noticeable and tried to cover that up, which they then felt was more obvious, and so on, until they'd worked themselves up into a state where they *were* obviously freaking out. The researchers decided to run the experiment again, but this time they explained the illusion of transparency to some of the subjects, telling them they might feel like everyone could see them losing it, but they probably couldn't. This time, the feedback loop was broken. Those told about the illusion felt less stressed, gave better speeches, and the audiences said they were more composed.

When your emotions take over, when your own mental state becomes the focus of your attention, your ability to gauge what other people are experiencing gets muted. If you are trying to see yourself through their eyes, you will fail. Knowing this, you can plan for the effect and overcome it.

When you get near the person you have a crush on and feel the war drums in your gut, don't freak out. You don't look as nervous as you feel. When you stand in front of an audience or get interviewed on camera, there might be a thunderstorm of anxiety in your brain, but it can't get out; you look far more composed than you believe. Smile. When your mother-in-law cooks a meal better fit for a dog bowl, she can't hear your brain stem begging you to spit it out.

If you are trying to communicate something complex, if you have vast knowledge of a subject and someone else does not, realize it is going to be difficult to get it across the gulf between your brain and theirs. The explanation process may become thorny, but don't take it out on the other person. Just because that person can't see inside your mind doesn't mean he or she is not so smart. You don't suddenly become telepathic when you are angry, anxious, or alarmed. Keep calm and carry on.

37

Learned Helplessness

THE MISCONCEPTION: *If you are in a bad situation, you will do whatever you can do to escape it.*

THE TRUTH: *If you feel like you aren't in control of your destiny, you will give up and accept whatever situation you are in.*

In 1965, a psychologist named Martin Seligman started shocking dogs.

He was trying to expand on the research of Pavlov—the guy who could make dogs salivate when they heard a bell ring. Seligman wanted to head in the other direction, and when he rang his bell, instead of providing food, he zapped the dogs with electricity. To keep them still, he restrained them in a harness during the experiment. After they were conditioned, he put these dogs in a big box with a little fence dividing it into two halves. He figured if the dog rang the bell, it would hop over the fence to escape, but it didn't. It just sat there and braced itself. They decided to try shocking the dog after the bell. The dog still just sat there and took it. When they put a dog in the box that had never been shocked before or had previously been allowed to escape and tried to zap it—it jumped the fence.

You are just like these dogs.

If, over the course of your life, you have experienced crushing defeat or pummeling abuse or loss of control, you convince yourself over time that there is no escape, and if escape is offered, you will not act—you become a nihilist who trusts futility above optimism.

Studies of the clinically depressed show that they often give in to defeat and stop trying. The average person will look for external forces to blame when he or she fails the midterm. People will say the professor is an asshole, or they didn't get enough sleep. But depressed people will often blame themselves and assume they are stupid. Seligman called this your explanatory style. You see events affecting your life along three gradients: personal, permanent, and pervasive. If you blame yourself or blame forces beyond your control, it hurts more. If you believe the situation will never change, sadness is stronger than if you believe tomorrow things will be better. If you think your problems affect every element of your existence instead of just a specific element of your life, once again, you feel far worse. Pessimism sits on one side of the gradient and optimism on the other. The more pessimistic your explanatory style, the easier it is to slip into learned helplessness.

Do you vote?

If not, is it because you think it doesn't matter because things never change, or politicians are evil on both sides, or one vote in several million doesn't count? Yeah, that's learned helplessness.

When battered women, or hostages, or abused children, or longtime prisoners refuse to escape, they don't because they have accepted the futility of trying. What does it matter? Those who do get out of bad situations often have a hard time committing to anything that may lead to failure. Any extended period of negative emotions can lead to you giving in to despair and accepting your fate. If you remain alone for a long time, you will decide loneliness is a fact of life and pass up opportunities to hang out with people. The loss of control in any situation can lead to this state.

In another study by Seligman, he grafted cancer cells into rats so they would develop fatal tumors. The rats were then given routine electric shocks, but some had an opportunity to escape by pressing a lever. Another group received no shocks at all. One month later, 63 percent of the rats who could escape rejected their tumors. By comparison, 54 percent of the group who were not shocked rejected theirs. The survival rate of the group forced to bear the shocks was only 23 percent. Rats suffering from cancer will die faster if placed in an inescapable situation.

A study in 1976 by Ellen Langer and Judith Rodin showed in nursing homes where conformity and passivity are encouraged and every whim is attended to, the health and well-being of the patients declines rapidly. If, instead, the people in these homes are given responsibilities and choices, they remain healthy and active. This research was repeated in prisons. Sure enough, just letting prisoners move furniture and control the television kept them from developing health problems and staging revolts. In homeless shelters where people can't pick out their own beds or choose what to eat, the residents are less likely to try and get a job or find an apartment. When you are able to succeed at easy tasks, hard tasks feel possible to accomplish. When you are unable to succeed at small tasks, everything seems harder.

Psychologist Charisse Nixon at Penn State Erie shows her students how learned helplessness works by having them complete word unscrambling tests. She asks her students to rearrange the letters in words so they create new words. She asks her class to do this one word at a time: "whirl," "slapstick," "cinerama." Try it yourself, but don't move to the next word until you finish the first. If you were in Nixon's classroom, as you were working on the first word she would ask for everyone who was already finished to raise their hands, and then you would look up and see half the class was ready to move on. Nixon then tells everyone to go to the next word, and once again everyone but you and a few others raises a hand. Again, she repeats this for the third word, and again half the class gets it quickly while the rest sits dumbfounded. The trick in her informal study is that half the class gets the words above, and the other half gets: "bat," "lemon," "cinerama." "Bat" is easily turned into "tab," and "lemon" becomes "melon" just as easily. So when the half with the easy words gets to "cinerama," they find it simple to unscramble it into American. If you acted like most people, you would feel weird and inadequate as the hands went in the air while you looked at "whirl" and turned it over in your head searching for another word to make from the letters. "If this is so easy, what is wrong with me?" Then comes "slapstick," and now you feel even dumber, as half your peers seem to have no problem figuring it out. Now, with learned helplessness in full effect, you see "cinerama" differently from the now confident others with the easy word tasks. Even though it shouldn't be too tough, learned helplessness tells you to give up. In Nixon's classes, this is what usually happens. The half with the impossible words gives in by the third word.

The leading theory as to how such a strange behavior would evolve is that it springs from all organisms' desire to conserve resources. If you can't escape a source of stress, it leads to more stress, and this positive feedback loop eventually triggers an automatic shutdown. At its most extreme, you think if you keep struggling you might die. If you stop, there is a chance the bad thing will go away.

Every day you feel like you can't control the forces affecting your fate—your job, the government, your addiction, your depression, your money. So you stage micro-revolts. You customize your ring tone, you paint your room, you collect stamps. You choose.

Choices, even small ones, can hold back the crushing weight of helplessness, but you can't stop there. You must fight back your behavior and learn to fail with pride. Failing often is the only way to ever get the things you want out of life. Besides death, your destiny is not inescapable.

You are not so smart, but you are smarter than dogs and rats. Don't give in yet.

38

Embodied Cognition

THE MISCONCEPTION: *Your opinions of people and events are based on objective evaluation.*

THE TRUTH: *You translate your physical world into words, and then believe those words.*

Imagine this scene.

You brush the snow off your shoulders as you step into a home where a fire crackles in the corner. You slip on a sweater, wrap your hands around a cup of steaming cider, and sit back in a comfortable chair across from the fireplace. Sound cozy?

As strange as this is going to sound, people think in metaphors—words like "warm" and "cold," "fast" and "slow," "bright" and "dark," "hard" and "soft." These words mean two things. "Cold" can be a physical sensation but also a mood, demeanor, or style. "Dark" can describe a shade of color, or the way a song sounds. "Hard" can be a type of bargaining technique or the resistance of a chair to your back.

The scene above is warm—physically warm—and as a result, all of your interactions and observations in such a setting will be interpreted as being emotionally warm. Warm sensations bring up word associations that include warmth, and those thoughts prime you to behave in a way that could be metaphorically described as warm.

In 2008, Lawrence Williams and John Bargh conducted a study where they had people meet strangers. One group held a cup of warm coffee, and the other group held iced coffee. Later, when asked to rate the stranger's personality, the people who held the warm coffee said they found the stranger to be nice, generous, and caring. The other group said the same person was difficult, standoffish, hard to talk to. In another round of research subjects held either a heating pad or a cold pack and then were asked to look at various products and judge their overall quality. Once they had done this, the experimenters told them they could choose a gift to keep for participating or they could give the gift to someone else. Those who held the heating pad chose to give away their reward 54 percent of the time, but only 25 percent of the cold pack group shared. The groups had turned their physical sensations into words, and then used those words as metaphors to explain their perceptions or predict their own actions.

There's a lot of research showcasing this phenomenon. You see people with bright clothes as being friendly and smart—bright. You see people who speak slowly as being less intelligent—slow. Whatever metaphors your culture uses will change the way you feel about the world around you, should it match up with those words. The sensation of touch is also a powerful form of this phenomenon—the way things feel to your skin can translate to how they feel to your heart.

In a 2010 study conducted by Josh Ackerman, Christopher C. Nocera, and their associates, subjects pretended to conduct job interviews. They took their interviewing job more seriously and saw résumés as being more impressive if those résumés were attached to heavy clipboards. Resumes attached to light clipboards were regarded as being from less-qualified applicants. The weight and heaviness of the participants' physical sensation translated not only into the weight and heft of their duty but the import of what they read. In another of the researchers' studies people pretending to buy a car who sat in hard-backed chairs haggled more and expected better bargains than did those who sat in cushioned ones. The chair was hard, so they drove a hard bargain.

In experiments where people sat in a cold room and watched videos of chess games, they later described the video in empirical terms. If they instead were seated in a warm room, they describe the video with emotions and anecdotes. The next time you watch a movie, notice how great filmmakers put words in your mind so you will interpret the following scenes with the emotions they want you to feel. If the angle is askew, you then see the characters or the situation as being off-kilter. If the room is empty and silent, you then see the characters as distant and lonely.

Settings prime you to see the world a certain way, and all it takes to see things differently is a change of temperature, or the sturdiness of a surface. Texture matters. The way something feels to your touch begins a series of associations in your brain. Your thoughts change based on the words you conjure. You should be aware, advertisers and retailers are already jumping on this bandwagon. The field of neuromarketing is keen to test embodied cognition and has been buzzing about its potential since Bargh's research began circulating the Internet. If you start to see products with shapes and surfaces designed to begin a long chain of thoughts and feelings, this research is probably the source.

The next time the doctor puts an ice-cold stethoscope on your chest, remember you are not so smart before you assume the MD is hard to get along with. Likewise, if someone asks you out for a cup of coffee, remember the cup in your hands can change the way your heart responds to that person's smile.

39

The Anchoring Effect

THE MISCONCEPTION: *You rationally analyze all factors before making a choice or determining value.*
THE TRUTH: *Your first perception lingers in your mind, affecting later perceptions and decisions.*

You walk into a clothing store and see what is probably the most bad-ass leather jacket you've ever seen. You try it on, look in the mirror, and decide you must have it. While wearing this item, you imagine onlookers will clutch their chests and gasp every time you walk into a room or cross a street. You lift the sleeve to check the price—$1,000.

"Well, that's that," you think. You have started to head back to the hanger when a salesperson stops you.

"You like it?"

"I love it, but it's just too much."

"No, that jacket is on sale right now for $400."

It's expensive, and you don't need it really, but $600 off the price seems like a great deal for a coat that will increase your cool by a factor of eleven. You put it on your card, unaware you've been tricked by the oldest retail con in the business.

One of my first jobs was selling leather coats, and I depended on the anchoring effect to earn commission. Each time, I figured it was obvious to customers the company I worked for marked up the prices to unrealistic extremes. Yet, over and over, when people heard the sale price, they smiled and wrestled with their better judgment.

The prices you expect to pay, where did those expectations originate?

Answer this: Is the population of Uzbekistan greater or fewer than 12 million?

Go ahead and guess.

OK, another question, how many people do you think live in Uzbekistan?

Come up with a figure and keep it in your head. We'll come back to this in a few paragraphs.

In 1974, Amos Tversky and Daniel Kahneman conducted a study and asked people to estimate how many African countries were part of the United Nations, but first they spun a wheel of fortune. The wheel was painted with numbers from zero to one hundred, but rigged to always land on ten or sixty-five. When the arrow stopped spinning, they asked people in the experiment to say if they believed the percentage of countries was higher or lower than the number on the wheel. They then asked people to estimate what they thought the actual percentage of nations was. They found people who landed on ten in the first half of the experiment guessed around 25 percent of Africa was part of the UN. Those who landed on sixty-five said around 45 percent.

The participants had been locked in place by the anchoring effect.

The trick here is no one really knew what the answer was. They had to guess, yet it didn't feel like a guess. As far as they knew, the wheel was a random number generator, but they still worked off of that number.

Back to Uzbekistan. The populations of Central Asian states probably aren't numbers you have memorized. You need some sort of cue, a point of reference. You searched your mental assets for something of value concerning Uzbekistan—the terrain, the language, *Borat*—but the population figures aren't in your head. What *is* in your head is the figure I gave you, 12 million, and it's right there up front. When you have nothing else to go on, you fixate on the information at hand.

The population of Uzbekistan is about 28 million people. How far away was your answer? If you are like most people, you assumed something much lower. You probably thought it was more than 12 million but less than 28 million.

You depend on anchoring every day to predict the outcome of events, to estimate how much time something will take or how much money something will cost. When you need to choose between options, or estimate a value, you need footing to stand on. How much should you be paying for cable? How much should your electricity bill be each month? What is a good price for rent in this neighborhood? You need an anchor from which to compare, and when someone is trying to sell you something, that salesperson is more than happy to provide one. The problem is, even when you know this, you can't ignore it.

When shopping for a car, you know it isn't a completely honest transaction. The real price the dealer can charge you and still make a profit is surely lower than what the dealer is asking for on the window sticker, yet the anchor price is still going to affect your decision. As you look over the vehicle, you don't consider how many factories the company owns, how many employees they pay. You don't pore over engineering diagrams or profit reports. You don't consider the price of iron or the expensive investments the manufacturer is making in safety testing. The price you are willing to pay has little to do with these considerations because they are as far from you at the point of purchase as the population of Uzbekistan. Even if you've done some research online, you don't know for sure exactly what the car is worth or what the dealer paid for it. The focus instead is the manufacturer's suggested retail price, and no matter how unrealistic it is, you can't help but be tethered to it. Any discussion of price has to start at that anchor.

The anchoring effect can also slip in unannounced. Drazen Prelec and Dan Ariely conducted an experiment at MIT in 2006 where they had students bid on items in a bizarre auction. The researchers would hold up a bottle of wine, or a textbook, or a cordless trackball, and then describe in detail how awesome it was. Then each student had to write down the last two digits of their social security number as if it was the price of the item. If the last two digits were 11, then the bottle of wine was priced at $11. If the two numbers were 88, the cordless trackball was $88. After they wrote down the pretend price, they bid. Sure enough, the anchoring effect scrambled their ability to judge the value of the items. People with high social security numbers paid up to 346 percent more than those with low numbers. People with numbers from 80 to 99 paid on average $26 for the trackball, while those with 00 to 19 paid around $9. The source of the number was irrelevant. Any number would have worked as the anchor.

The auction experimenters conducted another study in which they asked people to listen to annoying sounds for money. The researchers initially offered either 90 cents or 10 cents for a blast of awful electronic screaming, and then they asked the subjects how much would be the lowest possible price they would need to be paid to listen to the sound again. People who were offered 10 cents said it would take about 33 cents to continue. People offered 90 said it would take 73.

The researchers repeated the experiment in other ways, but no matter how they messed with the sounds or the payouts, those who were first offered a low payment consistently agreed to lower amounts than those used to better wages. People who got more money at first were unwilling to accept lower payments later.

If you move up to a nice car or a big house, a nice computer or an expensive smartphone, you become anchored and find it difficult to move back down later, even if you should. Those who buy expensive purses know they are being hornswoggled, at least at some level, yet the anchoring effect still reaches into their bank account. Does an $800 Louis Vuitton purse function better than a $25 hand-bag from Wal-Mart? No, not even if it was hand-made from giraffe leather and stitched by real, magical leprechauns. It's just a purse. But the anchor is set. Louis Vuitton bags are expensive, and that in itself has social value. People still buy them and are happy with their purchase. If Wal-Mart offered a purse at $800, it would never leave the shelf. The price would be so far from the anchors already set by the store it would seem like a bad deal.

Like most psychological phenomena, anchoring can be used to ma-nipulate people to do good. The best example is a 1975 study by Cata-lan, Lewis, Vincent, and Wheeler, where they asked a group of students to volunteer as camp counselors two hours per week for two years. They all said no. The researchers followed up by asking if they would volunteer to supervise a single two-hour trip. Half said yes. Without first being asked for the two-year commitment, only 17 percent agreed.

Remember this study when you are in a negotiation—make your initial request far too high. You have to start somewhere, and your initial decision or calculation greatly influences all the choices that follow, cascading out, each tethered to the anchors set before. Many of the choices you make every day are reruns of past decisions; as if traveling channels dug into a dirt road by a wagon train of selections, you follow the path created by your former self. External anchors, like prices before a sale or ridiculous requests, are obvious and can be avoided. Internal, self-generated anchors, are not so easy to bypass. You visit the same circuit of Web sites every day, eat basically the same few breakfasts. When it comes time to buy new cat food or take your car in for repairs, you have old favorites. Come election time, you pretty much already know who will and will not get your vote. These choices, so predictable—ask yourself what drives them. Are old anchors controlling your current decisions?

When you are parting with your money, know the person on the other side of the deal thinks you are not so smart and is depending on the anchoring effect when telling you how much you are about to save.

40

Attention

THE MISCONCEPTION: *You see everything going on before your eyes, taking in all the information like a camera.*
THE TRUTH: *You are aware only of a small amount of the total information your eyes take in, and even less is processed by your conscious mind and remembered.*

Think of the last time you were in conversation at a crowded party or in a nightclub. The guy in the corner doing the running man, the girl dropping it like it's hot, the pulse of low-budget techno—it all fades into the background as you strain to hear the other person's voice and picture the trip to Ireland he or she is describing. The room is still loud, but inside your head, things have changed. When you focus your attention on one thing, everything else blurs into the periphery.

In science fiction movies like *Minority Report* and *Strange Days* people's memories are played back for others, and they are usually depicted as short films. The way the camera captures the action is the way the memories are played back, but this isn't how you see and remember the scenes in your life. You tune out sounds all the time at work, in a city, watching television, turning down the volume on what you aren't interested in—but you don't notice it as much when you do it visually. When you single out one voice among many, the rest of what is happening is not only getting turned down; most of it is also slipping through your mind without clinging to memory. You accept this easily when it comes to sound, but the same thing happens with the information coming through your eyeballs. The things you pay attention to create your moment-to-moment perception of reality. Everything else is lost or blurred.

Not only do you see only what you're focused on, over time you can become so accustomed to seeing familiar environments, everything blends into the background. Where are those damn keys at? You left them right here, didn't you? Oh, man. You're running late. How can you lose your keys in your own house? No doubt, you've lost your purse, wallet, phone—something—and then found it sitting in plain sight. You go on a scavenger hunt among your own possessions wondering why your IQ has dropped thirty points.

Psychologists call missing information in plain sight inattentional blindness. You believe with confidence your eyes capture everything before them and your memories are recorded versions of those captured images. The truth, though, is you see only a small portion of your environment at any one moment. Your attention is like a spotlight, and only the illuminated portions of the world appear in your perception.

Psychologists Daniel Simons and Christopher Chabris demonstrated this in 1999. They had students divide into two teams and pass a basketball back and forth. Half wore white shirts, and the others wore black. Simons and Chabris recorded a video of the action and then showed it to subjects in the lab. Before the video began, they asked people to count while watching it how many times the ball was passed from one person to another. If you want to try it yourself, they put the video online at www.theinvisiblegorilla.com. You should check it out right now before reading on if you don't want me to spoil the experiment for you. Most people had no problem getting the answer as they stared intensely, hardly blinking. The researchers then asked the subjects if they noticed anything unusual during the action. Most people said they didn't. What the subjects failed to notice was a woman in a gorilla suit who walked into the middle of the players and waved at the camera before casually strolling out of frame. When people were asked what they could recall, they could describe the background, the appearance of the players, the intensity of the action, but about half missed the gorilla.

Simons and Chabris showed tunnel vision is a fact of life—it is your default setting. In their research, they point out how easy it is to miss people you recognize in a movie theater as you scan for a seat, or how often you fail to notice when someone gets a new haircut. Your perception is built out of what you attend to. In the gorilla experiment, people are more likely to see the bizarre intruder if they are just allowed to watch the video without expectations, but it doesn't guarantee they will see it. Your vision narrows to a keyhole view of the world when you are focused, but it doesn't widen to take in everything when you are relaxed. You are usually ignoring the periphery or thinking about something else. When you end up in the closet wondering why you walked in there, you stand there and blink like a sleepwalker who just awoke because in many ways, this is what you are when the spell of your attention breaks.

The problem with inattentional blindness is not that it happens so often, it's that you don't believe it happens. Instead believe you see the whole world in front of you. In any event where eyewitnesses or close inspection are key, your tendency to believe you have perfect perception and recall leads to mistakes in judgment of your own mind and the minds of others. Human eyes aren't video cameras, and the memories formed aren't videos.

The fraternal twin of inattentional blindness is change blindness. The brain can't keep up with the total amount of information coming in from your eyes, and so your experience from moment to moment is edited for simplicity. With change blindness, you don't notice when things around you are altered to be drastically different than they were a moment ago. Reality, as you experience it, is a virtual experience generated by the brain based on the inputs coming in from your senses. You don't get a raw feed from those inputs; instead, you get an edited version.

In another experiment by Simons and Chabris, subjects had to approach a man and sign a consent form before taking part in what they thought was the actual experiment. The man stood behind a tall desk, like a registration desk at a hotel, and once they signed, the man behind the desk ducked under it to put away the form. Another man then stood up and handed them a packet of information. Two-thirds of the subjects didn't realize it was a different person. They had no problem recalling other aspects of the room and the interaction, but the actual identity of the person was just an impression, a shorthand. Their brains registered it was a young, Caucasian male, and that's it. No more attention was paid to the person behind the desk, so the memory was no clearer. The fact that he changed into a new person raised no alarms.

In other experiments, Simons and Daniel T. Levin showed a conversation at a dinner table between actresses filmed in two separate shots. In one shot subjects saw one actress, and then the shot changed to show the other actress when she spoke. Between the shots, nine different aspects of the scene were changed. The color of the plates went from white to red, food items appeared and disappeared, and even the clothes changed as the camera cut from one perspective to the other. When subjects were asked if they noticed, most didn't remember any changes. When the experimenters asked the subjects to specifically look for differences, on average only two of the nine changes were caught. When they ran the experiment again, but this time had one actor hear a phone ring and then a second actor appear in the following shot and answer it, only 33 percent of the people watching the video noticed the actor had been switched.

Magicians build careers around perceptual blindness. It takes just a smidgen of misdirection to conceal a change in your visual field. You believe when something unexpected happens the security guard in your brain will spit out his coffee and call the boss, but there is no security guard and there is no boss. Magicians know your brain isn't a passive receiver of images from your eyes. Instead, you choose what to perceive. While driving and talking on a cell phone, how much of your world do you miss? The research findings suggest you could have your eyes wide open, but fail to see the car, the bike, or the deer about to cross your path.

In the late 1970s Richard Haines at NASA was testing heads-up displays on commercial airliners. His research showed how the unexpected doesn't jump out at you, not even when you are in a situation where your senses are on alert. A heads-up display is a semitransparent glowing series of images that appear as if they float between the pilot and the windshield of the cockpit. The display was meant to keep pilots looking through the windshield at all times instead of diverting their attention to the control panels below. Haines tested the display in a flight simulator where he had pilots practice landing with its assistance. He found when it was turned on, the pilots took longer to react to the sight of another plane on the runway, and some even missed it completely. The pilots were paying so much attention to the new technology, they missed something that before would have been hard to miss. The technology designed to help them actually hurt them. The more your attention is engaged, the less you expect something out of the ordinary and the less prone you are to see it even when lives could be at stake.

One strange twist on this research comes from Richard Nisbett and Hanna-Faye Chua at the University of Michigan. In 2005, they showed people who grew up in Western cultures and people from East Asian cultures photos with one object as the focus of the action surrounded by interesting backgrounds. When they tracked their eye movements, they discovered the Western observers tended to ignore the background and fixate on the focal object, while the Asian subjects took in everything. If the image was a jet flying over mountains, Western eyes more quickly darted to the airplane and then spent more time examining it. A similar experiment at the University of Alberta had Westerners and Japanese subjects watch cartoons with one character in the foreground and four in the background. The study showed that the Japanese subjects spent 15 percent of their time looking at the background characters, while the Westerners spent 5 percent of theirs. The research into cultural cognition is new, but these studies suggest that Western culture is less concerned with context and more concerned with the center of attention, which means it is possible Westerners are more susceptible to both change blindness and inattentional blindness.

The world outside your head and the world inside it are not identical. The information flowing into consciousness from your senses is not only limited by your attention, but also edited before it arrives. Once there, it mixes like paint with all the other thoughts and perceptions swirling inside your cranium. The way you feel, the culture you grew up in, the task at hand, the chaos of technology and society—it all creates a granular, busy visual world. Only a slice of it arrives in your mind. Despite this, the great circus of human activity and invention goes on. You choose what to see more than you realize, and then you form beliefs without taking into account your selective vision. You can't do much about it other than to choose wisely when it is important. Don't put faith in your senses when you wear a hands-free headset in the car or lose yourself in a book in a public place. The unexpected isn't guaranteed to jar you out of your daydream.

41

Self-Handicapping

THE MISCONCEPTION: *In all you do, you strive for success.*

THE TRUTH: *You often create conditions for failure ahead of time to protect your ego.*

Chances are you know someone who seems to be in a perpetual state of illness. Maybe it's you, but let's assume it isn't. This person, the hypochondriac, is always complaining about a cold or a fever, a sick stomach or an aching back. For those who habitually see themselves as unwell, there are a number of benefits. A true hypochondriac absorbs empathy like a flower does sunshine, but the real reward comes when life gets too hard. When a project or an obligation seems like too much to handle, a hypochondriac can conveniently become sick and avoid the risk of failing.

Like most aberrant behaviors, hypochondria is just an extreme version of something everyone thinks and feels occasionally. Everyone gets depressed, just like everyone gets obsessed with cleaning their surroundings occasionally. Major depressive and obsessive compulsive disorders take those normal tendencies and amplify them into unmanageable variants. You share with hypochondriacs the tendency to unconsciously contrive excuses ahead of time.

From time to time a project will come along that seems so big and challenging you start to question your ability to succeed. It could be as epic as writing a book or directing a major motion picture, or it could be something more pedestrian like passing a final exam or delivering an important speech to your corporate boss. Naturally, some doubts will float through your mind whenever failure is possible. Sometimes, when the fear of failure is strong, you use a technique psychologists call self-handicapping to change the course of your future emotional state. Self-handicapping is a reality negotiation, an unconscious manipulation, of both your perceptions and those of others, that you use to protect your ego. Like its cousins sour grapes, in which you pretend you don't want what you can't have, and sweet lemons, in which you convince yourself something unpleasant is actually not so bad, self-handicapping is what psychologists call an anticipatory rationalization. Self-handicapping behaviors are investments in a future reality in which you can blame your failure on something other than your ability.

As with many of the topics in this book, this behavior is all about keeping your all-important self-esteem strong and resilient. If you can always blame your failures on external forces, instead of internal ones, well, who's to say you really fail?

Self-handicapping was studied by psychologists Steven Berglas and Edward E. Jones in 1978. In their research, they had students take difficult tests and then told them they had made perfect scores on them, no matter how they had actually performed. They hypothesized these students, who now had boosted self-images, would choose to protect their egos if given the opportunity. When they then gave them the chance to take what they were told was either a performance-inhibiting or a performance-enhancing drug before a second exam, the majority took the inhibiting drug. The drug was fake, but the behavior was real. Berglas and Jones later said their research showed when you are successful but don't know why, you wonder inside if you are truly capable of success. The stakes on future tests of ability are raised, but so are the fears of failure. Instead of making excuses after the fact that feel like lies, you create conditions ahead of time so the excuses can be real.

You might wear inappropriate clothes to a job interview, or pick a terrible character in *Mario Kart*, or stay up all night drinking before work—you are very resourceful when it comes to setting yourself up to fail. If you succeed, you can say you did so despite terrible odds. If you fall short, you can blame the events leading up to the failure instead of your own incompetence or inadequacy.

Adam Alter and Joseph Forgas at the University of New South Wales discovered in 2006 that your mood is a powerful predictor of when you will self-handicap, but not in the way you think. They had people take tests of their verbal abilities and divided them into two groups. One was told they did very well, and the other was told they didn't. What participants actually scored didn't matter because the experimenters were just interested in boosting or deflating their egos. After priming one of the groups to have a positive self-image, they then showed them videos putting them in either a good mood or a bad one. One film was a British comedy, the other a documentary about cancer. After this, the subjects were told they would be taking another test, but first they were given the choice of two different tea drinks, one that would make them sleepy or one that would give them a jolt of alertness. This was the crucial moment in the study. Would people who were likely to self-handicap be even more likely to follow through with it if they were sad? Actually, no. The people in a good mood were much more likely to self-handicap. Those who watched the comedy and did well on the first test chose the calming tea 65 percent of the time. Those who did well and watched the depressing documentary chose the calming tea 34 percent of the time. To bolster their findings, they ran the experiment in several ways, eliminating and adding variables to be sure the subjects were truly self-handicapping. In the end, Alter and Forgas concluded the happier you are, the more likely you will be to seek out ways to delude yourself into maintaining your rosy outlook on life and your own abilities. Sad people, it seems, are more honest with themselves.

Your sense of self, your identity, is something you are always tending. When you see your performance in the outside world as an integral part of your personality, you are more likely to self-handicap. Psychologist Phillip Zombardo told *The New York Times* in 1984, "Some people stake their whole identity on their acts. They take the attitude that 'if you criticize anything I do, you criticize me.' Their egocentricity means they can't risk a failure because it's a devastating blow to their ego."

In this and many other studies, men tend to be much more likely to self-handicap than women. The reasons are unclear. Perhaps men feel more pressure from society to be seen as competent, or maybe men are more likely to associate external task success with an internal sense of worth. The reasons are as yet unknown, but the tendency is clear. Men use self-handicapping more than women to assuage their fears of failure.

Whenever you venture into uncharted waters with failure as a distinct possibility, your anxiety will be lowered every time you see a new way to blame possible failure on forces beyond your control. The next time you face a challenge, remember you are not so smart, and start preparing for it now.

42

Self-Fulfilling Prophecies

THE MISCONCEPTION: *Predictions about your future are subject to forces beyond your control.*

THE TRUTH: *Just believing a future event will happen can cause it to happen if the event depends on human behavior.*

The self-fulfilling prophecy is a concept that goes far back into the history of storytelling and narrative fiction in just about all human cultures, but it isn't fiction.

Research shows you are highly susceptible to this phenomenon because you are always trying to predict the behavior of others. The future is the result of actions, and actions are the result of behavior, and behavior is the result of prediction. This is called the Thomas Theorem. The sociologist W. I. Thomas postulated in 1928, "If men define situations as real, they are real in their consequences." Thomas noticed when people are trying to predict future events, they make a lot of assumptions about the present. If those assumptions are powerful enough, the resulting actions will lead to the predicted future.

The easiest example of this is the rumor of a shortage. If you believe there will be a shortage of toothpaste, you will go and try to buy some before the stores run out—just like everyone else. Sure enough, the shortage occurs.

The sociologist Robert K. Merton coined the term "self-fulfilling prophecy" in 1968. By his estimation, the initial phase is always a false interpretation of an ongoing situation. The behavior that follows assumes the situation is real, and when enough people act as if something is real it can sometimes make it so. What was once false becomes true, and in hindsight it seems as if it always was.

Self-fulfilling prophecies gain their power from social definitions of reality, and most of your life is defined socially, not logically. A perception depending on logic, like the number of albums sold by Foghat, can be measured. The perception of how good Foghat is, and whether or not they should play the halftime show at the Super Bowl, is socially determined. If the perceptions of others translate into actions, policies, and beliefs, the perceptions become reality simply because so much of life is ruled by behavior. Is bottled water better for you than tap water? Is a Snuggie better than a regular blanket? Are leisure suits the ultimate fashion statement? Is *Inception*, like, the best movie ever made? Without scientific analysis, ideas like these can go from true to false to maybe and back again because they are socially defined. They depend on subjective feelings and a vacillating consensus of beliefs. The social hive mind of the moment creates a reality all its own that is separate from the reality of things like lunar eclipses and the radius of a circle. You swim in a sea of social ideas and mental constructs shared by a culture both ancient and popular. When these ideas become beliefs, and then those beliefs become actions, the logical and measurable side of reality changes to match.

Psychologists Claude Steele and Joshua Aronson conducted a

study in 1995 where they had white and black Americans take the Graduate Record Examination. The GRE is a standardized test used by many colleges to determine whether or not to accept graduate students. It is a comprehensive and difficult test and the source of much anxiety every year in the halls of academia. Steel and Aronson told half of their subjects they were testing for intelligence, which they hypothesized would add an extra level of stress the other half wouldn't feel. When they got back the results, the white students performed about the same whether or not they were told it was a test of how smart they were. The black students, though, primed by the stereotype threat, performed worse in the group who believed the test would reveal their true intelligence. According to Steel and Aronson, the social stigma of being an African-American messed with their minds. Attempting to fight their stereotype, they had unwelcome thoughts walking around and making noise in their brains while they solved word problems and figured fractions. The white students, free from these fears, had more mind space in which to work. This same sort of experiment had been repeated with gender, nationality, and all sorts of conditions. Psychologists call it the stereotype threat. When you fear you will confirm a negative stereotype, it can become a self-fulfilling prophecy not because the stereotype is true, but because you can't stop worrying that you could become an example proving it.

This self-fulfilling prophecy, being only a matter of perception, can be easily sublimated. Another study by Steele measured the math abilities of men versus women. When the questions were easy, the women and the men performed the same. When they were difficult, the women's scores plummeted lower than did those of their male peers. When they ran the tests again with new participants, but this time before handing out the problems told the subjects that men and women tended to perform equally on the exam, the scores leveled out. The women performed just as well as did the men. The power of the stereotype—women are bad at math—was nullified.

In social psychology, a version of the self-fulfilling prophecy called labeling theory shows how when someone believes you are a certain kind of person, you tend to live up to those expectations. If your teacher thinks you are smart, the teacher treats you like a smart person. You get extra attention and respect. You react with more effort, more drive, and the positive feedback loop leads to the fulfillment of your label. In a 1978 experiment by William Crano and Phyllis Mellon, a set of random students were chosen from an elementary class. The teachers were told these random students had been shown to be possible child geniuses based on an IQ test. The test, of course, didn't exist, and the results were imaginary. Sure enough, those students performed better on homework and exams thanks to more attention from the teachers who believed the prophecy.

Think of the stock market. When people predict it will fail, they stop investing and start selling. Others hear about the selling, and they sell. People start to try and predict the future, assume everyone is going to sell, and they sell too. Once the media starts reporting, stocks plummet.

Research shows if you believe someone is going to be an asshole, you will act hostile, thus causing them to act like an asshole. This same research shows if people think their partner doesn't love them, they will interpret small slights as big hurts—and this will then lead to a feeling of rejection that causes the partner to distance him- or herself. The feedback loop will build and build until the prophecy is fulfilled.

In an experiment performed by Steven Sherman in 1980, two sets of people were asked over the phone to donate three hours of time to a cancer drive. One group was simply asked if they would do it. They said yes. Four percent showed up. The other group was asked if they thought they would show up if they were to be asked. Most said they would show up. Almost all of them did. The second group had made an assumption about their own personality, and once they had painted a portrait of what kind of person they were, they had to conform to the idea or risk cognitive dissonance.

When it comes to belief, you are not so smart, and the things you think are true will become reality if given enough time to fester. If you want a better job, a better marriage, a better teacher, a better friend—you have to act as if the thing you want out of the other person is already headed your way. It doesn't guarantee you'll see a change, but it's better than nothing. The point is this: A negative outlook will lead to negative predictions, and you will start to unconsciously manipulate your environment to deliver those predictions.

Don't go buying *The Secret* just yet. No, you can't just want something to be true and have it become so, but you can avoid the opposite scenario, which might be just enough to improve your life.

43

The Moment

THE MISCONCEPTION: *You are one person, and your happiness is based on being content with your life.*

THE TRUTH: *You are multiple selves, and happiness is based on satisfying all of them.*

Have you ever been so sick you spent a week in bed? What do you remember from that period of time? Mostly nothing, right? All throughout your life great big patches of experience are tossed aside and forgotten. You turn around sometimes and think, "It's March already!?" or "I've been working here for five years!?"

To understand the difference between experience and memory, you first need to understand a little bit about self. Your sense of self is just that—a sense. The person you imagine yourself to be is a story you tell to yourself and to others differently depending on the situation, and the story changes over time. For now, it is useful to imagine there are two selves active at any given time in your head— the current self and the remembering self.

The current self is the one experiencing life in real time. It is the person you are in the three or so seconds your sensory memory lasts, and the thirty or so seconds after that in which your short-term memory is juggling all your senses and thoughts. You taste the ice cream and it is good. Then, you remember you tasted the ice cream. Then, in five years, you have no memory of tasting it at all. Sometimes, rarely, something else happens that prompts you to move the memory into long-term storage. Think back now to all the times you have tasted ice cream. How many true memories do you have that aren't just dreamlike wisps? How many stories can you tell about tasting ice cream? The remembering self is made up of all those memories that have passed into long-term storage.

When you replay your life in your mind, you can't go back to all the things you have ever experienced. Only the things that went from experience to short-term memory to long-term memory are available to fully remember. Going to get ice cream is not about building awesome memories. It's about being happy for a few minutes. It's about gratification. The happiness derived from such an experience is fleeting.

The psychologist Daniel Kahneman has much to say on this topic. He says the self that makes decisions in your life is usually the remembering one. It drags your current self around in pursuit of new memories, anticipating them based on old memories. The current self has little control over your future. It can control only a few actions, like moving your hand away from a hot stove or putting one foot in front of the other. Occasionally, it prompts you to eat a cheeseburger, or watch a horror movie, or play a video game. The current self is happy when experiencing things. It likes to be in the flow.

It is the remembering self that has made all the big decisions. It is happy when you can sit back and reflect on your life up to this point and feel content. It is happy when you tell people stories about the things you have seen and done. Kahneman proposes this thought experiment: Imagine you are preparing to go on a two-week vacation. At the end of this vacation, you will drink a potion that will erase all the memories from those two weeks.

How will this affect your decisions? Knowing you won't remember any of it, what will you spend your time doing during those two weeks? That weird feeling you are having thinking about this is the conflict between your experiencing self and your remembering self. The experiencing self can easily choose what to do. Sex, skiing, restaurants, concerts, parties—all of these things are about being happy during the event. The remembering self is not so sure. It would rather go to Ireland and look at castles or drive from New York to Los Angeles just to see what happens.

Kahneman's research suggests there are two channels through which you decide whether or not you are happy. The current self is happy when experiencing nice things. The remembering self is happy when you look back on your life and pull up plenty of positive memories. As Kahneman points out, a two-week vacation may yield only a handful of lifelong memories. You will pull those memories out every once in a while and use them to be happy. There is a serious imbalance between the time you spend creating these memories and the time you spend enjoying them later.

The current self doesn't like sitting in a cubicle. It feels caged. It could be doing something fun. The remembering self doesn't like not having the opportunity to build new memories, so it is willing to grind away to earn money for food and shelter and delay gratification.

Life for you and many others is full of conflict between these two selves over how best to be happy. Kahneman's research shows that happiness can't be all one or all the other. You have to be happy in the flow of time while simultaneously creating memories you can look back on later.

To be happy now and content later, you can't be focused only on reaching goals, because once you reach them, the experience ends. To truly be happy, you must satisfy both of your selves. Go get the ice cream, but do so in a meaningful way that creates a long-term memory. Grind away to have money for later, but do so in a way that generates happiness as you work.

44

Consistency Bias

THE MISCONCEPTION: *You know how your opinions have changed over time.*

THE TRUTH: *Unless you consciously keep tabs on your progress, you assume the way you feel now is the way you have always felt.*

Imagine yourself in high school. What kind of person were you?

Some obvious things come to mind—your awful haircut, those stupid shirts, the questionable taste in music. You sure were a dork.

If you were into a subculture, it is probably even more painful to see your old self. Were you an emo kid, a flannel-clad grunge fan, or did you trade *Star Trek* novels in your chess club? Whatever you were into at the time, it is likely you aren't so into it now. You've probably learned how to tame your hair, which clothes are silly, and what music is truly good to you. You've figured out your personal politics, your taste in movies, what real friendship is all about. It's as easy to see the differences in who you were then as it would be with two photographs taken now and then. Some differences, though, are hard to see. Scientists have shown you are not so smart when it comes to comparing your current mental world to the one you lived in years ago.

The psychologist Hazel Markus at the University of Michigan says when you receive new information that threatens your self-image, you react quickly to reaffirm your identity. The self is something psychologists have known from the beginning to be both consistent and changing. At any given moment, you guard your convictions and introspective conclusions, but the self you guard can shift from one social situation to the next. As the psychologist William James said in 1910, there are for any individual "as many different social selves as there are distinct groups of persons about whose opinion he cares." Right now, all those selves are like the many surfaces of a prism; turn it one way or the other, and a different you is reflected back to the world. The consistency bias makes you think this prism has always been the same size and shape it is now, but it hasn't.

In 1986, Markus published a paper that showed how malleable the self was and how oblivious to change you really are. The paper covered two decades of research. Back in 1965, Markus and his colleagues collected political opinions from a group of high school seniors and their parents. He then returned to the same people in 1973 and again in 1982 to see how their opinions might have changed. The questions ranged from the legalization of drugs to the rights of prisoners and the validity of war. As you might expect, the younger people's attitudes changed a lot more between 1965 and 1973 than did their parents', and overall those young attitudes became more conservative over the course of seventeen years. Markus showed how when you are young you are more open to changing your opinions. Your partisanship has yet to solidify into a personal philosophy. After gaining enough life experience, you begin to settle into a view of the world and establish your moral outlook. It seems like common sense, but when he asked the people in the study what they used to believe, only about 30 percent could accurately recall their old answers. Instead, they tended to say they used to have the same political ideas they currently subscribed to. If, for instance, they believed the death penalty was a legitimate punishment, they thought they had always believed this, even when they had said the opposite as a teenager.

This same sort of experiment was conducted in 1998 by Elaine Scharfe at Trent University and Kim Bartholomew at Simon Fraser University, except they asked people to rate how happy they were in their relationships. Some of the subjects were dating, some were living together, and others were married. The questions ranged from how often the other person got on their nerves to how long they expected the relationship to last. They asked again eight months later, then asked the participants to recall their previous answers. Those whose relationships had stayed the same tended to remember their previous responses, but those whose relationships had gotten either better or worse did not see the past as clearly; 78 percent of the women and 87 percent of the men inaccurately recalled how they used to feel. Most of the people in the study had a good recollection of their original feelings, but for those who didn't, consistency bias altered their memories to make it seem as though they had always been as happy, or sad, as they now were.

In an experiment by George Goethals and Richard Reckman at Williams College in 1972, students were asked how they felt about racially segregated bussing. After recording their answers, they were led in a discussion of the issue a few weeks later by an actor who tried to change their minds. If they were pro-integration, the actor tried to get them to see the downsides. If they were anti-integration, the actor pointed out the harm. As in the other studies, when they were then asked their opinions from the original questionnaire, neither group responded correctly. They had been swayed, but they thought they had always held their new position.

One of the stranger facets of consistency bias is how it can be evoked on the spot. If you are primed to believe you are an honest person, you will then act as if you are.

In 2008, Dan Ariely, Nina Mazar, and On Amir at MIT had Harvard Business School students answer as many math problems as they could in five minutes. Afterward, one student would be randomly chosen in a lottery and win $10 for every correct answer. Before the test began, half of the students listed ten books they remembered reading in high school, and the other half listed as many of the Ten Commandments from the Bible they could recall. In both groups, half of the students were given an opportunity to grade themselves and cheat by simply telling the researchers how many answers they got right, while the other half had to actually turn in their papers. In the group that listed books, the total scores were 33 percent higher than the average, which indicated that they had cheated. In the group that listed the Ten Commandments, the scores were less than average; no one cheated. Half of the students had been primed to think about honesty, and since we all want to believe we are honest, the resulting behavior was an attempt at consistency.

You experience this sort of instant consistency bias all the time. If you sign a pledge to be honest and trustworthy, you tend to follow through. If you agree ahead of time to do something you later don't feel like doing, you do it anyway so you don't feel inconsistent or appear so to others. In any situation where you are primed to think of yourself in a certain way, you will be more likely to engage in behavior that proves you are. In 1978, Robert B. Cialdinia, John T. Cacioppo, Rodney Bassett, and John A. Miller at Arizona State conducted an study where they asked people if they would be willing to take part in an experiment for a good cause, and about half said they would. After they agreed, they were then told the experiment would begin at 7 A.M. Ninety-five percent of the people still showed up. When the researchers did the experiment again but told the people up front when they had to arrive, 24 percent agreed to take part. The people in the first experiment weren't psyched about coming in so early, but because they had said they would be willing to participate, they felt forced into making their behavior consistent, even though there were no repercussions to do otherwise. You have no desire to be a hypocrite.

Consistency bias is part of your overall desire to reduce the discomfort of cognitive dissonance, the emotions you feel when noticing that you are of two minds on one issue. When you say one thing and do another, the ickiness of feeling hypocritical must be dealt with or else you find it difficult to proceed. You need to feel that you can predict your own behavior, and so you rewrite your own history sometimes so you can seem dependable to yourself. If your life story includes self-improvement, and you find meaning in change, you suppress consistency bias. At other times you simply desire certain parts of your autobiography to have unfolded in a pleasing way and can't imagine having once been the sort of person you would argue with. If you are madly in love now, but once had your doubts, you simply delete the past and replace it with one less inconsistent with your present state. Older people tend to look at younger people as naive, and sometimes become amused when they see in them the same ignorance with which they once dealt. Sometimes they try to reason with the ignorance, as if to suggest it could be overcome with mere wisdom. This is consistency bias at work: believing if you knew then what you know now, things would be different. But people naturally change over time. Consistency bias is the failure to admit it.

45

The Representativeness Heuristic

THE MISCONCEPTION: *Knowing a person's history makes it easier to determine what sort of person they are.*
THE TRUTH: *You jump to conclusions based on how representative a person seems to be of a preconceived character type.*

Your friend goes out on a date and tells you the other person was spontaneous, unpredictable, funny, and maybe a little dangerous. Your friend thinks she is in love. When you ask what this date does for a living, your friend says he is a podiatrist. Would this surprise you? Probably so, but why? What do you really know about foot doctors anyway? Are they the kind of people who would go skydiving one weekend and gamble on an illegal cockfight the next? Does this seem like the kind of thing a foot specialist would do, or do you see the foot specialist relaxing with a cluster of cats while perusing photo albums of exotic toenail fungi?

Unless you have spent time as a secretary of state, chances are you don't know a lot about people who are different from you. For everyone else you haul around prejudices, some benign, some less so. It helps you think faster, to build models of the unknown in a way that allows you to make decisions effortlessly. Without filters, the world around you is chaos. Over time you develop shortcuts to cognition. Categories are a great way to make sense of things. When it comes to strangers, your first instinct is to fit them into archetypes to quickly determine their value or threat. These constructs are called the representativeness heuristic.

Daniel Kahneman and Amos Tversky published a paper in 1973 that ferreted out the representative heuristic from the cluster of cognitive biases squirming in your mind. The following example is a mishmash of their research and others into the behavior:

> Donald is a very intelligent college student and does well in all his classes, but he lacks creativity. He is extraordinarily tidy and feels compelled to bring order to every aspect of his life. When he writes, it lacks emotion and is filled with science fiction references. He doesn't like people but has high moral standards.

In their study, subjects read a paragraph like the one above and were told the description came from one of a set of interviews with thirty engineers and seventy lawyers. Now, pretend you are in this study and answer the following question: Is it more likely Donald is an engineer or a lawyer?

This is where the representativeness heuristic sends you down the wrong path. If you are like most people, you think Donald is probably an engineer. He certainly matches the general vision you see when thinking of one. You completely ignore the fact there is a 70 percent chance he is a lawyer because, out of one hundred people, they interviewed only thirty engineers. Kahneman and Tversky say you make predictions with representativeness—the degree to which new information matches the existing information you have in your head. Sometimes, this information in your head is just a caricature of the actual thing. You think of a sheik, and you see a man in white robes and sandals. You think of a cowboy, and you see a hat, chaps, lasso, and gunbelt. You see an engineer and a lawyer, and the image above matches the engineer better. You toss aside the numbers. Your mental models aren't accurate, nor do they usually need to be. They just need to pop right into your mind automatically and without effort. If your ancestors heard a rustling in the bushes, they were better off assuming something bad and hungry was headed their way. If you need medical attention, you would be correct to assume the big red cross above the sign that reads EMERGENCY indicates the right building to head toward, even though you can't be sure it isn't abandoned or some elaborate amusement park ride. Kahneman and Tversky's research suggests that intuition ignores statistics. Intuition is bad at math.

Try again with this description:

> Tom is a twice-divorced man who spends most of his free time playing golf. He enjoys fine suits and drives an expensive luxury car. He is quick to argue and has to win or he becomes furious. He went to college for longer than he wanted to and tries to make up for it by socializing as much as he can.

Now, pretend in this study they interviewed seventy engineers and thirty lawyers. Knowing how the representativeness heuristic works, is it more likely Tom is an engineer or a lawyer? That's right. It is more likely, statistically, that he is an engineer, no matter how well the description matches your heuristic model for lawyers.

The representativeness heuristic helps fuel several other cognitive missteps, like the conjunction fallacy. Here is another example from Kahneman and Tversky's research:

> Linda is a thirty-one-year-old woman who is single. She is considered outspoken and very bright. She majored in philosophy in college. As a student, she was deeply concerned with discrimination and social issues. She participated in several demonstrations.

Is it more likely Linda is a bank teller or that she is a bank teller and is active in the feminist movement? Most people who read the above description pick the second answer, although it is statistically more likely she is a bank teller. There are more bank tellers in the world than bank tellers who are feminists, no matter what sort of background they may have.

The conjunction fallacy builds on your representativeness heuristic. The more things you hear about which match your mental models, the more likely they seem. In the example above, you can match both bank tellers and feminists with the description, so it seems twice as likely. Statistically though, it goes in the other direction. You don't naturally think in statistical, logical, rational terms. You first go to your emotional core and think of people in terms of narratives and characters that match your preconceived notions of the sort of people you have been exposed to in the past or have imagined thanks to cultural osmosis.

Kahneman and Tversky proved this by trying the same sort of experiment on professional futurists—people who forecast the likelihood of future events. In 1982 they asked 115 forecasters to predict which of two options was more likely to happen in the next year.

They divided them into two groups, and asked one to estimate the chances of the United States and the Soviet Union suspending all relations. The other group estimated the odds Russia would invade Poland in addition to suspending diplomacy with the U.S. The second group said that their scenario, with twice the number of events, was more likely to happen. Their representativeness reserves had been tapped twice, which made it seem more possible than the single event.

Representativeness heuristics are useful, but also dangerous. They can help you avoid danger and seek help, but they can also lead to generalizations and prejudices. When you expect people to be a certain way because they seem to represent your notions of the sort of people in that category, you are not so smart.

46

Expectation

THE MISCONCEPTION: *Wine is a complicated elixir, full of subtle flavors only an expert can truly distinguish, and experienced tasters are impervious to deception.*

THE TRUTH: *Wine experts and consumers can be fooled by altering their expectations.*

You scan the aisles in the liquor store looking for a good wine. It's a little overwhelming—all those weird bottle shapes with illustrations of castles and vineyards and kangaroos. And all those varieties? Riesling, Shiraz, Cabernet—this is serious business. You look to your left and see bottles for around $12; to your right you see bottles for $60. You think back to all the times you've seen people tasting wine in movies, holding it up to the light and commenting on tannins and barrels and soil quality—the most expensive wine has to be the better one, right?

Well, you are not so smart. But don't fret—neither are all those connoisseurs who swish fermented grape juice around and spit it back out.

Wine tasting is a big deal to a lot of people. It can even be a professional career. It goes back thousands of years, but the modern version, with all the terminology like "notes," "tears," "integration," and "connectedness," goes back a few hundred. Wine tasters will mention all sorts of things they can taste in a fine wine, as if they were a human spectrograph with the ability to sense the molecular makeup of their beverage. Research shows, however, this perception can be hijacked, fooled, and might just be completely wrong.

In 2001, Frederic Brochet conducted two experiments at the University of Bordeaux.

In one experiment, he got fifty-four oenology (the study of wine tasting and wine making) undergraduates together and had them taste one glass of red wine and one glass of white wine. He had them describe each wine in as much detail as their expertise would allow. What he didn't tell them was both were the same wine. He just dyed the white one red. In the other experiment, he asked the experts to rate two different bottles of red wine. One was very expensive, the other was cheap. Again, he tricked them. This time he had put the cheap wine in both bottles. So what were the results?

The tasters in the first experiment, the one with the dyed wine, described the sorts of berries and grapes and tannins they could detect in the red wine just as if it really was red. Every single one, all fifty-four, could not tell it was white. In the second experiment, the one with the switched labels, the subjects went on and on about the cheap wine in the expensive bottle. They called it "complex" and "rounded." They called the same wine in the cheap bottle "weak" and "flat."

Another experiment, at Caltech, pitted five bottles of wine against one another. They ranged in price from $5 to $90. Similarly, the experimenters put cheap wine in the expensive bottles—but this time they put the tasters in a brain scanner. While they tasted the wine, the same parts of the brain would light up in the machine every time, but with the wine the tasters thought was expensive, one particular region of the brain became more active. Another study had tasters rate cheese eaten with two different wines. One wine they were told was from California, the other from North Dakota. The same wine was in both bottles. The tasters rated the cheese they ate with the California wine as being better quality, and they ate more of it.

So is the fancy world of wine tasting all pretentious bunk? Not exactly. The wine tasters in the experiments above were being influenced by the nasty beast of expectation. A wine expert's objectivity and powers of taste under normal circumstance might be amazing, but Brochet's manipulations of the environment misled his subjects enough to dampen their acumen. An expert's own expectation can act like Kryptonite on the expert's superpowers. Expectation, as it turns out, is just as important as raw sensation. The buildup to an experience can completely change how you interpret the information reaching your brain from your otherwise objective senses. In psychology, true objectivity is pretty much considered to be impossible. Memories, emotions, conditioning, and all sorts of other mental flotsam taint every new experience you gain. In addition to all this, your expectations powerfully influence the final vote in your head over what you believe to be reality. So when tasting a wine, or watching a movie, or going on a date, or listening to a new stereo through $300 audio cables—some of what you experience comes from within and some comes from without. Expensive wine is like anything else that is expensive: The expectation it will taste better actually makes it taste better.

In one Dutch study, participants were put in a room with posters proclaiming the awesomeness of high-definition and were told they would be watching a new high-definition program. Afterward, the subjects said they found the sharper, more colorful television to be a superior experience to standard programming. What they didn't know was they were actually watching a standard definition image. The expectation of seeing a better-quality image led them to believe they had. Recent research shows about 18 percent of people who own high-definition televisions are still watching standard definition programming on the set, but they think they are getting a better picture.

In the early eighties, Pepsi ran a marketing campaign where they touted the success of their product over Coca-Cola in blind taste tests. They called this "The Pepsi Challenge." Psychologists had already determined you choose your favorite products often not by their inherent value, but because the marketing campaigns and logos and such have cast a spell over you called brand awareness. You start to identify yourself with one marketing campaign over another. That's what happened in all the taste tests up until the Pepsi Challenge. People liked Coca-Cola's advertising more than Pepsi's, so even though they tasted pretty much the same, when they saw that bright red can with a white ribbon people chose Coke. So for the Pepsi Challenge, they removed the logos. At first, the researchers thought they should put some sort of label on the glasses. So they went with M and Q. People said they liked Pepsi, labeled M, better than Coke, labeled Q. Irritated by this, Coca-Cola did their own study and put Coke in both glasses. Again, M won the contest. It turned out it wasn't the soda; people just liked the letter M better than the letter Q.

You look for cues from our environment whenever you find things you like. These cues help you to get back to the good stuff by recognizing what got you the reward last time. For the testers, the two products tasted pretty much the same. So, forced to make a choice, they moved to another set of cues to make their decision—which letter was more pleasant. Apparently, M is better than Q, and in other research people tend to pick A instead of B and 1 instead of 2. Branding works the same way. Vodka, for instance, has no flavor. So advertisers can't sell you on how great it tastes. Instead, they hijack your natural affinity for visual shortcuts by pummeling your brain with advertising. When you are standing in front of all those vodka bottles in the liquor store, the brands hope their marketing campaign has built enough expectation in your consciousness to lead you to their product.

In blind taste tests, longtime smokers can't tell their brand from any of the competitors and wine connoisseurs have a hard time telling $200 bottles from $20 ones. When presented with microwaved food from the frozen food section in the setting of a fine restaurant, most people never notice. Taste is subjective, which is another way of saying you are not so smart when it comes to choosing one product over another. All things being equal—you refer back to the advertising or the packaging or conformity with your friends and family. Presentation is everything.

Restaurants depend on this. Actually, just about every retailer depends on this. Presentation, price, good marketing, great service—it all leads to an expectation of quality. The actual experience at the end of all this is less important. As long as it isn't total crap, your experience will match up with your expectations. A series of bad reviews will make the movie worse, and a heap of positive buzz can sway you in the other direction. You rarely watch films in a social vacuum with no input at all from critics and peers and advertisements. Your expectations are the horse, and your experience is the cart. You get this backward all the time because you are not so smart.

47

The Illusion of Control

THE MISCONCEPTION: *You know how much control you have over your surroundings.*

THE TRUTH: *You often believe you have control over outcomes that are either random or are too complex to predict.*

If you were to flip a coin and have it come up heads five times in a row, you would have a strong feeling deep in your gut the next toss would land on tails because it needed to. You think it must balance out.

This is called the gambler's fallacy, or the Monte Carlo fallacy after a casino roulette game there in 1913 where black came up twenty-six times in a row. As you can imagine, the betting on red got out of hand as black came up over and over again, fifteen, sixteen, seventeen times. It was unbelievable, and in the minds of the gamblers the odds became astronomical that black would come up again; red just had to be next. Order must be restored. The excitement, the clamoring, and the noise as the ball bearing bounced across the numbers and colors was a great fit of delusion, because the odds never changed. It was just as likely to come up black, as it had twenty-six times before.

In gambling, whether it be on a slot machine, a roulette table, or in a game of cards, you have the tendency to see yourself as being lucky or unlucky, on a streak or in a rut. You say things like "The cards are about to turn." You see a change of dealers as a positive sign, or you notice when people get up from the table and change the rotation of the deal. You get two out of three cherries and decide to go for another spin; you bet on red after black comes up ten times in a row, because you think red is due.

You might even have your own system devised to maximize your chances. You never sit in the outer seats in blackjack. You play only slot machines with real handles, or you blow on the dice before tossing them down the craps table. None of this, of course, has any real effect on the odds. The odds are fixed, but sometimes you think you can beat them, because you are not so smart.

When you watch someone play a slot machine for twenty minutes and then walk away, you might rush and take over because it seems as if the one-armed bandit is ready to pay off after so many losses, but it isn't. This is the gambler's fallacy, assuming the odds change based on the history of the outcomes so far. Sure, over a long enough period of time the odds will return to normal, but in the short run there is no way to outsmart random chance. If you flip a coin five hundred times, you'll come across runs of heads and tails, some very long, on your way to an overall split of something close to 50 percent. If you just flip five times, the chances are better you'll streak. This is how casinos always win; when you are winning, you find it difficult to walk away. The longer you play, however, the more the odds balance out, but you never know when a streak will begin or end.

Your ancestors lived long enough to meet a partner and have children one after the other, generation upon generation, for millions of years because they were great at pattern recognition. Predators, prey, friends, and foes all stood out from the background because your kin could see signals amid noise. Thanks to them, you've inherited the same powers, but you can't turn them off. Your brain is always looking for patterns and sending little squirts of happy throughout your body when it finds them, but like faces in clouds, you often see patterns where none exist.

If you roll a die and it lands on one, and then roll again and get a two, and again and see a three, there is no force in the universe that is pushing the odds of a four out of the realm of random chance. But wouldn't it feel like it *had* to be? That's pattern recognition messing with your judgment. Each roll of a die is statistically independent of the next roll. Despite this, a study by James Henslin in 1967 showed people tend to throw harder when they need high numbers in a game of craps and toss gently when they want low ones. Since you briefly control the action, you start to feel like the control extends beyond just the toss, into the randomness that results.

Have you ever crossed your fingers while watching someone shoot for a free throw in basketball? Have you ever wished someone would get hurt, and then they did? In 2006, Emily Pronin and Sylvia Rodriguez at Princeton, along with Daniel Wegner and Kimberly McCarthy at Harvard, decided to see if they could study this behavior in the lab.

They had college students agree to participate in a study on psychosomatic symptoms, those that arise from merely thinking about being sick. This wasn't really the goal of the study though. They actually wanted to see if under the right conditions normal people would believe their own thoughts could harm or help others.

Students were told they would be participating with a partner who was also a student, but the partner was really an actor. In one group, the actor was ten minutes late and wore a shirt that said STUPID PEOPLE SHOULDN'T BREED. He then proceeded to act rude and obnoxious to the experimenter and chewed gum with his mouth open. In the second group, the actor was pleasant and agreeable. The actors and the students pulled slips of paper out of a hat after reading about voodoo for a while. Both slips read "witch doctor," but the students were told that one slip read "victim." The actors then pretended to get the victim slips.

After all of this, the students were handed a voodoo doll and told to think of the other person as they stuck pins into it. Soon the actor started to complain of a headache. As you probably guessed by now, the people who were made to hate the actor more often reported they believed they had caused his pain than did the group who met with a polite confederate. Most people were skeptical, but the skepticism was diminished in the group who had been influenced to harbor negative thoughts about the actor. They saw an effect, and given all the possibilities, they saw their own thoughts as a possible cause.

The experimenters had people watch an athlete shoot basketballs into a basket in a second round of this study. The shooter was blindfolded with a trick blindfold he could secretly see through. In one group the researchers asked subjects to visualize the shooter making the shot for ten seconds before each time he launched the ball, and in the other group they asked the spectators to visualize the shooter lifting weights. They went so far as to have the player practice for a minute before they began and miss most of the shots.

The shooter tried to consistently make six out of eight tries, which he usually did. It was an astonishing feat for a person wearing a blindfold, and the two groups saw it differently. When questioned later, most people were skeptical, but those who had visualized the shooter making the basket were nearly twice as likely to say they believed they helped. As with any good magic trick, people wanted to believe that something otherworldly or telepathic might be afoot.

The researchers concluded most people engage in magical thinking to some degree, assuming their thoughts can influence things outside of their control. The people in the experiments knew they were in a study, so they likely were more skeptical than usual. This skepticism can dissolve away in the right conditions. If you are an avid sports fan, you can't help but think your mental cheerleading has some sort of positive effect on the game play. You take some credit when your team wins. You think you didn't cheer hard enough if they lose. This illusion of control is pervasive enough to show up when teachers take credit for the success of their students or people in war zones start to accumulate lucky charms or engage in rituals they think will keep them alive. You ask people to send well wishes and positive thoughts when someone is sick.

In 1975, Ellen Langer conducted a series of studies in which she had people engage in games of chance both with and without some control over how the games were played. In a card game she had people play against both nervous and confident actors, and although the outcome was random, the subjects bet more when they believed their opponents were weak. She had people either pick their own lottery numbers or have them assigned. Those who picked their own numbers asked for more money than those who did not when she tried to buy back the tickets. She also had people flip coins and predict if they would land on heads or tails, but her team manipulated the outcomes. Some subjects were made to believe they guessed correctly fifteen times in row at the beginning, some fifteen times in a row at the end, and a third group fifteen times spread out over all thirty tosses. Those who thought they did well at the beginning said they felt like they could practice to improve their performance on future runs. Those who thought they guessed poorly at the beginning or saw their fifteen correct guesses as being random were less confident. The number of correct guesses were the same in all three groups, but the people who experienced streaks early on believed they had some sort of control. They thought they could beat the odds.

Langer concluded the deciding factors were the cues in the games that made the participants feel as if some skill was involved. Seeing patterns, becoming more familiar with the games, having options as to how to play—all contributed to the illusion of control. As obvious as it should have been, the subjects tended to see randomness as something they could outwit. This is why you are far more likely to participate in games of chance when there are some customizable features. Allowing you to choose your own lottery numbers or pick the numbers to bet on in roulette affects how you see the results. You assume the cold hand of fate becomes a tad less potent if you have some say in how you tempt it.

Flipping a coin or winning at poker are relatively simple in comparison to giant monsters of randomness like stock markets and wars, corporate mergers and family vacations, yet no matter how complex a situation can be, there will be people who assume they can predict and control it. Those who hold power become delusional about how far the power extends.

In 2008, Nathaneal Fast and Deborah Gruenfeld at Stanford University conducted experiments designed to reveal how the illusion of control is created. They knew previous studies had shown those with high socioeconomic status or who came from cultures where power and influence were highly regarded were more likely to think they were better at predicting the future. People even fear death less when they have a college degree. What if, they asked, you were just asked to think about being powerful?

They divided subjects into three groups. One group wrote an essay about a time in their life in which they remembered being a leader. Another group wrote about a time when they were a follower. The third group served as a control and wrote about going to the supermarket. After the essays were finished, the groups played a game where they had to guess the roll of a pair of dice. If they guessed correctly, they would get $5. The catch was this: Choose yourself or another person to roll.

Sure enough, the illusion of control had been properly primed in the group that wrote about being leaders. A full 100 percent of them asked to roll the dice. In the subordinate group, 58 percent asked for control of the roll. The control group fell in between, with 69 percent asking to try their luck instead of handing the dice over to someone else. Of course the dice didn't care who tossed them. You start to assume you are imbued with gifts others do not possess if you find yourself at the helm of a great and powerful ship. You make plans and decisions assuming randomness and chaos are for chumps. The illusion of control is a peculiar thing because it often leads to high self-esteem and a belief your destiny is yours for the making more than it really is. This over-optimistic view can translate into actual action, rolling with the punches and moving ahead no matter what. Often, this attitude helps lead to success. Eventually, though, most people get punched in the stomach by life. Sometimes, the gut-punch doesn't come until after a long chain of wins, until you've accumulated enough power to do some serious damage. This is when wars go awry, stock markets crash, and political scandals spill out into the media. Power breeds certainty, and certainty has no clout against the unpredictable, whether you are playing poker or running a country.

Psychologists point out these findings do not suggest you should throw up your hands and give up. Those who are not grounded in reality, oddly enough, often achieve a lot in life simply because they believe they can and try harder than others. If you focus too long on your lack of power, you can slip into a state of learned helplessness that will whirl you into a negative feedback loop of depression. Some control is necessary or else you give up altogether. Langer proved this when studying nursing homes where some patients were allowed to arrange their furniture and water plants—they lived longer than those who had had those tasks performed by others.

Knowing about the illusion of control shouldn't discourage you from attempting to carve a space for yourself out of whatever field you want to tackle. After all, doing nothing guarantees no results. But as you do so, remember most of the future is unforeseeable. Learn to coexist with chaos. Factor it into your plans. Accept that failure is always a possibility, even if you are one of the good guys; those who believe failure is not an option never plan for it. Some things are predictable and manageable, but the farther away in time an event occurs, the less power you have over it. The farther away from your body and the more people involved, the less agency you wield. Like a billion rolls of a trillion dice, the factors at play are too complex, too random to truly manage. You can no more predict the course of your life than you could the shape of a cloud. So seek to control the small things, the things that matter, and let them pile up into a heap of happiness. In the bigger picture, control is an illusion anyway.

48

The Fundamental Attribution Error

THE MISCONCEPTION: *Other people's behavior is the reflection of their personality.*

THE TRUTH: *Other people's behavior is more the result of the situation than their disposition.*

You go to a restaurant and your server brings back something you didn't order. When you send it back, it takes forever for them to return with the correct dish. They forget to fill your glass and seem unable to remember what you are drinking when they do check on you. What sort of tip do you leave?

I waited tables for three years while in college, and I can tell you. If the kitchen got a table's order wrong, I knew my tip was ruined. It wasn't my fault, but people consistently punished me as if it was. If the food was cold, or burned, or rare when it should have been well done, the diners would communicate their dissatisfaction by leaving nothing or, worse than nothing, a single coin. Some people are polite right up until the moment of truth when they cast their monetary vote of nonconfidence. Others get violently angry and while still chewing will demand to see a manager. Waiting ta-

bles fosters a peculiar sort of acrimony among waiters and wait-
resses. I never met a server who didn't know when a bad tip was
coming. No one was ever taught a lesson from being shortchanged.
Over those three years, I knew the service had more to do with the
situation than my own disposition. I could dampen the fallout from
the circumstances outside my control by being nice and funny, or
striking up a conversation when I felt it was appropriate, but the
customers still blamed me when something went wrong.

So have you ever left a bad tip to show your exasperation?

When you are at a restaurant, you have a hard time seeing
through to the personality of the server. You place blame and assume you are dealing with a slacker. Sometimes you are right, but
often you are committing the fundamental attribution error.

Have you ever watched a quiz show like *The Weakest Link* or
Jeopardy and thought, however briefly, that the host was super-
smart? Perhaps there are a handful of musicians, or authors, or pro-
fessors in your life you've placed on a pedestal. You imagine how
difficult it would be to hold your own in conversation with these
people, as you imagine their towering intellect would crush you as
you resorted to prattling on about pasta recipes and your collection
of ornate spoons. When you don't know much about a person,
when you haven't had a chance to get to know him or her, you have
a tendency to turn the person into a character. You lean on archetypes and stereotypes culled from experience and fantasy. Even
though you know better, you still do it.

You put on and take off social masks all the time. You are a different person with your friends than you are with your family or
your boss. Somehow, you forget that your friends, family, and boss
are doing the same.

You perpetrate the fundamental attribution error just about every time you read a news story. For instance, every once in a while, someone snaps and goes on a killing spree at the post office. Going back to 1983, there has been a shooting near or in a U.S. post office about every two years. Often, the killer is a disgruntled employee. Sometimes they still work for the United States Postal Service, sometimes they are recently fired. There's even a phrase for the phenomenon: "going postal." This is part of the collective unconscious of America at this point. Movies, books, television shows, and even pop music continue to refer to postal workers going on rampages, as recently as 2010. The concept of going postal will remain part of English slang for decades.

Many explanations have been offered for the phenomenon, ranging from stress at the workplace to a frustrating bureaucratic grievance process and the copycat effect. The truth, however, is people are always snapping and going on shooting sprees in the modern United States. There are lists available online of three hundred or more incidents, and you can Google the term "shooting rampage" any time of the year and be guaranteed a mass murder will appear from within the last few weeks. Oddly enough, the homicide rate at post offices is actually lower than in retail, but that's probably because people in retail are more likely to be killed in a robbery. At any rate, the reason you are familiar with the idea of a lone postal worker killing all his coworkers is that the national media tends to cover these incidents no matter where they occur.

When you hear about a shooting like those at the post office or in a school or at an airport, what is the first thing you assume about the killer? The most comforting thought is that the murderer was crazy. He or she was nuts, and one day something just came over that person. In its own dark way, this is comforting. You don't want to think potential killers are all around you, or you yourself could lose it in such a grand and total way.

Yet, most of the time, the people who snap don't wake up one day with murder on the brain. The rage builds for years. They are usually frustrated and angry because of grievances at work. They build an identity around their jobs and think they've lost everything when they get fired. They often suffer from a sense of anomie and isolation and believe they can go out in a blaze of glory. Many feel as if they've been tormented and shamed for too long and want to settle a score. To them, life has become a relentless, depressing assault and they are powerless. The situation, in their minds, is driving them mad.

You see killers on a rampage as lunatics, but coworkers and family rarely agree. They say the job and the stress drove them to madness. Friends say if it wasn't for the job, things would have been different. For you, on the outside, it is easier to blame the personality of the murderer as if that person was bound to kill one day no matter what. As distressing as it may be, it is another way the fundamental attribution error drives you to jump to conclusions. You see the person, and ignore his or her surroundings, and then cast blame on only the individual.

If it could happen to anyone, it could happen to you. It's an unpleasant thought to imagine evil could be more the result of a series of terrible events and social pressures than the working of a deviant mind. Knowing this is so does in no way excuse those who harm others, but nevertheless it seems to be true. If this rattles you a bit, don't worry, it means you are still sane.

In your school there were geeks and nerds, jocks and princesses. There was a class clown and a slacker, a misanthropic poet and an energetic politician striving for grades. You love stories. Movies and books with a cast of characters make sense to you because in life you tend to turn everyone into a character whose behavior is predictable. The mind struggles to make sense of the world. You are always aware of the minds of others and are always searching for an explanation as to why people are behaving the way they do.

Psychologists know most behavior is the result of a tug-of-war between external and internal forces. People aren't characters without nuance who can be easily predicted. You seem like a different person at work than at home, a different character at a party than you are when you're with your family. On paper, this seems like common sense, but you easily forget about the power of the setting when judging others. Instead of saying, "Jack is uncomfortable around people he doesn't know, thus when I see him in public places he tends to avoid crowds," you say, "Jack is shy." It's a shortcut, an easier way to navigate the social world. Your brain loves to take shortcuts. It is easy to ignore the power of the situation. Seeing people through the lens of their situation is one of the foundations of social psychology, where it is referred to as attribution theory.

If someone walks up to you in a bar and offers to buy you a drink, the first thoughts in your mind won't be an analysis of the person's face or the temperature in the room. Your first thoughts will be assumptions as to the person's intent. Is this an attempt at seduction? Is this an act of kindness? Is this person a threat? To what, you ask, can this person's behavior be attributed? You can't be sure of the answer, so it shifts and bounces from one possibility to the next.

When you see a behavior, like a child screaming in a supermarket while the seemingly oblivious parents continue to shop, you take a mental shortcut and conclude something about the story of their lives. Even though you know you don't have enough information to understand, your conclusion still feels satisfying. Your attribution, the cause you believe to have preceded the effect, could be right on the money. Often, though, you are not so smart.

A study in 1992 by Constantine Sedikides and Craig Anderson had Americans explain why they thought other U.S. citizens would want to defect to the former Soviet Union. Most people rushed to judge, with 80 percent saying the defectors were probably confused or traitorous. They imagined them as characters whose personalities predicted their actions. America, after all, is the land of the free and the home of the brave. It is where these subjects grew up and enjoyed life. When the researchers then asked why a Russian might defect to the States, 90 percent said the Russian was probably fleeing horrible living conditions or looking for a better way of life. From an American state of mind, the Russians weren't motivated by their personalities, but by their environment. Instead of turning them into traitors, which would be deeply unsettling since they were coming to the subject's home country, Americans had to place the blame for their behavior on something external.

According to psychologist Harold Kelly, when you conjure an attribution for someone else's actions, you consider consistency. If one of your friends gets into a fight with someone you know, you first look to see if their behavior is consistent with their past behaviors. If they are always getting into fights over petty disagreements, you place the blame on their personality. If they are usually calm, you place the blame on the situation. Usually, this shorthand works, and in our evolutionary past it was easy to check for consistency among the people one saw every day. In the modern world, you can't check for consistency with your waitress or the people on the subway. You can't tell if the person on the shooting rampage was being consistent, or if the person who just cut you off in traffic is always an asshole. When you can't check for consistency, you blame people's behavior on their personality.

One of the first studies to uncover the machinations of the fundamental attribution error was conducted in 1967 by Edward Jones and Victor Harris at Duke University. They had students read speech transcripts of debaters both in support of and in opposition to the political ideologies of Fidel Castro. (Today they might have used Osama bin Laden.) The students correctly attributed the speechwriter's ideas as influenced by the speechwriter's internal feelings when told the person who gave the speech had chosen his own position. If, for instance, the debaters said they disagreed with Castro, the students said they believed them. When the students were told the debater had no choice in the matter and was assigned the position as either pro- or anti-Castro, the students didn't buy it. If the debater was assigned a pro-Castro position and then gave a pro-Castro speech, the students reading that speech told the researchers they thought the debater really believed what he or she was saying. The situation's influence didn't play into their assumptions; instead they saw all the debaters' words as springing from their character.

Variations of this experiment are still being conducted today. Each new twist of the variables leads to the same mistakes. In 1997, Peter Ditto had men meet with an actress working for the experimenters. She and the men would have short one-on-one conversations and then she gave a written report of her impressions. When Ditto told the men she had been instructed to give a negative report, the men said she was just following orders. When told she had been asked to give a positive report, the men said although they knew she was just doing her job, they felt that she really did like them.

You commit the fundamental attribution error by believing other people's actions burgeon from the sort of people they are and have nothing to do with the setting. When a man believes the stripper really likes him, or when the boss thinks all his employees love to hear his stories about fishing in Costa Rica, that's the fundamental attribution error.

It's hard to grasp just how powerful a situation can be, how much it can influence the behavior of you and people you think you know pretty well. In 1971, Philip Zimbardo conducted an experiment at Stanford University that would rattle him to his core and change psychology forever. Zimbardo was interested in the roles you play throughout your life, the characters you create and then pretend to be depending on the situation. He thought perhaps the brutality displayed in war and in prisons had less to do with evil than it did with unconscious role-playing.

He had twenty-four male students flip coins to see who would be prisoners and who would be guards in a pretend prison set up on campus. Those who were randomly selected to be prisoners wore prison smocks with numbers on the back and ankle chains. Guards wore full uniforms with mirrored shades and wielded wooden batons. The guards were told to refer to the prisoners only by their numbers but never physically harm them. Zimbardo had the local police arrest the mock prisoners at their homes and undergo searches in front of their neighbors. They then went through a simulated booking at the police station, complete with mug shots and fingerprints. After the prisoners had waited blindfolded in a real cell, the police then took them to campus, where they were strip-searched and deloused in the fake jail. After all this, the experiment was supposed to take two weeks. Participants would pretend to be guards and prisoners while psychologists videotaped them and took notes. It ended after six days.

There was a riot on the second day. One person had to be released on the third day after suffering so much emotional distress the researchers couldn't bear to keep him confined. What went wrong?

Zimbardo made sure his participants were middle-class college students with no history of violence or substance abuse. He told the guards to maintain order but didn't give specific instructions as to how to go about it. At first, both guards and prisoners didn't take the experiment seriously. They goofed around a bit and were slow to warm to the role-playing, but Zimbardo had the guards regularly wake up the prisoners with whistles and then count them, forcing the prisoners to recite their numbers one at time. Over time, the guards became more aggressive during these counts, more abusive, and cruel. If a prisoner broke a rule, the guards would force that person to do push-ups or place the prisoner in a closet as if it were solitary confinement. On the morning of the second day, the prisoners felt like they had endured enough and barricaded their cells with mattresses while yelling back at the pretend guards. In turn, the guards grabbed a fire extinguisher and doused the prisoners through the bars so they could force their way into the cells. They then stripped the prisoners naked, took away their beds, and began to insult and berate them. To prevent further insurrections, they allowed certain prisoners to wear clothes and sleep on beds if they maintained good, obedient behavior. They also were allowed better food and the indulgences of a toothbrush and toothpaste. After a few hours, the guards took all the privileges away from the compliant prisoners and had them switch places with the defiant ones in an attempt to scramble their minds and destroy any alliances they might have formed by creating doubt in their minds as to who was secretly cooperating with the guards. Before long, the guards were forcing the prisoners to relieve themselves in a bucket and forcing them to simulate sodomy on one another.

Zimbardo became overwhelmed by the power of the situation just as much as the students had. He started imagining himself as a warden, and when he heard rumors of a possible escape plan being hatched by the prisoners, he tried unsuccessfully to move his experiment into a real jail. Once he saw footage of the guards becoming physically violent when they thought the psychologists weren't looking, he realized that the situation was getting out of hand. When one of his graduate students visited for the first time and recoiled in horror at the conditions the prisoners were living in, Zimbardo finally saw through her eyes that things had gone too far. On the sixth day, they ended the experiment. The prisoners rejoiced; the guards complained.

In the interviews that followed, the students who role-played as prisoners said they felt as if they had lost their identity, and that the experiment had been replaced by a real prison. They questioned their own sanity. They forgot they could leave if they only requested for the experiment to end. The guards said they were only following orders.

Remember, all of these people were just average, middle-class college students the week prior. Nothing they or anyone else knew about them suggested they were capable of such malice or conformity. It all took place in a row of offices in a building on a college campus, and everyone knew this, but the situation, the external forces, were so powerful that the participants changed into monsters and victims in just one day.

Decades later, Zimbardo would reject the U.S. government's claims about the sadism displayed at the Abu Ghraib prison as being the result of the behavior of a few bad apples. The government was committing the fundamental attribution error, ignoring the power of the situation, turning the perpetrators into easy-to-dismiss characters. Although he doesn't absolve those who tortured and humiliated Iraqi prisoners at Abu Ghraib, Zimbardo suggests whenever people are put into a situation like the one he created in his experiment, the same results will unfold, as they did in 2004 in the Baghdad Correctional Facility and as they have in other prisons throughout history. People are not good at heart, Zimbardo says, but because their environment encourages it. Anyone, he believes, is capable of becoming a monster if given the power and opportunity.

When you interpret your loved one's coldness as his or her indifference to your wants and needs instead of as a reaction to stress at work or problems ricocheting in your loved one's own heart, you've committed the fundamental attribution error. When you vote for someone because that person seems likable and approachable, and ignore how much of their persona is contrived for the sake of votes, it's the same error at work. You commit it again when you assay friendliness as sexual interest, or poverty as the result of laziness. When you look for a cause for another person's actions, you find it. Rarely, though, do you first consider how powerful the situation is. You blame the person, not the environment and the influence of the person's peers. You do this because you would like to believe your own behavior comes strictly from within. You know this isn't true though. You shift from introvert to extrovert, from brainiac to simpleton, from charismatic to impish—depending on where you find yourself and who is watching.

The fundamental attribution error leads to labels and assumptions about who people are, but remember first impressions are mostly incorrect. Those impressions will linger until you get to know people and understand their situation and the circumstances in which their behavior is generated. Knowing this doesn't mean you must forgive evil, but perhaps it can help prevent it.

ACKNOWLEDGMENTS

A super-tight hug goes out to Erin Malone, who found my blog and believed it should exist in physical form. Through her confidence and hard work it now does. Thank you so much.

Thanks too to Patrick Mulligan, who "got it" early on and then slashed and questioned the original manuscript until it made sense. I'm fortunate to have had such a plugged-in editor.

Boundless thanks go out to my wife, Amanda, who read this book as it came together and kept it from going off the rails many times.

In many ways this book and the blog from which it sprang started in a psychology class I took seven years after graduating from high school.

After getting married, my wife and I sold all our possessions and traveled to Germany for no other reason than to see what would happen. We had both gone to a tiny school in a small town in Mississippi, and we both worked the sort of jobs that went along with those foundations—waiting tables, construction, selling coats. Escaping into a strange adventure made a lot of sense at the time. As tramps abroad, we were shocked at not only how naive we were, but how uneducated. We swore to each other when we got back to the States we would get college degrees.

One of our first college experiences was an incredibly challenging and life-changing course—Introduction to Psychology, taught by one extraordinary teacher, Jean Edwards.

Edwards's class wasn't like the other courses. Nothing about it was remedial. She came every day with a laptop and a projector and used videos, photos, animations, and diagrams to detail the intricacies of how the mind worked. The textbook was an afterthought, a supplement. In her class, she used presentations labored over for years to boggle our minds and shake us out of our delusions. She made us stand up and perform, she put us in and out of groups, she pointed at our faces and made us talk. When the tests landed on our desks, there was no memorization, there were no word banks. Every question was a puzzle that required a deep understanding of the material to unfurl and solve. Once we went on to a full university, my wife and I were astonished to find no course ever compared to hers.

In one class, she asked us to imagine a man who woke up every day and wrapped his entire body in newspaper before putting on his clothes. He worked hard, provided for his family, and hurt no one. At the end of the day, he would discreetly remove his wrappings before going to bed. She then asked, "Is this person crazy?" For an hour, the class argued about it. Most people's knee-jerk reaction was "Yeah, obviously." She nursed the conversation, pointing out our ignorance, asking us to examine our own quirks and neurotic habits. By the end of the class the students had reached a consensus: The newspaper man was as deluded as the rest of us, and therefore not crazy.

Every class with Edwards was revelatory, not just because of the overwhelming number of eye-opening facts and epiphanies, but also because she showed people like me and my wife there were kindred spirits out there. She had no problem losing an hour of her day to an after-class conversation, and she was always ready to subvert the norms and expectations of her pupils and peers. She made it safe and respectable to be different, and she provided her students with a role model they didn't know was an option before meeting her. She was a smart, successful, professional woman who questioned everything and dared you to join her. This book, and the blog that led to it, started in that class.

So, I thank you, Jean Edwards. You changed my life and tilted my view of the world permanently.

BIBLIOGRAPHY

Introduction

Nyhan, B., & Reifler, J. (2010). When corrections fail: the persistence of political misperceptions. *Political Behavior* 32(2), 303–330.

Munro, G. D., & Ditto, P. H. (1997, June). Biased assimilation, attitude polarization, and affect in reactions to stereotype-relevant scientific information. *Personality and Social Psychology Bulletin* 23(6), 636–653.

Munro, G. (2010). The scientific impotence excuse: discounting belief-threatening scientific abstracts. *Journal of Applied Social Psychology* 40(3), 579–600.

Priming

Bargh, J. A., & Chartrand, T. L. (1999, July). The unbearable automaticity of being. *American Psychologist* 54(7), 462–479.

Bargh, J. A., Chen, M., & Burrows, L. (1996). Automaticity of social behavior: direct effects of trait construct and stereotype activation on action. *Journal of Personality and Social Psychology* 71(2), 230–244.

Bargh, J. A., & Wyer, R. S. (1997). *The automaticity of everyday life*. London: Psychology Press.

Carey, B. (2007, July 31). Who's minding the mind? *New York Times*.

Friedman, R., & Elliot, A. J. (2008, November). Exploring the influ-

ence of sports drink exposure on physical endurance, Original
Research Article. *Psychology of Sport and Exercise* 9(6), 749–759.

Kay, A. C., Wheeler, S. C., Bargh, J. A., & Ross, L. (2004). Material
priming: The influence of mundane physical objects on situational construal and competitive behavioral choice. *Organizational
Behavior and Human Decision Processes* 95, 83–96.

Zhong, C., & Liljenquist, K. (2006). Washing away your sins: threat-
ened morality and physical cleansing. *Science* 313(5792), 1451–
1452.

Confabulation

Fiala, B., & Nichols, S. (2009). Confabulation, confidence, and introspection. *Behavioral and Brain Sciences* 32(2), 144–145.

Hirstein, W. (2005). *Brain fiction: Self-deception and the riddle of confabulation.* Cambridge, Mass: MIT Press.

Joseph, R. (1986). Confabulation and delusional denial: Frontal lobe
and lateralized influences. *Journal of Clinical Psychology* 42, 845–
860.

Mandler, G. (1985). *Cognitive psychology: An essay in cognitive science.*
Hillsdale, N.J.: L. Erlbaum Associates.

Nisbett, R. E., & Wilson, T. D. (1977, May). Telling more than we can
know: Verbal reports on mental processes. *Psychological Review*
84(3), 231–259.

Pantel, J. (2006, March). Brain fiction: Self-deception and the riddle of
confabulation: Review. *American Journal of Psychiatry* 163, 559.

Ramachandran, V. S. (2009, January 10). *Self-awareness: The last fron-
tier.* Retrieved December 2010 from http://integral-options
.blogspot.com/2009/01/vs-ramachandran-self-awareness-last.html.

Sapolsky, R. (1995, November 1). Ego boundaries, or the fit of my
father's shirt: A neuroscientist racks his brains to find where one

person ends and another begins. *Discover.* Retrieved December 2010 from http://discovermagazine.com/1995/nov/egoboundarie sort586.

Zaidel, E., Zaidel, D. W., & Bogen, J. E. (n.d.). *The split brain.* Retrieved December 2010 from http://www.its.caltech.edu/~jbogen /text/ref130.htm.

Confirmation Bias

Knobloch-Westerwick, S., & Meng, J. (2009, June). Looking the other way: Selective exposure to attitude-consistent and counter attitudinal political information. *Communication Research* 36(3), 426–448.

Krebs, V. (2008). *New Political Patterns.* Retrieved December 2010 from http://www.orgnet.com/divided.html.

Krebs, V. (2000, March). Working in the connected world: Book network. *IHRIM Journal,* 87–90.

LaMarre, H. L., Landreville, K. D., & Beam, M. A. (2009, April). The irony of satire: Political ideology and the motivation to see what you want to see in The Colbert Report. *The International Journal of Press/Politics* 14(2), 212–231.

Marks, M. J., & Fraley, R. C. (2006, January). Confirmation bias and the sexual double standard. *Sex Roles* 54(1/2), 19–26.

Nickerson, R. S. (1998). Confirmation bias: A ubiquitous phenomenon in many guises. *Review of General Psychology* 2(2), 175–220.

Owad, T. (2006, January 4). *Data mining 101: Finding subversives with Amazon wish lists.* Retrieved December 2010 from http://www .applefritter.com/bannedbooks.

Owings, J. (2009, February 24). *Confirmation bias and the internet.* Retrieved December 2010 from http://www.justinowings.com/b /index.php/me/confirmation-bias-and-the-internet.

Pratchett, T. (2000). *The truth: A novel of Discworld.* New York: HarperCollins.

Snyder, M., & Cantor, N. (1998). Understanding personality and social behavior: A functionalist strategy. In D. T. Gilbert, S. T. Fiske, & G. Lindzey (Eds.). *The handbook of social psychology: Vol. 1.* (4th ed., pp. 635–679). Boston: McGraw-Hill.

Hindsight Bias

Teigen, K. H. (1986). Old truths or fresh insights? A study of students' evaluations of proverbs. *British Journal of Social Psychology* 25(43–50), 18.

Vedantam, S. (2006, October 2). Iraq war naysayers may have hindsight bias. *Washington Post.* Retrieved December 2010 from http://www.washingtonpost.com/wp-dyn/content/article/2006/10/01/AR2006100100784.html.

The Texas Sharpshooter Fallacy

Abumrad, J., & Krulwich, R. (2009). Stochasticity. *Radiolab Podcast* 6(1). Retrieved December 2010 from http://www.radiolab.org/2009/jun/15/.

Altered Dimensions. (2005). *The prophecies of Nostradamus.* Retrieved December 2010 from http://www.spartechsoftware.com/dimensions/mystical/nostradamus.htm.

Forer, B. R. (1949). The fallacy of personal validation: A classroom demonstration of gullibility. *Journal of Abnormal Psycholog*, 44, 118–121.

Gawande, A. (1999, February 8). The cancer-cluster myth. *New Yorker,* p. 34.

Griffiths, T., & Tenenbaum, J. (2006, September). Statistics and the Bayesian mind. *Significance*, 3(3), 130–133.

Kurtus, R. (2006 November 24). *Similarities between the assassinations of Kennedy and Lincoln.* Retrieved December 2010 from http://www.school-for-champions.com/history/lincolnjfk.htm.

Novella, S. (2009, December 21). Autism prevalence. *Neurologica Blog.* Retrieved December 2010 from http://theness.com/neurologicablog/?p=1374.

Robertson, M. (1898). *Futility: Or the wreck of the Titan.* Retrieved December 2010 from http://www.daggy.name/cop/effluvia/twott-t.htm.

Shermer, M. (1998, January). The truth is out there and Ray Hyman wants to find it: An interview with a co-founder of Modern Skepticism. *Skeptic Magazine.* Retrieved December 2010 from http://www.theeway.com/skepticc/archives03.html.

Procrastination

Ariely, D., & Wertenbroch, K. (2002, May). Procrastination, deadlines, and performance: Self-control by precommitment. *Psychological Science* 13(3), 219–224.

Bloch, M., Cox, A., McGinty, J. C., & Quealy, K. (2010, January 8). A peek into Netflix queues. *New York Times.*

Milkman, K. L., Rogers, T., & Bazerman, M. H. (2010, March). I'll have the ice cream soon and the vegetables later: A study of online grocery purchases and order lead time. *Marketing Letters* 21(1), 17–35.

Milkman, K. L., Rogers, T., & Bazerman, M. H. (2009, June). Highbrow films gather dust: Time-inconsistent preferences and online DVD rentals. *Management Science* 55(6), 1047–1059.

Read, D., Loewenstein, G., & Kalyanaraman, S. (1999, December). Mixing virtue and vice: Combining the immediacy effect and the diversification heuristic. *Journal of Behavioral Decision Making* 12(4), 257.

Normalcy Bias

Azevedo, T. M., Volchan, E., Imbiriba, L. A., Rodrigues, E. C., Oliveira, J. M., Oliveira, L. F., Lutterbach, L. G., & Vargas, C. D. (2005, May). A freezing-like posture to pictures of mutilation. *Psychophysiology* 42(3), 255–260.

Barthelmess, S. (1988, March/April). Coming to grips with panic. *Flight Safety Foundation: Cabin Crew Safety* 23(2), 1–4.

Klingsch, W. (2010). *Pedestrian and evacuation dynamics 2008.* Springer.

Leach, J. (2004, June). Why people "freeze" in an emergency: Temporal and cognitive constraints on survival responses. *Aviation, Space, and Environmental Medicine* 75(6), 539–542.

Leach, J. (2005). Cognitive paralysis in an emergency: The role of the supervisory attentional system. *Aviation, Space, and Environmental Medicine* 76(2), 134–136.

Mikami, S., & Ikeda, K. (1985). Human response to disasters. *International Journal of Mass Emergencies and Disasters,* 107–132.

Ripley, A. (2005, April 25). How to get out alive. *Time.* Retrieved December 2010 from http://www.time.com/time/magazine/article/0,9171,1053663-6,00.html.

Ripley, A. (2009). *The unthinkable: Who survives when disaster strikes— and why?* New York: Three Rivers Press.

Schmidt, C. (Producer). (2006, October 17). The deadliest plane crash. (*Nova*). Boston: WGBH Educational Foundation.

Svenvold, M. (2006). *Big weather: Chasing tornadoes in the heart of America.* New York: Macmillan.

Introspection

Haigh, E. A. P., & Fresco, D. M. (n.d.). *Relationship of depressive rumination and distraction to subsequent depressive symptoms following successful antidepressant medication therapy for depression.* Retrieved December 2010 from http://www.personal.kent.edu/~dfresco /Fresco_Papers/AABT_05_Rum_Haigh.pdf.

Wilson T. D., Dunn D. S., Kraft D., & Lisle D. J. (1989). Introspection, attitude change, and attitude-behavior consistency: The disruptive effects of explaining why we feel the way we do. *Advances in Experimental Social Psychology* 22, 287–343.

Wilson, T. D., & Schooler, J. W. (1991, February). Thinking too much: Introspection can reduce the quality of preferences and decisions. *Journal of Personality and Social Psychology* 60, 181–192.

The Availability Heuristic

Glassner, B. (1999). *The Culture of Fear.* New York: Basic Books.

Stephens, R. D. (Executive Director). (2010, July 14). *The National School Safety Center's Report on School Associated Violent Deaths.* Retrieved December 2010 from http://www.schoolsafety.us /media-resources/school-associated-violent-deaths.

Tversky, A., & Kahneman, D. (1973). Availability: a heuristic for judging frequency and probability. *Cognitive Psychology* 5, 207–232.

The Bystander Effect

Darley, J. M., & Batson, C. D. (1973). From Jerusalem to Jericho: A study of situational and dispositional variables in helping behavior. *Journal of Personality and Social Psychology* 27(1), 100–108.

Darley, J. M. & Latane, B. (1968). Bystander intervention in emergencies: Diffusion of responsibility. *Journal of Personality and Social Psychology* 8, 377–383.

Gansberg, M. (1964, March 27). Thirty-eight who saw murder didn't call the police. *New York Times*.

Latane, B., & Darley, J. (1969). Bystander "Apathy." *American Scientist* 57, 244–268.

Manning, R., Levine, M., & Collins, A. (2007, September). The Kitty Genovese murder and the social psychology of helping: the parable of the 38 witnesses. *American Psychologist* 62(6), 555–562.

Shotland, R. L., & Straw M. K. (1976) Bystander response to an assault: When a man attacks a woman. *Journal of Personality and Social Psychology* 35, 990–999.

The Dunning-Kruger Effect

Burson, K. A., Larrick, R. P., & Klayman J. (2006, January). Skilled or unskilled, but still unaware of it: how perceptions of difficulty drive miscalibration in relative comparisons. *Journal of Personality and Social Psycholog,* 90(1), 60–77.

Kruger, J., & David D. (1999). Unskilled and unaware of it: How difficulties in recognizing one's own incompetence lead to inflated self-assessments. *Journal of Personality and Social Psychology* 77(6), 1121–1134.

Apophenia

Littlewood, J. E., & Bollobás, B. (1986). *Littlewood's Miscellany*. New York: Cambridge University Press.

Brand Loyalty

McClure, S. M., Li, J., Tomlin, D., Cypert, K. S., Montague, L. M., & Montague, P. R. (2004, October 14). Neural correlates of behavioral preference for culturally familiar drinks. *Neuron* 44(2), 379–387.

The Argument from Authority

Acharya, H. J. (2004, March). The rise and fall of the frontal lobotomy. *Proceedings of the 13h Annual History of Medicine Days,* 32–41.

Goodman, B., & Maggio, J. (Producers). (2008). The Lobotomist (*American Experience*). Brooklyn, NY: Ark Media. Retrieved December 2010 from http://www.pbs.org/wgbh /americanexperience/films/lobotomist/.

The Just-World Fallacy

Andre, C., & Velasquez, M. (1990, Spring). The just world theory. *Issues in Ethics* 3(2). Retrieved December 2010 from http://www .scu.edu/ethics/publications/iie/v3n2/justworld.html.

BBC News. (2010, February 15). *Women say some rape victims should take blame—survey.* Retrieved December 2010 from http://news .bbc.co.uk/2/hi/uk_news/8515592.stm.

Campbell, R., & Raja, S. (1999). Secondary victimization of rape victims: insights from mental health professionals who treat survivors of violence. *Violence and Victims* 14(3), 261–75.

Hafer, C. L., & Bègue L. (2005). Experimental research on just-world theory: problems, developments, and future challenges. *Psychological Bulletin* 131(1), 128–167.

Haidt, J. (2010, October 16). What the tea partiers really want. *Wall Street Journal.* Retrieved December 2010 from http://online.wsj .com/article/SB10001424052748703673604575550243700895762 .html.

Janoff-Bulman R., Timko, C., & Carli, L. L. (1985, March). Cognitive biases in blaming the victim. *Journal of Experimental Social Psychology* 21(2), 161–177.

Lerner, M. J. (1980). *The belief in a just world: A fundamental delusion.* New York: Plenum Press.

Miller, F. D., Smith, E. R., Ferree, M. M., & Taylor, S. E. (1976, December). Predicting perceptions of victimization. *Journal of Applied Social Psychology* 6(4), 352–359.

Neal, J. (1998, Spring). Belief in a just world for the self as it relates to depression, stress, and psychological well-being. *Living in a Social World: Psy 324: Advanced Social Psychology.* Retrieved December 2010 from http://www.units.muohio.edu/psybersite /justworld/selfmh.shtml.

Springer Science+Business Media (2010, November 11). Swedish teens say individual traits are the main reasons for bullying. *ScienceDaily.* Retrieved December 2010 from http://www .sciencedaily.com/releases/2010/11/101111101404.htm.

Thornberg, R., & Knutsen, M. A. (2010). Teenagers' explanations of bullying. *Child and Youth Care Forum.* DOI 10.1007/s10566-010 -9129-z.

The Public Goods Game

Ariely, D. (2008). *Predictably irrational: The hidden forces that shape our decisions.* New York: Harper.

Davis, D. D., & Holt, C. A. (1992). *Experimental economics.* Princeton, N.J.: Princeton University Press.

Hardin, G. (1998, May 1). Extensions of "The Tragedy of the Commons." *Science* 280(5364), 682–683.

The Ultimatum Game

Crockett, M. J., Clark, L., Tabibnia, G., Lieberman, M. D., & Robbins, T. W. (2008, June). Serotonin modulates behavioral reactions to unfairness. *Science* 320(5884), 1739.

Güth, W., Schmittberger, R., & Schwarze, B. (1982, December). An experimental analysis of ultimatum bargaining. *Journal of Economic Behavior and Organization* 3(4), 367–388.

Forsythe R., Horowitz, J., Savin, N. E., & Sefton, M. (1994). Fairness in simple bargaining experiments. *Games and Economic Behavior* 6, 347–369.

McMillan, S. (2007, November 19). Monkeys have sense of fairness. *Emory Wheel*. Retrieved December 2010 from http://www.emory wheel.com/detail.php?n=24747.

Cult Indoctrination

Myers, D. G. (2005). *Social psychology*. New York: McGraw-Hill.

Groupthink

Fox News (2004) *"Group Think" led to WMD assessment*. Retrieved December 2010 from http://www.foxnews.com/story /0,2933,125123,00.html.

Janis, I. L. (1972) *Victims of groupthink*. Boston: Houghton Mifflin Company.

Meyers, D. G. (2005) *Social psychology*. New York: McGraw-Hill.

Weiten, W. (2002) *Psychology: Themes and Variations*. Belmont, CA: Wadsworth.

Supernormal Releasers

Associated Press. (2006). *Food servings are bigger than 20 years ago, but most unaware, study says.* Retrieved December 2010 from http://www.msnbc.msn.com/id/16076842/ns/health-diet_and_nutri tion/.

Buss, D. M. (1994). *The evolution of desire: strategies of human mating*. New York: BasicBooks.

Johnson, K. L., & Tassinary, L. G. (2005, November 1). Perceiving sex directly and indirectly: Meaning in motion and morphology. *Psychological Science* 16(11), 890–897.

Singh, D. (2002, December). Female mate value at a glance: relationship of waist-to-hip ratio to health, fecundity and attractiveness. *Neuroendocrinology Letters* 23(Suppl 4), 81–91.

The Affect Heuristic

Abumrad, J., & Krulwich, R. (2008). Choice. *Radiolab Podcast* 5(1). Retrieved December 2010 from http://www.radiolab.org/2008/nov/17/.

Bechara, A., Damasio, H., Tranel, D., & Damasio, A. R. (1997, February). Deciding advantageously before knowing advantageous strategy. *Science* 275(5304), 1293–1295.

Denes-Raj, V., & Epstein, S. (1994). Conflict between intuitive and rational processing: When people behave against their better judgment. *Journal of Personality and Social Psychology* 66(5), 819–829.

Funicane, M. L., Alhakami, A., Slovic, P., & Johnson, S. M. (2000, January/March). The affect heuristic in judgments of risks and benefits. *Journal of Behavioral Decision Making* 13(1), 1–17.

Timarr. (2010, May 26). Risk, Stone Age economics and the affect heuristic. *The Psy-Fi Blog*. Retrieved December 2010 from http://www.psyfitec.com/2010/05/risk-stone-age-economics-and-affect.html.

Wallis, J. D. (2006). Evaluating apples and oranges. *Nature Neuroscience* 9, 596–598.

Weinschenk, S. (2009). *Neuro web design: What makes them click?* Berkeley, CA: New Riders.

Winkielman, P., Zajonc, R. B., & Schwarz, N. (1997). Subliminal af-
    fective priming attributional interventions. *Cognition and Emotion*
    11(4), 433–465.

Dunbar's Number

Dunbar, R. I. M. (1992, June). Neocortex size as a constraint on group
    size in primates. *Journal of Human Evolution* 22(6), 469–493.

Dunbar, R. (1998). *Grooming, gossip, and the evolution of language*.
    Cambridge, Mass: Harvard University Press.

Gladwell, M. (2000). *The tipping point—how little things can make a big
    difference*. Boston: Little, Brown and Company.

Selling Out

Heath, J., & Potter, A. (2005). *The rebel sell: Why the culture can't be
    jammed*. Chichester, Quebec, CA: Capstone.

Self-Serving Bias

Hoorens, V. (1993). Self-enhancement and superiority biases in social
    comparison. *European Review of Social Psychology* 4(1), 113–139.

Kruger, J. (1999, August). Lake Wobegon be gone! The "below-
    average effect" and the egocentric nature of comparative ability
    judgments. *Journal of Personality and Social Psychology* 77(2),
    221–232.

Meyers, D. G. (2005). *Social Psychology*. New York: McGraw-Hill.

Wilson, A. E., & Ross, M. (2001, April). From chump to champ:
    people's appraisals of their earlier and present selves. *Journal of
    Personality and Social Psychology* 80(4), 572–584.

The Spotlight Effect

Gilovich, T., Kruger, J., & Medvec, V. H. (2002). The spotlight effect revisited: Overestimating the manifest variability of our actions and appearance. *Journal of Experimental Social Psychology* 38(1), 93–99.

Gilovich, T., Medvec, V. H., & Savitsky, K. (2000). The spotlight effect in social judgment: An egocentric bias in estimates of the salience of one's own actions and appearance. *Journal of Personality and Social Psychology,* 78(2), 211–222.

The Third Person Effect

Bryant P., Salwen, M. B., & Dupagne M. (2000). The third-person effect: A meta-analysis of the perceptual hypothesis. *Mass Communication and Society* 3(1), 57–85.

Johansson, B. (2005). The third-person effect. Only a media perception? *Nordicom Review* 26(1), 81–94.

Perloff, R. M. (1993). Third-person effect research 1983–1992: A review and synthesis. *International Journal of Public Opinion Research* 5(2), 167–184.

Catharsis

Baumeister, R. F., Bushman, B. J., & Feenstra, J. S. (2008). *Social psychology and human nature.* Belmont, CA: Thomson Higher Education.

Berkowitz, L. (1977). *Advances in experimental social psychology, Vol. 10.* New York: Academic Press.

Bushman, B. J. (2002, June). Does venting anger feed or extinguish the flame? Catharsis, rumination, distraction, anger, and aggressive responding. *Personality and Social Psychology Bulletin* 28(6), 724–731.

Bushman, B. J., Stack, A. D., & Baumeister, R. F. (1999). Catharsis, aggression, and persuasive influence: Self-fulfilling or self-defeating prophecies? *Journal of Personality and Social Psychology* 76(3), 367–376.

Carey, B. (2009, February 3). The muddled track of all those tears. *New York Times,* p. D1.

Landers, R. N. (2010, May 19). Playing violent video games for a release that never comes. *Thoughts of a Neo-Academic.* Retrieved December 2010 from http://neoacademic.com/2010/05/19/playing-violent-video-games-for-a-release-that-never-comes/.

The Misinformation Effect

Bartlett, Sir F. C. (1967). *Remembering: a study in experimental and social psychology.* London: Cambridge University Press.

Berkowitz, S. R., Laney, C., Morris, E. K., Garry, M., & Loftus, E. F. (2008). Pluto behaving badly: False beliefs and their consequences. *American Journal of Psychology* 121(4), 643–660.

Bernstein, D. M., Laney, C., Morris, E. K., & Loftus, E. F. (2005). False memories about food can lead to food avoidance. *Social Cognition* 23(1), 11–34.

Heaps, C. H., & Nash, M. (2001). Comparing recollective experience in true and false autobiographical memories. *Journal of Experimental Psychology: Learning, Memory and Cognition* 27(4), 920–930.

Loftus, E. F. (2003, November). Make-believe memories. *American Psychologist* 58(11), 867–873.

Loftus, E. F. (2001, September). The advertisers are coming for your childhood. *Independent.* Retrieved December 2010 from http://www.independent.co.uk/opinion/commentators/elizabeth-loftus—the-advertisers-are-coming-for-your-childhood-668019.html.

Loftus, E. F., & Ketcham, K. (1996). *The myth of repressed memory: False memories and allegations of sexual abuse.* New York: St. Martin's Griffin.

Loftus, E. F., & Palmer, J. C. (1974). Reconstruction of automobile destruction: An example of the interaction between language and memory. *Journal of Verbal Learning and Verbal Behavior* 13, 585–589.

Roediger, H. L. III, Meade, M. L., & Bergman, E. T. (2001). Social contagion of memory. *Psychonomic Bulletin & Review* 8(2), 365–371.

Saletan, W. (2010, June 4). The Memory Doctor: The future of false memories. *Slate.* Retrieved December 2010 from http://www.slate.com/id/2256089/.

Conformity

Asch, S. E. (1956). Studies of independence and conformity: A minority of one against a unanimous majority. *Psychological Monographs* 70(416).

Latane, B., & Darley, J. (1969). Bystander "apathy." *American Scientist* 57, 244–268.

Milgram, S. (1963). Behavioral study of obedience. *Journal of Abnormal and Social Psychology* 67, 371–378.

Wolfson, A. (2005, October 9). A hoax most cruel. *Courier-Journal* (Louisville, KY).

You are a conformist (that is, you are human). Recognize that conformity is inevitable and avoid its pitfalls. (2010, December 5). *Psychology Today.* Retrieved December 2010 from http://www.psychologytoday.com/blog/insight-therapy/201012/you-are-conformist-is-you-are-human.

Extinction Burst

Behavior: Skinner's Utopia: Panacea, or Path to Hell? (1971, September 20). *Time*. Retrieved December 2010 from http://www.time.com/time/magazine/article/0,9171,909994,00.html.

Social Loafing

Ingham, A.G., Levinger, G., Graves, J., & Peckham, V. (1974). The Ringelmann Effect: Studies of group size and group performance. *Journal of Experimental Social Psychology* 10, 371–384.

Karau, S. J., & Williams, K. D. (1993). Social loafing: A meta-analytic review and theoretical integration. *Journal of Personality and Social Psychology* 65, 681–706.

Latane, B., Williams, K., & Harkins, S. (1979, June). Many hands make light the work: The causes and consequences of social loafing. *Journal of Personality and Social Psychology* 37, 822–832.

Myers, D. G. (2005). *Social psychology*. New York: McGraw-Hill.

The Illusion of Transparency

Gilovich, T., Medvec, V. H., & Savitsky, K. (1998). The illusion of transparency: Biased assessments of others' ability to read one's emotional states. *Journal of Personality and Social Psychology* 75(2), 332–346.

Savitsky, K., & Gilovich, T. (2003, March 25). The illusion of transparency and the alleviation of speech anxiety. *Journal of Experimental Social Psychology* 39, 618–625.

Learned Helplessness

Abramson, L. Y., Seligman, M. E., & Teasdale, J. D. (1978, February). Learned helplessness in humans: Critique and reformulation. *Journal of Abnormal Psychology* 87(1), 49–74.

Langer, E. & Rodin, J. (1976). The effects of choice and enhanced personal responsibility for the aged: A field experiment in an institutional setting. *Journal of Personality and Social Psychology* 34, 191–198.

Magnusson, D., & Ohman, A. (1987). *Psychopathology: An interactional perspective*. New York: Academic Press.

Myers, D. G. (2005). *Social psychology*. New York: McGraw-Hill.

Seligman, M. E. P. & Maier, S. F. (1967). Failure to escape traumatic shock. *Journal of Experimental Psychology* 74, 1–9.

Servan-Schreiber, D. (2008). *Anticancer: a new way of life*. New York: Viking.

Embodied Cognition

Ackerman, J. M., Nocera, C. C., & Bargh, J. A. (2010, June 25). Incidental haptic sensations influence social judgments and decisions. *Science* 328(5986), 1712–1715.

Lawrence, E. W., & Bargh, J. A. (2008, October). Experiencing physical warmth promotes interpersonal warmth. *Science* 322(5901), 606–607.

The Anchoring Effect

African nations in the U.N. Retrieved December 2010 from http://en.wikipedia.org/wiki/File:UN_Member_Countries_World.svg.

Ariely, D., Loewenstein, G., & Prelec, D. (2006). Tom Sawyer and the construction of value. *Journal of Economic Behavior & Organization* 60, 1–10.

Cialdini, R. B., Vincent, J. E., Lewis, S. K., Catalan, J., Wheeler, D., & Darby, B. L. (1975). Reciprocal concessions procedure for inducing compliance: The door-in the face technique. *Journal of Personality and Social Psychology* 31(2), 206–215.

Kahneman, D., Slovic, P., & Tversky, A. (1982). *Judgment under uncertainty: heuristics and biases*. Cambridge: Cambridge University Press.

Attention

Chabris, C., & Simons, D. (2010). *The invisible gorilla: and other ways our intuitions deceive us*. New York: Crown.

Chua, H. F., Boland, J. E., & Nisbett, R. E. (2005). Cultural variation in eye movements during scene perception. *Proceedings of the National Academy of Sciences* 35, 12629–12633.

Levin, D. T., & Simons, D. J. (1997). Failure to detect changes to attended objects in motion pictures. *Psychonomic Bulletin and Review* 4, 501–506.

Masuda, T., Akase, M., & Radford, M. H. B. (2008). Cultural differences in patterns of eye-movement: Comparing context sensitivity between the Japanese and Westerners. *Journal of Personality and Social Psychology* 94(3), 365–381.

Simons, D. J., & Chabris, C. F. (1999). Gorillas in our midst: sustained inattentional blindness for dynamic events. *Perception* 28(9), 1059–1074.

Simons, D. J., & Levin, D. T. (1998). Failure to detect changes to people during a real-world interaction. *Psychonomic Bulletin and Review* 5, 644–649.

Self Handicapping

Alter, A. L., & Forgas, J. P. (2007). On being happy but fearing failure: The effects of mood on self-handicapping strategies. *Journal of Experimental Social Psychology* 43, 947–954.

Berglas, S., & Jones, E.E. (1978). Drug choice as a self-handicapping strategy in response to noncontingent success. *Journal of Personality and Social Psychology* 36 (4), 405–417.

Carey, B. (2009). Some protect the ego by working on their excuses early. *New York Times*.

Goleman, D. (1984). Excuses: New theory defines their role in life. *New York Times*.

Kay, A. C., Jimenez, M.C., & Jost, J. T. (2002). Sour Grapes, Sweet Lemons, and the Anticipatory Rationalization of the Status Quo. *Personality and Social Psychology Bulletin* 28(9), 1300–1312.

Kolditz, T. A., & Arkin, R. M. (1982). An impression management interpretation of the self-handicapping strategy. *Journal of Personality and Social Psychology* 43, 492–502.

Smith, T. W., Snyder, C. R., & Perkins, S. C. (1983). The self-serving function of hypochondriacal complaints: Physical symptoms as self-handicapping strategies. *Journal of Personality and Social Psychology* 44(4), 787–797.

Self-Fulfilling Prophecies

Burger, J. M. (1999). The foot-in-the-door compliance procedure: A multiple-process analysis and review. *Personality and Social Psychology Review* 3(4), 303–325.

Crano, W. D., & Mellon, P. M. (1978, February). Causal influence of teachers' expectations on children's academic performance: A cross-lagged panel analysis. *Journal of Educational Psychology* 70(1), 39–49.

Spencer, S. J., Steele, C. M., & Quinn, D. M. (1999). Stereotype threat and women's math performance. *Journal of Experimental Social Psychology* 35, 4–28.

Steele C. M., & Aronson, J. (1995, November). Stereotype threat and the intellectual test performance of African Americans. *Journal of Personality and Social Psychology* 69(5), 797–811.

The Moment

Kahneman, D. (2010, March). The riddle of experience vs. memory. Retrieved December 2010 from http://blog.ted.com/2010/03/01/the_riddle_of_e/.

Consistency Bias

Ariely, D. (2008). *Predictably irrational: The hidden forces that shape our decisions*. New York: HarperCollins.

Burger, J. M., & Petty, R. E. (1981). The low-ball compliance technique: Task or person commitment. *Journal of Personality and Social Psychology* 40(3), 492–500.

Cialdini, R. B., Cacioppo, J. T., Bassett, R., & Miller, J. A. (1978, May). Low-ball procedure for producing compliance: Commitment then cost. *Journal of Personality and Social Psychology* 36(5), 463–476.

Dean, J. (2008, February). *How the consistency bias warps our personal and political memories*. Retrieved December 2010 from http://www.spring.org.uk/2008/02/how-consistency-bias-warps-our-personal.php

Goethals, G. R., & Reckman, R. F. (1973, November). The perception of consistency in attitudes. *Journal of Experimental Social Psychology* 9(6), 491–501.

Markus, G. B. (1986). Stability and change in political attitudes: observed, recalled, and explained. *Political Behavior* 8(1), 21–44.

Markus, H., & Kunda, Z. (1986). Stability and Malleability of the Self-Concept. *Journal of Personality and Social Psychology* 51(4), 858–866.

Scharfe, E., & Bartholomew, K. (1998). Do you remember? Recollections of adult attachment patterns. *Personal Relationships* 5(2), 219–234.

The Representativeness Heuristic

Kahneman, D., Slovic, P., & Tversky, A. (1982). *Judgment under uncertainty: heuristics and biases.* Cambridge: Cambridge University Press.

Tversky, A., & Kahneman, D. (1983, October). Extension versus intuitive reasoning: The conjunction fallacy in probability judgment. *Psychological Review* 90(4), 293–315.

Yudkowsky, E. (2007, September 19). Conjunction fallacy. *Less Wrong.* Retrieved December 2010 from http://lesswrong.com/lw/ji/conjunction_fallacy/.

Expectation

Advertising: Coke-Pepsi Slugfest. (1976, July 26). *Time.*

Bertolucci, J. (2008, November 24). HD or standard def? One in five HDTV owners don't know the difference. *PCWorld.*

Brochet, F. (n.d.). *Chemical object representation in the field of consciousness.* Retrieved December 2010 from http://www.enophilia.net/writable/uploadfile/chimica%20della%20degustazione.pdf.

Goldstein, R., Almenberg, J., Dreber, A., Emerson, J. W., Herschkowitsch, A., & Katz, J. (2008, Spring). Do more expensive wines taste better? *Journal of Wine Economics* 3(1), 1–9.

Lehrer, J. (2007, November 2). The subjectivity of wine. *Frontal Cortex.* Retrieved December 2010 from http://scienceblogs.com/cortex/2007/11/the_subjectivity_of_wine.php.

Lehrer, J. (2008, February 24). Grape expectations: What wine can tell us about the nature of reality. *Boston Globe.*

Logan, M. (2009, June 11). The pull of cigarette packaging. *The Star.*

Morrot, G., Brochet, F., & Dubourdieu, D. (2001 November). The color of odors. *Brain and Language* 79(2), 309–320.

Simonite, T. (2009, October 7). Think yourself a better picture. *New Scientist*.

Woolfolk, M. E., Castellan, W., & Brooks, C. I. (1983). Pepsi versus Coke: Labels, not tastes, prevail. *Psychological Report*, 52, 185–186.

The Illusion of Control

Fast, N., Gruenfeld, D. H., Sivanathan, N., & Galinsky, A. D. (2008, December 1). Illusory control: A generative force behind power's far-reaching effects. Stanford University Graduate School of Business Research Paper No. 2009. Available at SSRN: http://ssrn .com/abstract=1314952.

Jarrett, C. (2010, November). Can psychology help combat pseudo-science? *British Psychological Society Research Digest*. Retrieved December 2010 from http://bps-research-digest.blogspot .com/2010/11/can-psychology-help-combat.html.

Jenkins, H. H., & Ward, W. C. (1965). Judgement of contingency be-tween responses and outcomes. *Psychological Monographs* 79, 1–17.

Kluger, J. (2009, March 10). Why powerful people overestimate them-selves. *Time*. Retrieved December 2010 from http://www.time .com/time/health/article/0,8599,1883658,00.html.

Langer, E. J. (1977). The psychology of chance. *Journal of Personality and Social Psychology* 7(2), 185–203.

Langer, E. J. (1975). The illusion of control. *Journal of Personality and Social Psychology* 32(2), 311–328.

Langer, E. J., Roth, J. Heads I win, tails it's chance: The illusion of con-trol as a function of the sequence of outcomes in a purely chance task. *Journal of Personality and Social Psychology* 32(6), 951–955.

Pronin, E., Wegner, D. M., McCarthy, K., & Rodriguez, S. (2006). Everyday magical powers: The role of apparent mental causation in the overestimation of personal influence. *Journal of Personality and Social Psychology* 91(2), 218–231.

Tijms, H. C. (2004). *Understanding probability: Chance rules in everyday life.* New York: Cambridge University Press.

Ward, W. C., & Jenkins, H. M. (1965). The display of information and the judgment of contingency. *Canadian Journal of Psychology* 19, 231–241.

The Fundamental Attribution Error

Ames, M. (2005). *Going postal: Rage, murder, and rebellion: From Reagan's workplaces to Clinton's Columbine and beyond.* Brooklyn, NY: Soft Skull Press.

Dreifus, C. (2007, April 3). Finding hope in knowing the universal capacity for evil. *New York Times.*

Kluger, J. (2007, April 19). Inside a mass murderer's mind. *Time.*

Weir, B., Horng, E., Kotzen, J., & Sterns, O. (2008, Februrary 9). What pushes shooters over the edge? ABC News. Retrieved December 2010 from http://abcnews.go.com/GMA/story?id=4267309&page=1.

Zimbardo, P. G. (2010). A simulation study of the psychology of imprisonment conducted at Stanford University. Retrieved December 2010 from http://www.prisonexp.org/.